BECOMING THE NATURAL

BECOMING THE NATURAL

My Life In and Out of the Cage

Randy Couture
with Loretta Hunt

First paperback edition published in the UK in November 2009
(Also in hardback - Collectors Limited Edition)

First published in the US by Simon Spotlight Entertainment -
A division of Simon & Schuster - in hardback July 2008

ISBN: 978-0-9562586-0-1 Paperback
ISBN: 978-0-9526586-2-5 Hardback

Designer: Martin Jennings
Publisher: Fiaz Rafiq
Published by: HNL Publishing Ltd - A division of HNL Media
Group - Suite 185, 6 Wilmslow Road, Manchester, M14 5TP,
United Kingdom

Front cover photo copyright Scott Haney/ Xtreme Couture

THIS BOOK IS DEDICATED:

To my mother, who has been an example of hard work and integrity for as long as I can remember—you have always been my hero.

To my sisters, Yolanda and Traci, who have endured life's challenges by my side, kept their heads, and came out better people for the adversity and the experience.

To my coaches, John Casebeer, Dave McAboy, Floyd "Bad News" Winter, Joe Seay, Bruce Burnett, and Bob Anderson. You gentlemen, each in your own way, have exemplified what it means to be a man. Thank you! You fostered a passion for the sport of wrestling that has carried me through my competitive life. A boy and young man could never ask for better.

To my father, Ed. With time and an understanding heart I see you in a different light and am thankful for all the ways you've affected my life. They have helped make me the person I am.

To my stepfather, Marco. Thanks for all your support, most of which was done stealthily behind the scenes, but I knew you were there.

To all my workout partners over the years. "Iron sharpens iron, so one man sharpens another." I never would have accomplished anything at any level if it weren't for all of you who toiled and bled with me every step of the way and challenged me to improve and work for what I wanted.

To all my staff at Natural Couture Inc. and Xtreme Couture, without whom I would be buried somewhere under a pile of God knows what!

To my children, Ryan, Aimee, and Caden, who have carried much of the burden of my chosen path with grace and honour. I see the reflection of all that is good about me in your eyes and in your hearts. You make me very proud! I love you very much.

Contents

Foreword

THEY SAY THE hardest thing to do in professional sports is to hit a fastball. I might have to disagree.

Imagine you're inside the Octagon, with 20,000 rabid fans packed into the surrounding arena, screaming wildly. You're about to do battle with the UFC heavyweight champion, who is seven inches taller than you and outweighs you by thirty-five pounds. You are the underdog. And oh yeah, I forgot. You're forty-three years old. "Ready? Fight!"

I was first introduced to the UFC back when it began in 1993. My buddies and I would get so pumped full of adrenaline when we watched that I'll admit, for an extremely brief period of my life, I entertained (or rather, fantasised) about becoming a UFC fighter and climbing into the Octagon. I trained for a bit and actually felt pretty good about myself. Then one night, while sparring another student, I got hit with an undetected short uppercut that caught my nose pretty square.

I'm going to be real honest and say it wasn't even the hardest of punches. He actually may have just been stretching. But as soon as it made contact, I saw a white flash, my eyes watered up and I went down—hard.

The second I regained control of my bodily fluids, I managed to get back to my feet and said to myself, "I need to write jokes." Oh, I still love the sport of fighting, I just love it from *outside* the Octagon…with a bag of chocolate-covered pretzels.

Through my job, I've been lucky enough to have had the opportunity to meet some of my sport's heroes. But the risk in meeting one of them is that they may not live up to who you have imagined them to be. Well, Randy Couture far exceeded any of my expectations. Simply put, he's great. Just a regular guy, who's very down-to-earth.

That's why it's always weird to me, when we grab a dinner or just hang out, that this guy, who I'm proud to call my friend, *is* the forty-three-year-old "underdog." The night I mentioned earlier, Randy went on to display one of the greatest performances in UFC history. The only thing that might be more impressive was that, in his next fight, "the Natural," once again an underdog, dominated his twenty-eight-year-old opponent at the age of forty-four. Yeah, you heard me, forty—FOUR!

One day, Randy and I were talking about what it's like in the Octagon when you have a 265-pound animal trying to stomp a mud hole in your head. We talked about the decisions you make in those tough moments and how they extend into your everyday life. We also talked about "fight or flight" and what you do when the hard stuff goes down.

Me? I run—metaphorically of course, because, let's face it, I get tired. But Randy fights, no matter what. He fights.

Whatever Randy chooses to do in life, he'll find a way to win. And like he's done in the Octagon so many times before, he'll win with class. That's what I admire so much about him. He never talks trash about his opponents. In fact, he usually says something complimentary about them. Randy is so low-key and soft-spoken, he's truly one of the nicest guys I know. He's like Andy Griffith, if Andy Griffith could ground-and-pound the crap out of you.

-Kevin James

Round One

WRESTLING
FROM WITHIN

1

1

CHAPTER ONE:
SAYING GOOD-BYE

ENTERING THE MANDALAY BAY EVENTS CENTRE IN Las Vegas on February 4, 2006, felt like a thousand gentle, little pricks all over, like there was a static electricity in the air, making every one of my hairs stand up on end. Every clap, every cheer, felt like a lightning bolt shooting from all directions instantly to a conductor, and the conductor was me.

I suppose it's adrenaline, but it's not like the rush you feel when you're standing at the edge of a 300-foot cliff with only a rope tied around you, or the rush you get hurling yourself out of an airplane thousands of feet above solid ground. I should know. I have bungee jumped and skydived as well.

A crowd 11,000 strong stood on its feet, some hanging their bodies over the stands with their palms outstretched to me, others reaching past the wall of security guards that lined the snaking path to the Octagon as I made my way down it. The background roar sounded like a seashell placed up to my bumpy cauliflowered ear, and even though snippets of individual voices broke through the white noise, I couldn't stop my stride long enough to hear any specific one as I passed.

An Ultimate Fighting champion five times in my nine-year career, I'd made this walk twenty-one times before. Each time had been memorable, but this time was the one I really wanted to savour. Win or lose tonight, I would never make this walk again.

A life of professional cagefighting had not been my first choice, but I readily welcomed the card God had dealt into my hand. As I'd always done in my walk, I raised my index finger to the sky to thank the man upstairs, as cameras flashed against the black backdrop like fireflies dancing.

For the last nine years, I had been a part of the evolution of a pariah sport once dubbed "human cockfighting." From small-town one-thousand-seat auditoriums to swanky Las Vegas arenas brimming with high rollers and crowds of 15,000 fans or more, I watched mixed martial arts brush with extinction, then make one of the greatest comebacks of all. I saw many of my colleagues elevate the sport to an art form, and also witnessed just as many of them fall to serious injury and laughable paydays. I proudly did my part to help nurture a fragile, infant sport, taking a chance on something unproven that few would give a moment's thought to, something I believed in with every fibre of my being.

My own personal journey through mixed martial arts had come full circle to this one night. I had one more shot to win back the title from a man that had been quicker than me a year and a half before. It was quite a challenge—but the kind of challenge I live for.

When I reached the centre, I hustled up the three steps to the silver ramp surrounding the cage. I slid off my flip-flops, the touch of cold metal tingling my feet, then stepped over the threshold into the Octagon. The spongy blue canvas sank beneath my weight.

The music faded and the lights dimmed to pitch-black. The audience crescendoed into a howl. In a few minutes, UFC light heavyweight champion Chuck Liddell would stand only a few feet across from me. The gate would close with its familiar clang. The crowd would hush. And then the bell would sound one last time. Then I would say good-bye.

Retiring wouldn't be an easy break. Becoming a professional fighter had enriched my life in both obvious and unforeseen ways. I had tried four times in thirteen years to gain a slot on the U.S. Olympic wrestling team and not making the squad had been one of my greatest disappointments. In fighting, I learned that you have to embrace opportunities that sometimes find their way in front of you by chance, even if they don't seem the obvious path and nobody thinks you should go for it. Some people call them obstacles. My life has been a winding road of such opportunities and choices.

I'm not scared to fail. I'm not scared to lose. I'm not scared to die, for that matter. I've done a lot of stupid shit that probably could have killed me, but it's gonna happen when it happens and it's gonna work out the way it's supposed to work out, and you just have to go ahead and do what you think you're supposed to do. I think I was meant to fight.

In recent years, I've been able to make a nice living by mastering my own way of combining the disciplines of wrestling, boxing, kickboxing, jiu-jitsu, and others into one cohesive force. As I got older and kept winning way past the age considered "normal" to fight, I garnered more attention and popularity then I'd ever thought possible, more than I ever really wanted. I even had strangers follow me into the bathroom. But I learned to adjust as the sport shed its negative connotations and the fans started flocking.

I found an occupation I was good at, one that defined me as an athlete and a person. That's why it would be hard to let it go. In some way, shape, or form, I had felt I was never good enough until I started fighting. I was always striving to show my worth and value, to one man in particular.

★　★　★

MY FATHER, ED, left when I was three years old. My sister Yolanda was one and Traci was a newborn. I couldn't tell you much about my life before that moment, about my sisters' births or any memories of my mom and dad in happier times.

I remember my father storming out the door. Clinging to his pants leg, my small frame couldn't muster the strength to stop him. He ignored my cries and paused just long enough to peel me off of him, knocking me to the living room floor in the process.

I raced to the window and watched intently as he climbed into his car and sat there for what seemed like hours. I didn't know what he was doing. I pressed my face against the glass each time I climbed up the couch to see if he was still there. Finally, I stared out onto an empty street.

There wasn't an argument or any screaming back-and-forth or the slamming of doors or the crashing of broken dishes. I couldn't even tell you where my mother was at the time. I often question if this memory is 100 percent accurate, or something my mind conjured up to document a childhood trauma. All I know is that it's a memory that has stayed with me all these years, a marker for many of the decisions I've made in life, whether they were right or wrong.

I do know I was born twenty-five miles north of Seattle in the seacoast town of Everett, Washington. It was the first of a cluster of suburbs surrounding the city that my family and I would jump around. You can say I was a fighter from the opening bell, a heavyweight at ten and a half whopping pounds, barrelling my way into the world. Doctors had to dislocate one of my collarbones to get me out without performing a Caesarean. My mom would not allow them to use forceps or tongs on my head, which was partially the reason I couldn't be extracted easily. It was a very strenuous labour.

After they finally pried me free and wiped me off, a nurse laid me on the scales. I immediately propped myself up on my elbows.

"Give that kid directions to the nursery and just point which way to go," the doctor teased my weeping mother.

I was a fearless, curious baby. As soon as I could walk, my mom says, I ventured off the front porch and crashed onto the lawn, already oblivious to the general principles of human mortality.

My adventurous spirit complemented the Pacific Northwest lifestyle, where people embraced the term *outdoorsmen* wholeheartedly. Taking full advantage of the thick-wooded countryside and neighbouring shores of Puget Sound, Pacific Northwesterners embody a do-it-yourself mentality. They fix their own cars. They mow their own grass. They hunt, camp, and fish. That was the kind of neighbourhood I grew up in after my mom, sisters, and I moved to Edmonds, Washington.

On her own with three mouths to feed, my mother went to work as a bookkeeper and bartender for Marco Courounes, who owned a chain of taverns in the area. My sisters and I were left with babysitters, and one experienced firsthand my unabashed ways. At four years old, I stood in front of the television watching an Indian get stabbed by a heroic cowboy, then I picked up a paring knife left next to an apple on the coffee table and dug it into my ribs. I don't remember the blood or even being fazed by it. My mom rushed home from work to take me to the hospital, and somehow, I walked away unscathed. But after that incident, knives were kept out of reach.

My inquisitiveness far outweighed any rules any adult could ever tell me. At four years old, I wandered around my neighbourhood looking for other kids to play with, though I'd been instructed in no uncertain terms to stay inside the safety of my backyard's fence. All it would take was the sound of another kid's laugh in the distance, and I'd take off to find him.

My mom had good reason to worry about me (other than my interest in knives). One of the kids I played with got hit by a car riding his bike on the busy two-lane road off the cul-de-sac down a ways from our house. It was a big happening for my street as the ambulance pulled up into the neighbourhood, its red-and-blue flashing beacon lighting up what was supposed to be a lazy summer evening. I remember watching the boy's brother frantically pedal up Edmonds Way crying out for help. The neighbourhood was swept up into an emotional chaos, and panicked adults raced across the street. The next week, the boy reappeared. His head was shaved; his eyes were little less full of life, but he was home. The sight of him should have taught me a lesson in caution, though it didn't slow me down at all.

In my neighbourhood, everybody knew everybody, and with my mom away so often, I think many of the adults understood and had taken it upon themselves to help keep an eye on me. I remember many of them like colourful characters out of a book, and they each faded in and out of my life, shaping the person I became.

On my block, there was a lady I called Auntie Red, though she wasn't my aunt or any relative that I knew of. Auntie Red's parents lived a block away at the end of the cul-de-sac. Red's dad had huge fingers like sausages he'd thump on my head every time he saw me. He thought it was funny and I'd flash him a smile because he had the coolest yard any kid could ever want, with an elaborate in-ground fish pond he spent all of his spare time fussing over. Wrapped along the front and side of the house were giant stalks that sprouted out of the earth with green elephant ear leaves that flapped about in the breeze. I thought these leaves were the greatest things, so my friends and I picked a bunch one day and waved them in the air like kites, running around the yard. We didn't know that our homemade airplanes were rhubarb and that we had ruined the patch. I got my arse spanked for that one.

Outside of the neighbourhood folk, my mother's boss Marco spent a lot of time with my family. Although I was too young to understand it at the time, Marco was more than just my mom's employer, though he had a wife and family of his own to go home to. Marco was a successful local businessman who, at his peak, owned nine pubs in the area.

Marco was a fixture of my childhood. On my fourth birthday, I was given a shiny yellow bike. It was way too big for me, so Marco and my mom put blocks on the pedals so I could ride it. They used tyre inner tubes to secure the blocks and keep them in place, and I was game to try it out. I came crashing down in a heap of metal.

My mom, Yolanda, and I rode around in Marco's Cadillac often. We didn't have car seats back then, so I stood on the back seat, anxiously leaning over the front to get a good view of where we were going next.

We'd often drive to a little restaurant called the Cascade Inn, where I'd order pancakes and syrup. Sometimes they'd take us out to Snohomish, where my mom grew up. My mom's friend had a goat tied up in the backyard that I was just fascinated by. I'd roughhouse with the goat just like any other of my playmates, pulling its horns and head-butting it. Every time the goat head-butted me back, I thought it was the funniest thing. After one of these visits with the goat, I head-butted Marco in the back of head as we drove home. He wasn't as amused as I was.

My father's mother, Grandma Powell, also lived in Snohomish, out in the country. My Grandma Powell had divorced my grandfather, Robert Couture, when my father was young, and later remarried William Powell. Like me, my dad's father had left him at an early age. My dad always referred to his father as "Pop" in a detached, bitter sort of way.

Grandma Powell owned an old house on a sprawling piece of farmland. In my father's absence, Grandma Powell went out of her way to spend time with us. She took us to church on Easter, and had us over on the weekends so my Grandpa Powell could take me fishing. Grandpa Powell also took me to the Safeway Distribution Centre where he worked as a truck driver and let me climb around the monstrous eighteen-wheelers.

In the summer between kindergarten and first grade, my mom moved us into a much larger, split-level house in neighbouring Lynnwood. Surrounded by a lush fir tree forest common in Washington's rainy climate, this is the house I grew up in until I graduated from high school. It had an above-ground swimming pool in the backyard, which made us an instant hit with our new neighbourhood. The house was certainly a step up for a single mother with three kids. Looking back, I imagine Marco helped get us there by co-signing for it.

I LOVED BEING outdoors. On the other side of a public utility department road that ran next to our house, the woods were undeveloped land for miles. That was my playground.

My bike and my neighbours were my best friends and fellow explorers. Down the street lived Jack Thomas, a year older than me and just as daring. We rode our bikes endlessly and fixed them tirelessly. Our favourite pastime was to go around "left turn," which was this huge series of roads that made a big loop. Every turn was to the left and brought you back to where you started.

"We're going down 'left turn,' Mom," I'd yell over my shoulder, a packed lunch in my hands as I burst out the door and onto my trusty steed alongside Jack. On the backside of the road there was an area called "the Bridle Trails," which were big dirt roads where we performed our jumps. There were two little mini-markets at the top of the hill. After a day of collecting soda bottles all the way around "left turn," we'd reward ourselves with candy. That was our adventure.

When Jack and I weren't on our bikes, we'd play hide-and-seek and "kick the can" at the elementary school across the street. I met Bobby Stevenson through the school's soccer programme there. Bobby had six brothers, all older than him, which gave us enough players for our very own soccer games. Bobby's brother would call the games in a thick British accent like the announcers we heard on TV. We played a lot of soccer, especially when it rained. We *liked* getting muddy.

Would I have been such a physical kid had I lived somewhere else? It's hard to say. I happened to be in an environment that encouraged my rough-and-tumble ways. Probably not by coincidence, I had friends who were also constantly pushing the envelope with what kids our age could do in our spare time.

No one ever guessed that I had bad bouts with asthma as a young boy and spent a lot of nights in a clear plastic oxygen tent. I had a vaporiser that travelled with me everywhere, even on overnights at Grandma's. I think I outgrew my asthma by the time I hit kindergarten, although as I've gotten older, it has come back around.

I had a happy childhood with an endless supply of friends and a mother who encouraged me into sports. And though she was supporting us mostly on her own, I never suffered for want of anything. When I started playing baseball in grade school, I had a hard time getting to first base once I cracked the ball. I didn't have cleats like the other kids. I looked like I was moving in slow motion as I rounded the bases.

One day, my mom pulled up in the car after practise to take me home. I opened the car door, and on the seat were a pair of black spiked cleats with white stripes running up the sides. I knew my mom hadn't bought them, but I didn't care where she she'd gotten them. They were my first pair of Adidas sneakers. In fact, they were the first brand-name shoes I ever remember getting.

Whatever I needed seemed to mysteriously appear. I figured that was because of Marco, who always seemed to be lingering in the background, looking over my family.

Christmas mornings were sponsored by our own Secret Santa. Waking up in the goofy red caps my mom would make us wear to bed, Yolanda and I would come tearing upstairs to wake up mom, only to stop in our tracks at the top of the steps because the living room was covered with presents.

Christmas and my birthdays were the times I looked forward to most, because that's when I would get to see my father, Ed. Dad would come on my birthday and usually take me shopping to get a gift. Sometimes he'd show up at our house for Christmas, or we'd go to my Grandma Powell's house to see him. One year, he bought me a telescope at Kmart. I was so proud to get it because it was made of real metal with an elaborate tripod, so it didn't really seem like a toy at all. My friends and I took it up on the sundeck and looked up at the stars at night. I kept that gift until I was eighteen.

I was always excited to see my father. He was a big, commanding man, six-foot-three and barrel-chested with arms like meat hooks. My dad had brown hair, brown eyes, and an olive complexion like my sister

Yolanda, from the little bit of Native American Indian in his blood. He had a very physical presence that I admired. He showed up often in his work clothes, which had holes burned through from his welding jobs. He had that smell about him a man gets after a hard day's work, that sweaty, metallic odour mixed in with tobacco, which he loved. To me, it was the most comforting smell in the world.

My love of hunting came from my dad. All through grade school, the highlight of my year came when he showed up in his "beater" truck wearing his black and red plaid, buttoned-up wool jacket to take me into the wilderness. He had a different truck every time.

"What happened to your truck?" I'd ask him.

"Oh, I had to tear the motor out of it to fix her up," he'd say like clockwork, packing our supplies into another unsuspecting car that would end up on the chopping block in couple months time.

We were never very successful on our hunting trips. I can't remember ever shooting a deer or elk, which was mainly what we went for. In fact, I don't think I ever saw one with him. It didn't matter to me, though.

Don't get me wrong. I loved the thrill of the hunt. One time we went with my uncles and my grandfather to Whidbey Island to hunt rabbits and drove around in trucks in the pitch-black night, using spotlights to pick them off. My uncles jumped off the trucks and ran after the swift creatures, trying to catch them midair as they bounced in and out of the brush.

My hunting trips with my dad were about something else though. I got to spend time alone with him. He never took my sisters, not that he ever paid much attention to them anyway. It was just us.

We never said a whole lot. My father never needed to fill the moments with chatter. He was content to breathe in the concentrated scent of pine, to watch and listen to the wildlife as it tossed and turned and went about its business. My father never spoke about himself, announced his accomplishments, or tried to get others' attention. He was satisfied just to be. People tell me I am the same way.

On one trip when I was ten years old, we went hunting in Ellensburg, Washington, on a very cold, damp day. We camped in a national forest area where you couldn't start fires and we'd slept outside in front of the truck under the stars. My dad had only brought coffee and beer to drink and the coffee had long turned cold, so I drank my very first beer that day. It was early in the morning and we were packing up our stuff, getting ready to leave.

We had no idea that a black bear had been rummaging through a Dumpster in the parking area next to us. It came out of the Dumpster and ran right through our camp, yards away from where we'd just slept. I'd never seen my dad move that fast. He grabbed me and we sprinted for the truck. It wasn't terrifying. It was exhilarating. We sat in the cab of the truck watching the bear to see what he'd do next, if he'd go for our food. He poked his snout in and out of our supplies, and not seeing anything he fancied, he eventually drifted away.

We hunted all day long. I didn't have very good boots, and my feet got so wet and cold that I cried out from the throbbing pain. My dad stopped me and sat me down on a rock. Then he took my shoes and socks off. At first, I didn't understand what he was doing. My feet were frozen, and I didn't see how taking off my boots would fix them.

He took my bare feet and put them on his chest and rubbed, massaging them until they warmed up. Then he put on dry socks and slid sandwich bags over them before putting my boots back on. My feet stayed dry and toasty the rest of the day.

When we got back to the truck, a couple parked next to us had shot a black bear, the same black bear that had run through our camp that morning. Tagged and motionless, this black bear lay mere feet away from me. It was the first wild animal that I'd ever been close to. I reached out and touched its dense, soft coat, remembering the power it had exuded only a few hours earlier.

SHORTLY AFTER THAT trip, my dad married a woman named Pat and moved to Bellevue, a town in the next county over and a couple of hours away. My sisters and I visited my dad, Pat, and her three kids Joanna, Bud, and Robby, there a few times. It was always a war for attention between the two sets of children, but I found my allies in my sisters, Yolanda and Traci.

My visits with my father always ended much faster than I wanted them to, but my mom went out of her way to keep me preoccupied at home. When I was old enough, she took me across the street to the grade-school gymnasium and signed me up for the Boy Scouts. This is where I met Tim Detschman, another one of my neighbours who became one of my closest friends. Tim's dad was very good with his hands. Mr. Detschman built wood cabinets and had handmade boxes lying around his garage, filled with every tool a young boy would find interesting.

Mr. Detschman was someone I looked up to my entire childhood. He used to give his kids a short, tight haircut in the summer called "the butch," but he called me "Randallina" or "Rosey" because I kept my longer locks. I thought it was a big compliment because I loved Roosevelt "Rosey" Grier, a famous football defensive tackle for the New York Giants who went on to become a successful TV and film actor. Of course, Mr. Detschman didn't know that, but he was such a kind man that I liked to pretend that he did.

I got my first glimpse of college wrestling in pictures hanging on the walls of the Detschman house. Mr. Detschman had been a college wrestler in Minnesota, and I stared closely at the old school uniforms and the proud faces staring back at me.

I tagged along with Tim and his dad to the Boy Scouts events. At the father-son soccer games, Mr. Detschman and the other parents never made a big deal that my dad wasn't there with me, though it bothered me inside. I was introverted about stuff like that, about how it made me feel, and never said a word.

I had always been shy around adults in general. I had a soft voice and kept quiet most of the time. I was less shy around my friends and opened up around them as far as my personality, but I didn't talk to them about my dad either, except for one time.

In fourth grade, my sisters had a sleepover and invited our neighbour Sherry Dormer. Lying in our sleeping bags on the living room floor in the dead of night, Sherry told us her parents were getting a divorce and her dad was moving out. My sisters started to cry and I teared up as well. It was the first time I had cried in front of another person and admitted I missed my dad.

Getting older and watching the other boys with their fathers, my interest in my own dad naturally grew, to the point where I finally asked my mom about him. I had never understood why he left and couldn't get a straight answer to why my parents had divorced, but I never once put the blame on myself. I just wanted to know what my dad was like.

"Your dad was a great father, a very smart guy," my mom told me before pausing briefly, then continuing. "When he went into the service, he started drinking and became a different person. He was a religious man and thought about going on a mission, but he went into the service instead and that's when he changed. He never liked to stay in one place for very long."

I knew my father was smart. I'd watched him interact with my aunts and uncles, and though he never said a lot, he voiced his own opinion when he needed to. He knew how to fix cars and was always leaning over a fixer-upper, tinkering below the hood. That took smarts.

On our hunting trips, I'd never noticed that my father had a problem with alcohol. Sure, he'd drink a beer or two, but he never got drunk. Still, I had no reason not to believe my mother, so I just nodded my head.

One of my math teachers, who'd also taught my dad told me what a good football player he was. This was how I heard about my father— in trickles and spurts. This little piece of insight into his life piqued my interest more than anything. I raced home to question my mom about it. She told me he had wrestled, then boxed when he joined the navy.

She said my dad was an exceptional athlete, a tough competitor who didn't go down lightly.

She then told me that my dad had come to see her one day during his lunch hour at Marco's tavern, where she tended bar. My father was furious with my mother, though she didn't mention why. He grabbed her, shaking her and slapping her across her jaw so hard the curlers in her hair came loose and tumbled to the floor around her. Several regulars rose from their barstools to come to her aid, but my dad levelled them all, knocking down each of them before walking out the door just as quickly as he'd come in.

Ironically, my mom told me this story to show me how physically gifted my dad was. It made me all the more in awe of him. Though I thought it not like my father to hit my mom—I'd never seen him strike her before—all I could think of was how strong he must have been to handle all those guys all at once. I was so enamoured with this feat, it never dawned on me to think what had motivated my dad to do what he did.

I clung to this swashbuckling story of my dad for years, never fully comprehending its true meaning. Back then, all I knew was that my dad was gone and likely not coming back, and I would simply have to move on.

Years later, as an Ultimate Fighting Championship icon entering the last fight of my career, it felt like I had the entire world's attention. But as a young boy, I would have traded that all in to have one particular man notice me.

2 CHAPTER TWO:
PIECES OF
THE PUZZLE

I WAS LUCKY ENOUGH TO HAVE MANY PEOPLE WHO loved and cared about me, who floated in and out of my early years. I was a puzzle waiting to be put together, and each piece represented a person who influenced me in a particular way. Each piece had its significance, whether it taught me a life lesson, exposed a bad habit, or helped me develop a redeeming characteristic.

My mother Sharan was a big piece of my puzzle. Our relationship has always been close, and her incredible work ethic heavily contributed to the man I am today. At five-foot-ten with dark hair and green eyes, my mother was always very long and lean, no doubt from a mix of good genes and the fact she was always on the go. I suppose most men found her very attractive. I remember years later, when she got a job in a meat market, my buddies would comment how buff her arms and shoulders looked from lifting heavy trays all day long.

As a child, I didn't really know what a single mother was. It seemed normal for my sisters and me to be left with a babysitter while my mom ran off to work. Being the only male and the oldest of all the kids, I took on the "man of the house" role. It was up to me to make sure that my sisters were up and ready to go to school and that the chores were completed.

You know what they say about idle hands? My mother wouldn't have any part of that. When she wasn't at work, she toiled around the house or in the yard, and we all helped. I remember dragging chain link around to smooth out the dirt so we could plant grass. I pushed the lawnmower along at the age of six or seven, even though my hands could barely reach the handle. I helped erect a six-foot cedar fence. Weeding was also my job, and there was always plenty of planting and tending to the flower beds.

Inside the house, when my mother was gone, I was in charge of the chore list, which included loading the dishwasher, dusting, and vacuuming the floors. My sisters and I learned to do the wash and the ironing, and as I got older, I learned to cook for myself. I was the one responsible for implementing the schedule between me, Yolanda, and Traci, which gave me my first taste of leadership.

We were always doing something, and my mother was right beside us with her sleeves rolled up. She decorated the house. She hosted Avon parties. She always had a goal or project in front of her to accomplish, and that's where I learned to become industrious.

My mother's schedule was hectic not by choice, but by necessity. Because of that, she spent a lot of time away from us, and I think that worried her. In response, my mom put me in every single sport you could think of. I started with T-ball and soccer, then I had tennis lessons. I went roller-skating and bowling, and I got to go to camp every summer where I played soccer, basketball, and baseball.

I competed in club soccer (my favourite) with the same group of boys from sixth grade through high school: Mark Baggerly, Jeff Lind, Robert Anderson, and Bobby Stevenson. Our bond is so great that these guys were all in my hotel room the night before my third fight with Chuck Liddell, laughing about the good old days.

The only sport my mom wouldn't allow me to try was boxing, which she thought was too dangerous. When she found out I'd snuck over to the Elks Club a couple of times with a neighbourhood kid to hit some bags in junior high, she told his dad the gym was off limits to me.

"I should have let you do it then, to let you get it out of your system," she joked years later.

Sports were my mom's attempt to keep me occupied and out of trouble, and I will always be grateful that she encouraged me to try almost all of them. I don't know how she did it, but my mom managed to get to all my games, even when I played two sports at a time. She was always there, cheering me on. It didn't matter how much I played, I always felt like I was the priority.

My physicality made me a fearsome rival on and off the sports fields. It probably helped that I never had a sense of fear the way other kids do. Nothing seemed to rattle my cage.

I wasn't afraid to stick up for others, and got into my very first fight protecting my younger cousin Craig on the baseball field. Craig and I weren't blood relatives, but our moms had been best friends through high school, and I called his mom Aunt Money. Craig had been playing in the dirt field by the baseball diamond when our classmate Boonie ambushed him and beat him up, then pushed his face in a puddle for good measure.

Boonie was a bit of roughneck, already puffing on cigarettes at eleven years old. His house butted up against our baseball diamond, so Boonie only had to hop over the school fence to get to Craig, then hop back for a quick getaway. I heard about the attack when I got home after baseball practise.

The next day at school, I walked up to Boonie on the playground and beat the shit out of him in retaliation, punching him in the face and bruising him up pretty badly. But then after school, I found two of Boonie's two older brothers waiting for me. They knocked me down and proceeded to show me the same hospitality I had afforded their little brother earlier.

The next day, I returned the favour and beat up Boonie again. This went on for four days. Neither side would budge. Finally, my mom had enough. She marched over to Boonie's house, threatening to press charges because Boonie's brothers were three and five years older than me.

I had felt a deep sense that what Boonie had done to Craig was wrong, that beating up someone smaller and weaker simply because he could was cowardly. Boonie was a bully, pure and simple, and I wasn't going to stand for it. Fighting back seemed like the right thing to do. I wasn't a grade-school guardian angel. I stood up for my friends when I could, but I wasn't exactly a saint.

I made a big mistake once, that I'll never forget, because I learned a great lesson from it. When the temperature dropped into the thirties and a fresh blanket of snow covered the ground, we'd drive to our great-grandparents' house to bake Christmas cookies and decorate them with all different coloured sprinkles and icing. My sisters and I would each get a coffee can to fill with cookies to bring home with us.

On one particular visit, when I was ten, my mother and I stopped at the store to pick up flowers for Great-grandma Griggs, who by that time lived in a nursing home. My mom picked a nice bunch and we brought them to the checkout counter. I can't tell you what came over me, but as I stood behind my mother, I picked up a pack of gum and stuck it in my pocket. The checkout lady saw me do it and signalled to my mom, who whipped around to face me.

I was caught, red-handed. "Empty your pockets," she ordered in a stern tone, a distraught look on her face.

We didn't speak the entire trip until we got home and she sent me downstairs to my bedroom, which was in the basement next to the garage. I knew my mom had called Marco, so I sat on the edge of my bed until I heard the sound of his car tyres slide into our driveway.

Marco entered my room quietly, and full of purpose. I had no reason to steal and I knew it. Marco had bought my sisters and me packs of gum countless times. I was used to being spanked—my mom had always used a belt or a thin piece of cedar kindling—but I wasn't prepared for what Marco did. He knocked me around, threw me against the wall, bounced me off the bed and slapped me with his open hand. He really roughed me up, something no one had ever done to me before. I was too astonished to move.

Because he owned so many bars, Marco knew practically every

policeman in town. He had one of his buddies come pick me up and take me to the sheriff's office, tour me through the jail, and scare the living shit out of me for stealing that pack of gum. Marco told me if I stole again, that's where I'd end up. I don't know if my mom ever knew how Marco handled me that day, but I have never forgotten even the slightest detail of it. It was the only time Marco ever really disciplined me.

MARCO HAD BEEN in my life as long as I could remember, albeit always behind the scenes. He never slept over, though he seemed to come whenever my mother called. I had met Marco's two children, Nick and Irene, during Little League, but our two families never interacted together.

I always liked Marco. He was a short, stout Greek man who greeted me with a great big bear hug and said, "How ya doing, kid?" in a funny voice he put on for us. To me, it didn't seem out of the ordinary to have Marco around. He was just a part of our lives.

I don't remember when things changed, but one day Marco stopped coming around. I was around eleven years old and going into sixth grade. Around the same time, my mom brought another guy home and introduced him to us as her boyfriend. His name was Don Elstead. Don took us up to the beach to dig for clams, and we had a blast. The next thing I knew, Don was moving in with us and my mom told us he was going to be our new dad.

A few months later, I found out my mom and Don had gotten married—they left a pack of pictures on the kitchen counter that showed them celebrating with our neighbours Sharon and Mike Sloy. It looked like they must have gotten married at City Hall, then went to a bar afterwards. Obviously, kids hadn't been invited.

Don was a good-sized man, about six-foot-three and 230 pounds with strawberry-blonde hair, a fair complexion and freckles, typical of his Norwegian heritage. He was a shift worker at Scott Paper Mill, which meant his hours changed each week. He punched buttons and ran the equipment that bleached pulp and spit it out as paper.

Don's presence changed the dynamic of our home immediately. Not long after he moved in with us, the police showed up at our front door. Suddenly, the whole family was escorted to a Travelodge motel, where we spent the night. On our way there, Don began to weep. It was the first time I'd seen a grown man cry. I didn't understand what was going on although I knew it had to be something big.

The next day, we returned home and my mom sat us down at the kitchen table. Marco had done something illegal, she said, and the police were trying to arrest him. For whatever reason, the police had fed Marco misinformation that Don was physically abusing us, to try to bait him into doing something about it. Marco responded by putting out a contract hit on Don. The police then picked up the contract themselves, and the whole scenario played out the night we stayed at the hotel.

Later, my mom told me the whole case was taken to court. I really don't know why the authorities were trying to take Marco down. The whole case eventually got thrown out because it was called a form of entrapment and Marco was exonerated. But he lost a bunch of his businesses and had to spend a chunk of time in counselling. I never held a grudge toward Marco for what he did, and oddly enough, my mom didn't seem to be upset with him either. I was so young; the whole situation felt like make-believe, like something you'd see on TV.

Though it was a rocky start, there was a definite upside when Don entered our lives. With the combined incomes of two full-time jobs, my family was able to enjoy the great outdoors even more. We bought a camper and a boat and started going on family vacations. Don's parents had a beach house on the coast of Tacoma, where we'd go water skiing and fishing in the summers. He and I started going on weeklong hunting trips every year for deer and elk.

There was another side to Don, however, a side that undermined my self-esteem. Don was an incessant tease. He tormented all four of us about anything and everything, and seemed to be exceptionally jealous of my close relationship with my mom. Watching my mom move heaven and earth to get to all of my sports games made him resentful because I don't think Don ever had that kind of relationship with his own parents. To retaliate, Don would embarrass me in front of my friends every chance he got and he used something that was completely out of my control.

"He can't spend the night at your house," he'd tell my friends. "He still wets the bed."

It was true. I wet the bed until I was in eighth grade. It wasn't every night, but it happened often. My mom was adamant that I go to the bathroom before I went to sleep, but that didn't help. She took me to a chiropractor, and the wetting would stop, but only for a few days at a time. None of my other friends wet the bed, so I thought I was freak. Slumber parties were out of the question, except in very controlled situations where my mom would speak to the parents first to take precautions. I was extremely shy around people because of it.

It wasn't until seventh grade when I started peeing blood, that the doctors finally figured out that I had an enlarged bladder, after a battery of tests. They determined that I must have been bursting blood vessels every time I held my bladder in too long playing sports. This came on top of me breaking my wrist and shoulder, and having to sit out the rest of the wrestling season. My confidence was at its lowest, but Don didn't care. It was a big joke to him.

I wasn't the only one who felt Don's wrath. Don told Traci she was a little boy turning into a girl because she had a little extra body hair on her arms. Traci was only eight years old at the time. He called her "Orville Pete," a name he made up to drive her crazy about it. After the three of us caught the chicken pox, Yolanda's back broke out with shingles, which was very rare for a child. Don ridiculed Yolanda by calling her a "baby elephant" and a "Shetland pony," referring to the short, stocky horse breed.

Don harassed Traci to the point where she packed up his stuff on the porch and was sitting on it when my mom came home from work one day. Traci looked up at my mom and said, "Either he leaves or I do." This was coming from an eight-year-old child.

To this day, I don't open up as well with guys because of the way Don harassed me. I'm always wary of being judged, or opening myself up to an attack. I guess I feel I was let down by certain men in my life as a child, and Don was one of them.

Don fancied himself a practical jokester, but his "pranks" were always taken too far. Coming back from a hunting trip, Don bribed me with an ice cream cone to get me to chew a tobacco plug in front of my mother. She was less than amused when her eleven-year-old son, his head spinning, painted the living room with chocolate ice cream.

Don didn't let up his torturous tendencies in front of my mom, and she was also a victim of his name-calling and callous high jinks. As a couple, my mom and Don seemed affectionate, but companionship came with a price.

Don was more of a bully when he had a few, and a twelve-pack of Schlitz stood at attention in the fridge at all times. It was standard for Don to down a six-pack in one night's sitting. When he and my mom split up years later, she called Don a "functioning alcoholic."

Don had his shortcomings, but he also had the same work ethic as my mother. At home, Don spent a lot of his free time in the garage with his projects. There was always a lot of stuff going on, so I followed him in there every chance I got. He always seemed to be bent over a tool bench, twisting and cranking on some contraption. Together, we built hutches and raised rabbits, slaughtered them, then tanned the hides. He whittled on wood all the time. He tuned the cars up. He even taught himself how to play the harmonica.

He was always a very good cook, and baked *lefse*, a deliciously sweet Norwegian crepe we'd spread butter on. He baked pies and made popcorn balls. He made his own jam and jellies. Don even made his own wine. He had a hunting dog named Nod, but got frustrated trying

to train it because it was so stupid. Nod—Don spelled backwards—
became my pet.

Don's introduction into my life signalled the end of my visits from
my dad. My dad had moved up to Alaska to weld on the pipeline, and
it was too expensive for him to come down to the Lower 48. I think my
mom was after him for child support at the time, so a sense of
resentment was growing in me anyway.

On one of our final hunting trips together, I walked behind my dad,
dragging my feet and cracking sticks, even though he'd asked me to
stay quiet. He turned around repeatedly and hit me on the top of my
head with the butt of his gun. I pulled my stocking cap down over my
forehead, covering my eyes so I could barely see, but I needed a little
padding because I knew another butt stroke would be coming. I came
home that day shattered, but I couldn't tell my mother. I buried that day
away in my mind. I still haven't told her, or anyone else for that matter,
until now.

I started hunting with Don. He was always the tormenter, but we
often had Mr. Detschman, who had struck up a friendship with Don,
and his son Tim with us so the trips took on a more light-hearted tone.
We got to swear on our hunting trips, which was big, because I was
never allowed to swear around the house. Around the campfire, we
passed around the "kill bottle," usually blackberry brandy, after we shot
a deer or elk. Don chewed tobacco and he'd always offer me a chew.
"Hey, you want some man's candy?" he'd ask. I always turned him
down.

Hunting had a different feel with Don than it did with my father. I
didn't have the same sentiment towards Don, though our success rate
on these trips was much higher—we always brought home a deer or
elk. The trips with my father were more about spending time together.
With Don, it was just about the hunt.

I never felt like Don and I had a father-son relationship, though I
wasn't sure what that even meant. I didn't get to see the private time
my friends spent with their fathers, so it was hard to tell. I was an

outsider looking in. I sensed that my relationship with Don didn't have the same emotional connection my friends had with their dads. I don't think Don ever really appreciated me or felt a strong bond with me. I don't know if he thought I was a pain in the arse or what. I don't know how he felt about me. He never told me he loved me.

Still, I don't remember hating Don. He was an enigma. There were two sides to him—one I thrived on and looked up to, and another I had no control over. Don wasn't my father and never tried to be. So I learned to move on without the love he could have given, trying to feel as little resentment in my heart as I could.

3 CHAPTER THREE: BOY TO MAN

BECOMING "THE NATURAL" HAS TAKEN FORTY-FIVE years…and counting. I was not born "the Natural." I believe champions are made. I think some people are born with a certain set of gifts, but if they're not taught how to use them, they'll never rise above a certain level. I see talented fighters all the time who don't understand how to take advantage of what they've been blessed with. They don't have the work ethic, the drive, or the passion. Sadly, lots of guys work their butts off, but just don't have the ability to match their ambition. Still, I'll take a guy who will work hard over one with natural talent any day of the week.

I consider myself one of those guys—one who sweats and toils at his craft, and moves up the ladder, rung by rung. I realise now that my work ethic probably wouldn't have been enough. I was lucky that I also found the guidance I needed to hone my gifts. It came at the age of nine, with my introduction to wrestling and one of the most influential people of my life.

I found wrestling—or should I say, wrestling found me—on a whim. If my friend's older brothers hadn't been looking for a laugh, who knows if I would have ever stepped onto the mat?

Bobby Stevenson's brothers, John and David, wrestled for Alderwood Junior High, and they dragged us along to their matches, where we'd buy bubblegum and hang around in the stands. One day they entered us in the novice tournament for shits and giggles. We were only nine, and Bobby's brothers probably thought we would fall flat on our faces, but on the mat, something came over me. I had not an ounce of direction nor any clue what I was doing, but my body seemed to take over. It shifted and torqued around my opponent's torso, and my arms instinctually found his neck and wrapped around it, squeezing till the referee pried us apart. I wasn't really sure what had happened, but the junior high school coach, John Casebeer, approached me as I walked off the mat.

"That move you used is called a headlock," he said. I wasn't quite sure what he was talking about, but my little heart beat with excitement.

I was so preoccupied with other sports that I didn't try wrestling again until Bobby and I entered the same tournament the next year. I still didn't know what I was doing, but it gave that coach another chance to look at me. When we started junior high school in the fall, Coach Casebeer also happened to be my new gym teacher. He walked up to me in class and told me to report to wrestling practise after school. I didn't argue.

You know when you find something that just feels right? For me, wrestling was that something. It was an immediate challenge, filled with technical moves we learned and drilled over and over. Coach Casebeer made big signs listing each takedown, escape, and reversal technique, and I would do my darnedest to memorise them. When I went home, I'd lie in bed and break the lists down into which ones I knew and which ones I didn't have a grasp of yet, so I could drill them the next day.

In the gym, we laid the wrestling mats out on the stage. On the wall, there was a wooden pegboard with handles that you'd inch your way up with by inserting them into the holes one by one. We had contests to see who could climb all the way up and around and back down the other side. Competitions like this really motivated me.

My immediate passion for wrestling followed me all the way home like a little puppy dog. I'd fly through the front door and demonstrate the moves I'd learned that afternoon on my mom or sisters. I'd show my guinea pigs what a half nelson or what a quarter nelson or reversal was. I'm sure they all appreciated my enthusiasm.

The workouts were gruelling, even for a team of energetic twelve-year-olds. We started with jumping rope, and then did push-ups and callisthenics. When we were worn down enough and gasping for each breath, we'd wrestle each other. Coach Casebeer was very fair and straightforward, a no-nonsense kind of a guy. We worked our butts off, but he always made it fun. He taught us all kinds of funny sayings like, "When in doubt, get out!" that we wrote in huge black letters on his tag boards of wisdom. I think we had a rhyme for every different situation we could get into on the mat.

By ninth grade, I was part of an undefeated team, so Coach Casebeer took us to a wrestling meet at Lynnwood High School. Bobby's brothers were on the varsity team by then, and they were taking on Rogers High School, who'd won the state championship the year before. I'll never forget that team because they had a particular intensity and seemed to move as one. They did everything as a team, and were so organised, almost militant. Coach Casebeer wanted us to see how serious they were and how hard they worked.

"Now that's what a state championship team looks like," he told us, as we watched them kick the dogsnot out of Lynnwood.

Before our own matches, Coach Casebeer walked by every anxious wrestler in the line-up—he'd rub our shoulders and stretch our arms out a bit. Then he'd give us a bear hug from behind, picking us up and cracking our backs. And just before we'd walk out to the mat, he'd smack us on the arse. He smacked so hard that half of us walked out rubbing our arse cheeks, it hurt so bad. But the sting distracted us. Coach didn't want us going out there all worried about our opponent, or about being out on the mat all by ourselves.

Though we never talked about anything more than wrestling, Coach Casebeer filled a void for me and became a great father figure. He taught me how to give it my all and win. He also taught me how to lose. He was never upset if I lost—instead, he would talk to me about the mistakes I made in the match and what I could do better next time. I learned to focus on the problems, correct them and not get emotional about it.

I began at 102 pounds and lost more matches than I won, but I kept at it.

At the district meet in eighth grade, I had to wrestle my best friend, Mark Baggerly, and I felt conflicted. We'd wrestled at different weight classes the entire season, and for some reason they paired us together in the final meet. It was difficult to wrestle somebody that I liked, and it got in the way of competing to my full ability. When I lost the match I was angry, and disappointed that I hadn't wrestled as hard as I could. I didn't know if Mark was better than me or not, and my hesitation left that question unanswered. This feeling was much worse than actually losing, and I vowed to always do my best from there on out.

In ninth grade, our team was undefeated and I won a majority of my matches, but my progress was short-lived. In tenth grade, I only won about five matches the entire year. By junior year, I was struggling to make the varsity team, and wrestled with the junior varsity squad for half the year. I challenged at 141, 148, 158, then 168 pounds and got beat by all those guys. Finally, I went all the way up to the 178-pound division. I only weighed 158 pounds, so I drank gallons and gallons of water to weigh in and earn the varsity slot. I wrestled the rest of the season at 178, and I had to fill myself like a camel every time, so I'd be no more than 20 pounds under on competition day.

Years later in the UFC, I would make a name for myself by taking on opponents who were 30 and 40 pounds heavier than me. But I'd actually had plenty of experience being the "little guy."

The move up in weight classes worked. I went .500 in my junior season and ended up qualifying to be an alternate for the state championship. In my senior year, I wrestled at my natural weight of 168 pounds and lost only four matches the whole year. I quit my job as a grocery bagger to concentrate on that season and won the state title—

the first one ever for my high school. It was one of those great moments when the whole team rushed out onto the mat and hoisted me up on their shoulders.

In the off-season, I played other sports. I went out for the basketball team, and it was the only time I ever got cut because I was too small. I was disappointed that I didn't make the team, though, because most of my wrestling buddies did. The basketball coach told me I could still come and be a manager or a statistician, and I thought, *the hell with that. That's for geeks*.

I wasn't going to be a number cruncher, so me and a kid named Paul Schmidt, who hadn't tried out for basketball, joined the girls' gymnastics team. It was a small, mostly disorganised programme, but they couldn't keep us from trying out. They didn't even have the men's apparatus like the pummel horse or high bar, but that didn't matter. We practised on the rings and vault, and when we got bored with that, we practised climbing the trusty peg board. Mostly though, we hung out with the girls.

I WAS POPULAR with the girls. You could say I epitomised the "strong, silent type," and since I'd grown up in a house with three women, being around them didn't faze me as much as it did the less experienced guys.

In junior high, my friends' parents hosted Halloween and Christmas-themed parties with dance contests in their basements. There was never any alcohol, but there was plenty of making out. I had a pretty unique group of friends at that time. Me and my best friend Mark had a group of girls we both pretty much dated at one point or another. Before the famous movie came out, we called ourselves "the Breakfast Club," because we'd meet on Fridays at a different house and that person would have to cook for the whole group.

Jodi Morrison was my first girlfriend and we kept it pretty simple, holding hands and kissing. Her mom drove us to the movies, and one summer I went on vacation with them to the ocean. Mrs. Morrison was a bubbly and vivacious single mom who loved hanging around us kids. She had one of those old station wagons with the back seat facing in the opposite direction. At stop lights, she'd call "Chinese fire drill!" and everybody would pile out of the car and switch their seats. I think it made her feel young. "You're always trying to feel Jodi's apples, aren't ya?" she would ask me playfully.

In high school, I guess I was a jock, but I moved through almost all the social circles. I went on bible retreats with the religious kids. I was also welcomed down at the "mud pits," an open lot in the middle of nowhere where the party crowd lit a bonfire and chugged beer on Saturday nights after the football games.

Mark and I played just about every sport together until high school, when he decided he liked basketball better than wrestling. I think his parents pressured him to stick with hoops. But senior year, Mark came back—he made the varsity wrestling team and got all the way to the district meet. We did everything together, and Mark's house became my home away from home. I called Mark's parents "Ma and Pa Bags" and they were like my surrogate parents. Pa Bags worked on my car with me all the time.

Some of my old friends had gotten more into the party scene, but Mark and I stuck primarily to sports and academics. We experimented a little bit here and there, drinking beer and smoking pot a couple of times. Our friend Vince Grant's mom used to let us have keggers, so on weekends we'd usually sneak out to his house. Mrs. Grant would collect everybody's car keys, thinking it was better for us all to be in front of her partying where she could keep an eye on us. Vince's band, Reign, provided the entertainment and kids would come from all over. Reign were pretty good—they won a local "Battle of the Bands" contest a few years later beating out Queensryche! Vince would always sing "Wild Thing," which brought the house down.

Mark and I liked to stand out front on Vince's deck, drinking beers.

Occasionally, we'd see Pa Bags cruising by, and we'd have to dive for the hedges.

"Oh, shit, that's your dad!" I'd whisper. "You think he saw us?" We never thought he did, but Pa Bags seemed to know what Mark and I were up to all the time. He taped our window once from the outside so we'd rip the seal when we escaped out of it. The next morning, he confronted us with the evidence.

He never got mean or angry about disciplining us, but whatever punishment was handed down to Mark, my mom would inflict on me too.

I spent a lot of time over at the Baggerly's house, as tensions had grown in my own home that drove me away. In my junior year of high school, my mom's marriage with Don began to unhinge.

Don had bought property up in Smokey Point, about forty or forty-five minutes from our home. He was building his dream log cabin and wanted my mom to move up there with him. I still had two more years left of school, so we discussed how I could stay. I wanted to move in with my friend Donny, who was an only child and had the room to take me in, while the rest of the family moved up to the cabin.

I'd known Donny since the first grade. His parents were very loving and generous. They treated us to season tickets to see our local pro soccer team, the Seattle Sounders, and they took me skiing with them all the time. Donny was on the ski team at Stevens Pass, a local resort. His family did well, so Donny had three pairs of skis and a ski pass, and spent a lot of time up in the lodge during the ski season. I secretly envied him. As a kid, my heroes were Olympic skiers like the dashing Frenchman Jean-Claude Killy, and the brooding "Austrian Astronaut," Franz Klammer. I couldn't afford the lessons to race, but I liked to go fast down the moguls. I flipped off chairlifts and built ramps in the woods so I could practise jumping all day.

My family hardly had the means to support my love of skiing, but Donny's did. He graduated early so he could pursue skiing full-time. He was en route to making the U.S. Ski Team when he had an accident.

He flew off a ski course, hit a tree, and broke his back. The injuries left him paralysed from the chest down and confined to a wheelchair for the rest of his life.

I remember going to the hospital in eastern Washington to visit him. He was strapped into one of those huge beds that rotated to keep him from getting pneumonia. His head was split open and he looked a mess. When I left the room, I cried my eyes out.

But Donny's spirit was remarkable. "What are you going to do?" he'd ask me. "Write to your congressman?" He went right on to play wheelchair basketball and race four-wheeled Odyssey go-carts. He went back to skiing in toboggans the next year as soon as he was healthy enough. I'd go to his house and we'd fly around the neighbourhood together, me in his extra wheelchair. That was his workout, like he was going running. He'd just take his chair out, and I'd be right beside him. Years later, he raced the Boston Marathon in his chair. I'm sure he had his down moments, but I certainly never saw them. Donny gave me perspective.

In the end, I never stayed with Donny. My mom got cold feet with the cabin, and that's when the whole marriage soured. She kicked Don out, but he came back one evening after he'd been drinking. My mom asked Don to leave and he called her a bitch. I shoved him off the front porch, and things escalated. I persuaded him to leave and that was that. Don ended up moving up to the cabin, and he and my mom got divorced. I was thankful to not have to move away, but at that point, it didn't affect me on an emotional level. Plus, I got the car out of it. Mom wasn't as fortunate. She felt like she had failed.

WITH DON'S EXIT, I happily finished out my last two years at Lynnwood High School. Things got interesting when I met Sharon Kumma.

It was attraction at first sight. Blonde, with a fair complexion, blue eyes, and a five-foot-two athletic build, she'd caught my eye at a girls' soccer game. She was one of the star players, and also a standout in fast-pitch softball. Her sports prowess was definitely a turn-on. Sharon was one of six kids whose parents loved sports, and they sponsored teams through their local upholstery store. Her bedroom was a trophy case.

In the hallway, I asked her to one of the school dances. She'd just broken up with her longtime boyfriend, Bill Wilkins, but she said no, and ended going back to him any way.

In the summer between my junior and senior year, I took a school trip to Europe, romping through France, Austria, and Italy. When I got back, Sharon's brother Norm told me that she and Bill had broken up, so I asked her out again. This time she said yes.

Sharon had an adorable giggle. Her parents were devout Lutherans, and she was shy, reserved, and somewhat conservative. She worked hard for her grades and became valedictorian. She and I were both named Athlete of the Year our senior term.

Sharon and I dated our entire senior year, but we broke up right before graduation. I had just turned eighteen, and I spent the summer dating other people and partying like a madman. I saw Sharon occasionally, but I was busy working as a custodian at the local mall, hanging out with my friends, and getting into typical teenage trouble.

Neither of my parents had been to college, so it wasn't even discussed until my senior year. I had gotten offers to some two-year junior colleges, but I wanted the experience of a big school campus. I decided to walk on to Washington State University in Pullman, the only Division I school in the state that still had a wrestling programme.

I sold my car to pay for my first year, and my mom drove me across the state and dropped me off. I rolled right into training with the wrestling team, and a month later, the coach announced that there would be wrestle-offs for the varsity slots to compete in the first tournament of the year right before Thanksgiving. I wrestled for the

190-pound weight class and was beat out by a returning team member. He travelled with the team to the tournament, while I was left behind on campus. It was very cold outside and I was all alone in the dorm, so I got on a Greyhound bus and rode home for Thanksgiving.

Over the long weekend, I went on a date with Sharon, who had enrolled at the University of Washington in Seattle. Three weeks later, the phone in my dorm rang. It was Sharon and she had big news. She was pregnant.

I stood there in shock, the receiver frozen to my face. I didn't know what to think. First I asked her if she was sure. Then I mustered up the courage to ask her what she wanted to do. Sharon was petrified. Coming from a strict Lutheran family, she had never even gone to a movie before she started dating me. I had corrupted her. I suggested an abortion, and she said no, that she would have the baby with or without me. That was that. I asked her to marry me right there. She said yes.

My first thought was that I wasn't going to be like my dad. I would have to marry her. When I told my friends on the dorm floor, they tried to convince me that I didn't have to. They were dead set against it, but I had made up my mind. Sharon drove to Washington State with her sister and brother-in-law, picked me up, and we made a silent, five-hour drive back to Lynnwood.

I showed up on my mom's front porch unannounced This was the first time my mom had gotten wind of my decision and there was a huge blow-up. Like my friends, my mom was adamant that I not marry Sharon. She told me to go back to school, and that Sharon could join me back up there so I could get my degree. I didn't see how that was going to work. What about Sharon? She had been in school too. Why should she have to give that up? We talked in circles the whole evening, and I felt the apron strings were cut that night for sure.

My mom called my father the next day. Over the phone, he told me he didn't think I should marry this girl. He had no idea that at the time, what concerned me most was that I wouldn't abandon my child the way he had.

We had my bachelor party at Donny's house, and sitting there in his living room next to him in his wheelchair, I tried to put things in perspective. Maybe it wouldn't be so bad. Of course, I had my reservations. That night, a friend and I drove over to an ex-girlfriend's house. A little tipsy, I knocked on her window at three in the morning. I spent the rest of the night sitting in her room talking to her about what I should do. She saw my hesitation and agreed with the others who thought getting married was a mistake. I felt even more confused.

Sharon and I were married by her uncle, a minister, at his church in Edmonds, Washington, on February 13, 1982. We had a traditional ceremony with around a hundred family members and friends. We honeymooned at Ocean Shores, a small beach town on the coast of Washington with little bungalows. We stayed for a long weekend, eating dinner, renting mopeds, and playing in the sand. I think Sharon was happy. She was in love. Honestly, I couldn't say I was as sure, but there was no way of getting out of it now.

4 CHAPTER FOUR:
WHAT'S MEANT TO BE

ADVERSITY COMES IN ALL SHAPES AND SIZES. OVER the last eleven years, my opponents have gotten younger and fresher, while I just seem to get older. As one of the lighter competitors in the heavyweight division, I've stared across the cage at monsters 40 to 60 pounds heavier than me, thinking to myself, *how am I going to get out of this one?* It's just the nature of the game. The truth is, we all face adversity in our lives, through our work or our relationships with family and friends. No one is immune.

My trick has always been to work backwards. Sometimes I have to minimise all the negative thoughts and worries surrounding a situation and get right to the heart of the problem. I figure out what the solution is, and then I quickly develop a plan to get myself there. I concentrate on getting it done and nothing else.

It's how I've always tackled life's twists and turns. When I wanted to go to Europe with my buddies the summer between my junior and senior years of high school, my best friend Mark and I worked at a chicken farm for six bucks an hour, cleaning the barns and catching chickens. We did it all between football and soccer practise after school, until we had the money.

Of course, chasing chickens wasn't going to solve the very real problems I now faced as a 19-year-old college dropout with a pregnant wife. For the first time in my life I was truly scared. My mother desperately wanted me to go back to school, and Sharon's family had offered for us to come and live with them, so they could help raise the baby. But I didn't want to be dependent on anyone, so I devised my own plan.

Before I married Sharon, my mother had convinced me to go back up to college that January to take my finals and finish out the semester. Walking around the small town of Pullman alone, I contemplated what had happened and how I could possibly find a way to cope with it all. My feet stopped in front of a U.S. Army recruitment office.

I took the Armed Services Vocational Aptitude Battery (ASVAB) and qualified for any job in the military I requested. Of all people, I credit former president Ronald Reagan for the one I chose. It was 1982. A year before, President Reagan had taken a stand by firing nearly 12,000 members of the Professional Air Traffic Controllers Organisation when they had gone on strike for better pay and conditions. The walkout had crippled the aviation industry overnight, and the Federal Aviation Agency (FAA) had to compensate by pulling qualified military personnel out of the service to fill the vacant civilian positions that would keep commercial air travel going.

This caused a ripple effect, and the U.S. army offered a $5,000 signing bonus to anyone who qualified to become an air traffic controller. I had always been interested in aviation, thinking I might become a helicopter pilot. The recruiter told me flight schools didn't take in civilians directly, so I was better off joining the service and then trying to get into flight school. I didn't know if it was a bunch of malarkey or not, but that bonus sure sounded good. Best of all, it would get Sharon and me out of Lynnwood and away from the tug-of-war between our parents. That was reason enough for me.

I guess the army managed to convince quite a few people with the same pitch. The schools were so backed up that they put me on delayed entry until October, which was seven months away. In the meantime, Sharon and I rented a tiny one-bedroom apartment in Everett, just north from where we'd both grown up. Marco had floated back into my mother's life, and helped me get a job as a groundskeeper at Shriner's Golf Course in Aurora Village, about twenty minutes from our apartment. I mowed and tended to the greens to pay our rent, and my mom gave us a used Audi Fox station wagon.

Both our families had become accustomed to the idea that we were going to handle our lives our own way and backed off quite a bit. Everyone's attention soon turned to the arrival of the baby.

Ryan Duane Couture was born at Virginia Mason Hospital in Seattle on August 27, 1982. Like his father, Ryan was a fairly large baby at a hearty 8 pounds, 12 ounces. Since Sharon was so petite, Ryan got stuck in her pelvis during delivery and his head wouldn't pop out. They put a monitor on him, and during contractions, his heart rate began to drop. Standing there in the delivery room in my paper booties and cap, I was petrified.

I'd had a nightmare that something bad was going to happen and that Sharon might die. When I was eleven years old, my Aunt Yvonne had passed away during childbirth, and the news had unglued me. I was lying in bed when my mom got the call late at night, and I remember crawling out from underneath my covers to get a better listen. Aunt Yvonne had come to live with us for a few months while my uncle was in the navy and deployed on a ship. We used to stay up late and watch Elvis Presley movies together, and I had grown especially close to her She had two little boys, Cary and Shawn, and was giving birth to their third boy, Jamie, when there were complications. She didn't make it through the birth alive.

The dread of that loss loomed over me as I waited there in the hospital, watching Sharon suffer. Twelve hours passed, and nothing happened. The doctors concurred that an emergency Caesarean would be needed, and I followed helplessly as they raced Sharon down the hallway to the operating room, trying to keep up with her gurney.

A few minutes later, Ryan was on Sharon's chest nestled in a blanket. I crouched down next to my wife and son, feeling that odd sense you only get from experiencing something surreal. I had watched the surgery and the mess that came from it. That was real, but having my son Ryan in the same room as me wasn't quite fathomable. He had a cone-head from being stuck in there so long and his skin was a faint yellow tint from a slight case of jaundice, but otherwise, he was perfect.

Ryan stayed in the hospital an extra three days, and then he came home. Knowing he'd never have the ability to experience what I just had, I asked my friend Donny to become Ryan's godfather.

I HARDLY HAD any time with my newborn son before I was called to basic training that October at Fort Bliss in El Paso, Texas. One of my last nights in Washington, my friends threw me a party at Donny's house and shaved my head so the army wouldn't have to. I wanted to do it on my own terms. When I got to boot camp, the drill sergeants dubbed me "Rockhead" because my scalp took on a shade of blue in the places where my hair had once been. A couple of weeks in, it was shortened to "Rock." It just seemed more fitting.

You know how in the movies the bus pulls up and the clueless-looking guys file off, dragging their duffle bags to get into formation as drill sergeants blast orders into their ears every inch of the way? The army was exactly like that.

I loved it. I thought it was cool. I wasn't used to having drill sergeants yell at me the way they did, and it was a little intimidating, but the army was the right fit at the right time in my life.

Once I got through the first few days in the reception station, collecting my uniforms and gear, going through medicals and getting my shots, and then settling into my barracks, the army was just one big exercise in physical fitness. It was countless push-ups, running in bulky combat boots in formation, and obstacle courses every day—and I felt right at home. Compared to the gruelling physical training of any wrestling practise, the military was a cakewalk.

Of course there was more to learn: how to set up mines, how to break down a weapon, how to brush your teeth the military way. A lot of it was tedious and just common sense, and they had us up at four in the morning until eight or nine at night, sometimes past that, pulling guard duty.

They pushed me and they motivated me, and I appreciated the routine. It was almost a luxury, to be told what to do and not have to make my mind up for myself. Hell, I got in more trouble for smiling in basic training than anything else! They'd get in my face and yell, and it would always make me grin. I couldn't tell you how many push-ups I did for cracking a smile.

The parallels between the army and wrestling went far beyond the physical grunt work and mental stamina. Like wrestling, the army provided familiarity. The guys in my unit became comrades I could depend on, a team. The same group of guys went through the same experiences, and I felt a sense of safety because I wasn't alone.

Basic training lasted ten weeks, but they released us in eight so we could go home for Christmas, then we'd return to complete the last two. I was looking forward to seeing Sharon and my son Ryan, but something else was brewing inside of me.

After finding out Sharon was pregnant, I had gone on auto pilot. I don't say this to explain my actions or make light of them or justify them. I had focused on becoming a father and finding a way to support Sharon and the baby, working toward my solution. But I think in the process, I also began to compartmentalise my life, separating aspects of myself from other parts.

Over that Christmas break, I found myself over my ex-girlfriend Roxanne's house. I had dated Roxanne in high school until she moved away after our sophomore year. She came back to our town the summer after I'd gotten married. I remember Sharon had been very jealous when we had all gone out together with a group of friends and Roxanne and I slow-danced together for a song.

I sat in Roxanne's living room, confiding to her how I regretted that we'd never gotten together. I thought Roxanne was the cat's meow, and

I found myself very attracted to her. Looking at her, and feeling the heat, I became a nineteen-year-old boy again. I broke my bond of marriage that day.

It was the first of two occasions during this time when I had strayed from Sharon. Another girl who had fancied me all throughout high school tracked me down during my break at home to tell me about all these feelings she had for me. She even told me she'd been trying to find me the night before I got married. Later, when I went back to army training, she wrote to me saying she'd gotten pregnant after our brief affair and had gotten an abortion. I was blown away, but Sharon never found out, and the girl just drifted out of my life.

I WENT ON to my advanced training at the monstrous Fort Rucker, stretched out on some 61,300 acres of Alabama countryside known as Wiregrass County. Recognised as the central hub for army aviation training, this is where I began to learn the special skills needed to become an air traffic controller. This time, Sharon and Ryan came with me and stayed in a little house not far from the base. I used my pay from the army to cover rent for the next five months of training.

Back in the recruiters' office a year and a half before, I jotted down two places I wanted to be considered for placement: Hawaii or Alaska, where my dad was living. I didn't expect to get my wish. In June, with my advanced training completed, I was shipped off to Erlensee, Germany. Sharon and Ryan went back to Seattle and waited for me to send word when I'd found a place for us to live.

It took me most of the summer to find an apartment. The waiting list for on-post housing was very long, so I walked through the streets around the *kaserne* (German for "base"), trying to find an apartment for the three of us to live in. During those three months, I turned twenty-one and I met a girl on the base named Barb, who I spent a lot of my free time with. We went to the movies and she took me out on my twenty-first birthday. We kissed, but it never went any further. I just didn't want to be alone.

I finally found a little place, an absolute dump of an apartment, in the back of a Citroën junkyard. (A Citroën is a compact French car.) We had to walk through a maze of twisted metal and glass, then behind a derelict gas station to get to the tiny attachment. It was substandard, but I was going on three months by myself, and I was anxious to see my family. Once I could provide an address, the army cut orders for Sharon, Ryan, and all our household goods to be shipped over.

Our first night in the junkyard we placed Ryan in a low bed in the room adjacent to ours. In the morning I was up early, preparing to leave, when I heard Sharon screaming from his bedroom. Ryan had disappeared. Fearful that he had been kidnapped, we ransacked the apartment until we could hear his soft, muffled cries. He had fallen out of the low bed and dozed back to sleep underneath it. The commotion we created looking for him had woke him up and he had bumped his head on the bed.

It took us a few months to find better accommodations. We finally located an apartment above a bakery in the next town over, and I rode my bike to the *kaserne* every morning in twenty minutes flat, almost as fast as I drove the car. We became friends with another military couple staying in a nicer basement apartment in a town called Langendiebach, only about five minutes outside the main gate of the base. When the couple got transferred stateside, we moved into their basement place and lived there the rest of our time in Germany.

Living off the base exposed us to the German culture and its people, and Sharon and I soaked up the opportunity to experience something different than our small-town lives. The military gave us a decent cost-of-living allowance, and we took advantage of the USO tours offered to Austria, Switzerland, Bavaria, Italy, and France. We joined the ski club and explored as many new slopes as we could on three- and four-day weekends.

Our landlord, Ken Schaeffer, an American GI, had married a

German girl named Anita. Ken had been there so long he had forgotten how to speak English. Anita's mother lived on the third floor, Ken and Anita took the second floor, and we occupied the basement. Grandma Schaeffer or "Oma," as we called her, babysat Ryan when we travelled. My mom and sister visited from America and went on trips with us well.

I had enlisted to become an air traffic controller, and there were two types that I was trained for. Tactical air traffic control simulated wartime procedure. I had to be able to set up an "LZ," or landing zone, in a farmyard or a field or just about anywhere. Fixed-base air traffic control was more like a stationary airport, with a runway and a tower. The unit that I was stationed at in Hanau, Germany, handled both.

This was at the peak of the Cold War, and every year we participated in the "Exercise Reforger," derived from REturn of FORces to GERmany. This annual event simulated the Russians coming over through the mountains to invade western Europe. The exercise tested the army's ability to handle such a threat, and it was a war game that involved the one million U.S. soldiers serving in Europe at the time.

If that was all I did during my military service, I probably would have been content. I had my family and was supporting them on my own, something my father had not been willing to do himself. But sometimes life throws you more.

I always like to say that what's meant to be is meant to be. I believe sometimes what first appears as a problem is really an opportunity to embrace something new, a chance to take a different road and see what happens. If I hadn't joined the army, I might never have wrestled again. Luckily, wrestling seemed to be looking for me.

I WAS IN Germany for less than two weeks when a field artillery lieutenant approached me while I was lifting weights at the gym on the base.

"You look like a wrestler. You work out?" he asked. I hadn't earned my bumpy, mat-torn cauliflower ears yet, so I'm not quite sure how he knew. I told him I'd wrestled in high school. The lieutenant invited me to the local wrestling club, Taurnigemain Langendiebach, the next night. I enjoyed getting back on the mats. After we worked out, the group told me they were heading to a tournament the next weekend and asked me if I wanted to join them.

"What kind of wrestling?" I asked.

"Freestyle."

I'd never wrestled freestyle before, but they threw me in and I did just fine, enough to rekindle my interest again.

I now had a club I could practise with, and a new goal. Many of my new teammates had the goal to make the All-Army wrestling team, a prestigious squad with stringent auditions whose athletes competed at the national and international level, including the Olympics.

To earn a position on the All-Army team, you first had to gain the attention of its coach by placing well in a succession of army tournaments held throughout the year. If he saw what he liked, you got an invitation to try out for the team. With wrestlers being recruited into the army just to fill the team, invitations from within were scarce and highly selective. Until you made the All-Army team, you practised in the club and prepared for the next tournament in addition to your regular military duties.

I learned quickly that army wrestling was rooted in history and technique. I also learned there were three major wrestling styles: freestyle, folkstyle (or collegiate), and Greco-Roman. The United States has a long heritage of folkstyle wrestlers (which is what I wrestled in high school), dating back to the early 1900s.

Much like sumo wrestling is primarily practised in Japan, the United States is the only country that practises folkstyle (it is not represented in the Olympics). Like freestyle wrestling, folkstyle utilises leg attacks, where the opponent can perform a "shot," or dive, on his target. All Greco-Roman holds and throws take place while holding your opponent's frame from the waist up, making it much more upright and subtle.

Since folkstyle is taught and practised in high schools and colleges nationwide, many wrestlers transition to freestyle when they hit the national and international levels of competition. Very few American wrestlers are coached in Greco-Roman at the start.

Wrestling freestyle was technically an easier adjustment for me. I saw the Greco matches going on but had never tried it. With a few competitions under my belt, I entered the 1983 Fifth Core Regional Championships in Germany in the freestyle bracket. I stood on the sidelines waiting for my match to start, when I heard my name called out on the Greco mat. I was stunned. I ran over to the official's table and told them there must have been a mix-up.

"Well, you're listed here," the official said, gazing down at the clipboard in front of him. His eyes rose to meet mine. "Are you wrestling or not?" he asked.

That was all I needed.

I felt like I was ten years old again, on the mat for the first time in the Alderwood Junior High School gym. I didn't know what I was doing. I just knew I couldn't go for his legs. I kept thinking I could grab him any way from the belt up to get him down and score. It became a fun challenge and my body adapted well. I went through all my opponents one by one to win the tournament.

My name eventually got called for the freestyle bracket, and I won that tournament as well. It was a good day.

Winning the Fifth Core Regional Championships qualified me for the All-European tournament, called the USAREUR (U.S. Army Europe). This time, I entered both the freestyle and Greco-Roman competitions. I won the freestyle and took second in the Greco after I was thrown on my head in the finals. The All-Army coach, Floyd Winter, was watching. He had a Greco background so he looked especially hard at that category. But he invited the guy that had beaten me to the tryouts instead.

I wasn't disappointed. I was motivated. I had found an outlet again for my competitive spirit. I went back to my unit as a regular soldier and trained even harder on the side at my local German club. My teammates decided to speak to me only in German, so I picked up a lot of the language as well.

FOR THE FIRST two years in Germany, I spent most of my time pulling shifts in the radar tower. One of my co-workers, Henry, was a competitive powerlifter and he exposed me to proper weight training. I had lifted on a plastic Universal gym at Lynnwood High School, so my knowledge was limited. He taught me to squat and explained what a deadlift was.

Henry was an animated guy, constantly frustrated that he couldn't break into the top three of his competitions. He suspected most of his competitors were doing steroids. He began bringing all this literature in, reams and reams of paper with information on all different steroids, how they worked and what they did to your body. Later in my career, it was always reputed that the Russians were getting special "vitamins" from their coaches as part of their programmes. But I never really knew about steroids until I met Henry.

He eventually dabbled in them, and as they go, I think he handled them fairly safely, because they didn't seem to change him that much. In wrestling, a weight class sport, it just didn't make sense to me to even think about using steroids. I never felt like I needed to get bigger or stronger. The guys who used them reminded me of ticking time bombs. One minute, a guy was Superman, lifting incredibly heavy weight and acting super confident. But when the season would come around, he'd have to get off them to make his weight class, and his bench-press numbers would go down again. Then he felt like he was a piece of shit. It was a vicious cycle I wanted no part of.

Outside my tower duties, I trained hard with my wrestling club to prepare for another crack at the next round of competitions. Sharon and I also decided to have another child, and she quickly became pregnant. If you can ever have a kid in the military, I would recommend it. My daughter Aimee Jean was born October 10, 1984, in a Frankfurt hospital—a 7-pound, 13-ounce bundle for a bargain $25. Her big brother Ryan's birth had run us $2,500 two years before.

The climb up the wrestling pyramid began again that year when I came back and won both the freestyle and Greco-Roman brackets, again in the Fifth Core tournament. At the USAREUR Championship, I placed first in freestyle and took second in the Greco finals again, but I showed a lot of improvement in a really close match. The guy that had beaten me, Lonnie Shelton, had already been to the All-Army trials before, so the coach invited us both this time.

I was released on temporary duty to fly to Fort Dix, New Jersey, for the tryouts, three of the most ball-breaking weeks I've ever been through. We trained "two-a-days," with a session in the morning, and another at night after we'd ate and rested. I had rashes up and down my forearms, inside my legs, and around my waist from drilling gut-wrenches over and over, but in the end, it paid off. Coach Winter selected me for the team.

I had made it onto the squad through the back door. Coach Winter had recruited most of the team from college standouts and from scouting tournaments in the United States and in Europe. Here I was, a guy who didn't even know you could wrestle in the army, getting a spot. Special TDY, or temporary orders, were cut for me to leave my unit, and I was assigned to the All-Army wrestling team training for six months in Fort Dix. My commander was very supportive about the move. He was an athlete himself, and he often let our unit play football and softball in our downtime.

My life in the army was now about wrestling. The army was just as serious about getting its athletes to the Olympics as any other private coach—who would charge a fortune to train with—so I felt confident in the programme.

Six-foot-two, 220 pounds, but wiry and nimble, Coach Winter was the first American to win a Greco-Roman gold medal in world competition at the 1972 World Military Championships in Ankara, Turkey. He shepherded three army athletes to the Olympics in his eight years coaching the team. He had also served in the 101st Airborne division during the Vietnam War. I liked Coach Winter from the start. He was funny, personable, and always smiling, with a quick wit. He had an anxious energy that made him almost stutter. I later listened to him deliver a speech about Pankrationists, the world's first mixed martial artists, at a banquet. I was blown away. He didn't even seem like the same guy, he spoke with such eloquence and passion.

The All-Army wrestling programme was based on merit. As long as you kept winning you got to stay. I wanted to stay more than anything. I didn't mind the air traffic control duty, but wrestling was way more fun. I hardly ever wore a uniform, wrestled all the time, and hung out with the guys.

During those six months at Fort Dix, I wrestled at national and international tournaments—basically wherever the coach sent the team. My first international trip lasted three weeks as we toured through Sweden, Norway, and Bulgaria to compete in three different tournaments. Wrestling tournaments were taken seriously in these parts, complete with elaborate opening and closing ceremonies, although our accommodations differed vastly. In Sweden, at the Malar Cup, the food was as good as the top dogs who came out to compete. In Bulgaria, still under Eastern Bloc rule, we stayed in a dingy, run-down hotel with faucets that barely dripped water and ate cold mashed potatoes, pickles and cold cuts. A Politburo member escorted us around at all times. Moving from tournament to tournament, I didn't know what my living situation would be like or how it would affect me. But I always stepped onto the mat with the best in the world and was expected to deliver.

In Europe, I really got to a sense of where I stood. I watched two little Scandinavian boys, both no more than ten years old, throw each other around with techniques I hadn't even learned yet. It was an eye-opener and I got my arse kicked as the resident throwing dummy, never coming close to placing. In the next three years, I made some sixty trips and soaked up all the technique and knowledge I could.

While I travelled between the New Jersey barracks and to competitions around the world, Sharon took the kids home to Seattle and came to visit me at the meets she could get to stateside. Those six months culminated at the Concord Cup, the only Class A Greco-Roman international tournament held each year in Concord, California. Afterward, I was sent back to Germany, and Sharon and the kids followed me back overseas.

I eventually spent less and less time in my air traffic control unit and became more involved as an athlete for the army. I spoke at high schools back in the States, ran wrestling seminars, and performed other tasks for the recruiting command as my athletic career progressed.

Joining the army team was a serious endeavour. I spent a lot of time in the barracks with the other wrestlers. There were only a couple of them who were married, so I basically hung around all the single guys. During the competition cycle, I would leave Germany for Fort Dix or West Point or wherever the army's training camp was that year for six-month stretches. I'd see Sharon maybe once a month. She'd come to a tournament, or I'd get time off to go home for a weekend. Sharon often took the kids back to Washington to stay with my folks or her folks. That's how we got along.

The first couple of years it seemed okay. I didn't think that much about our relationship. I had a job to do and just plugged away.

With the army team, I travelled anywhere from California to Russia. During this time, I met other women, and acted on my emotions a few times. It made me realise I was missing something. I felt guilty, and I knew what I was doing was wrong, but at the same time, I was beginning to realise the marriage I was in wasn't right either. When it came time to decide whether I was going to stay in the army or leave, I started analysing whether I was happy or not with the decisions I'd made with Sharon. The more time I spent away from my wife, the more I strayed from her.

At the end of my service, I had amassed a substantial résumé of national and international victories, and a path had cleared in front of me, with the Olympics a possibility on the horizon. It was 1986, and the Olympic Trials were nearly two years away. If I re-enlisted and continued to train with the army team, I had a shot. I'd never been stationed stateside and wanted to experience what that was like. So I signed up again, and Sharon, Ryan, Aimee and I headed home.

5 CHAPTER FIVE:
DOUBLE LEGS, DOUBLE LIFE

I DIDN'T HAVE A CHANCE. NOT IN A MILLION YEARS. AT least that's what everybody around me seemed to think. If I had listened, I would have ETSed, or exited, out of the army in 1986, but I thought I had a shot at taking wrestling all the way. As long as I believed in myself, that was all that mattered. I'd convince the rest in due time.

I extended my enlistment for two years. Timing was everything— it was sixteen months out from the 1988 Olympic Trials. If I remained in the service, the army would cover all my training and support my family financially while I wrestled to qualify. It just didn't make sense to walk away now.

I was stationed at Fort Campbell, which extends over both Tennessee and Kentucky, about sixty miles northwest of the cradle of country music in Nashville. Trying to put my best foot forward, I entered the 101st Airborne Division's Screaming Eagles, the only air assault division in the world. Instead of landing helicopters, I would now enter the battlefield rappelling out of them. I thought it would look better to my new commander if I committed to this esteemed programme.

To continue wrestling, I had to be released from my duty station to attend training camp. My commander had other plans. In his opinion, the army had spent enough money to train me as an air traffic controller, and he wanted them to recoup every penny.

"I'm not releasing you from shit," he said. "You're gonna pull duty in the motor pool and everything else just like every other soldier in this unit. I don't care what you've done or who you are."

But the army wrestling coach wasn't going to let me go that easily, either. He had invested a lot of time in me. Three years of making the team and moving up the national rankings was not something he could quickly replicate in another wrestler.

Stepping over my commander's head, he appealed to the Department of Defence that I was one of his best athletes and needed to be released. It was a fight, but one he eventually won.

I was assigned to a garrisons unit that handled bureaucracy at Fort Campbell and went to work for the sports department.

Fort Campbell was a massive base. I think there were five or six sports centres on the post, and each one had its own baseball diamond and soccer field. Football was played in a massive stadium where they also held parades. I was placed at one of these centres and put in charge of equipment inventory, engraving medals for the tournaments, coordinating soccer leagues for morale, and whatever else was needed. I essentially became a gopher, and that was kind of the point. It got me out of the air traffic control unit and freed up my time so I could go to every wrestling camp available.

I trained twice a day, when I wasn't travelling to a tournament, and went home to Sharon and the kids in our small house right off the base. It was the first time since I'd been in the service that my family was right where I trained and wrestled. Instead of going back to the barracks and hanging out with all the guys, I just went home. Ryan had gone to kindergarten in Germany, where he'd picked up the language, but we decided to enrol him again, this time in English. Aimee started pre-school. Sharon worked as a paralegal for a lawyer in town and we bought a new car. Although Fort Campbell lacked the exotic charms of Europe, we had a lot of our worries taken care of.

Through 1986 to 1988, my focus became the Olympics. Only four years earlier, I hadn't even known what the Olympic wrestling styles were. By 1987, I focused solely on Greco-Roman. I wasn't placing in freestyle anymore, and the coach would pack the Greco tournaments with twenty guys or more, so I had a much better chance. I was always trying to place in the next tournament, which raised my rankings and qualified me for the next one.

To get there, I made sacrifices. In Europe, I had wrestled steadily at 198 pounds. As soon as I rolled into the stateside army camp, the coach looked at me and said,"You're a 180-pounder. You're gonna wrestle 180." I walked around at about 6 percent body fat at 207 pounds. How the hell was I going to make 180?

For the next two years, I ran every day to keep my weight down, clocking in a slew of "road work" hours. I was also extremely restrictive about what I ate. I didn't know much about diet back then, so I consumed mostly greens and a lot of fruit because I knew it wasn't very calorie-rich. I was basically starving myself. I put on plastic suits and ran, and when it got down to the wire, I'd get in the sauna and ride a bike to sweat it out.

In twenty-four months, I missed weight only once. It was at my first U.S. Olympic Festival appearance in 1987 in Durham, North Carolina. Each year, the Olympic Festival hosted all sports, forming East, West, North, and South teams based on where the athletes lived. It was a test of competition, but more importantly, it often doubled as the trials to decide which wrestlers would make the World team that year.

I'd cut eighteen pounds of water weight the day before and wrestled at 180.5 pounds to win the mini-tournament qualifier, which put me in the top three. That gave me the chance to continue on to compete for the World team, but I had to weigh in that afternoon for the next day of competition. Because my bracket had overflowed, I wrestled in the last match of the mini-tournament, which left me with exactly ninety minutes to shed eleven pounds. Others had finished the tournament earlier and had more time to spare. Huffing and puffing away, I got down to within one pound of making weight when my time ran out. The weigh-in procedures were always changing as USA Wrestling tried to tweak the system, and this time out, it hadn't worked in my favour at all.

I had wrestled in about fifty to sixty tournaments during the three years I lived in Germany. When I moved back to the States, the number of tournaments diminished, but the level of competition rose substantially. The army coach sent the teams out to top-notch tournaments. We faced the best guys in the world at events like the Michigan Open or the Eastern Open, and also at international tournaments like the Concord Cup in California, or overseas.

By 1988, I was cracking into the top three in the country. I took third that year at the Nationals, which was the highest I'd placed up to that point. But by the time the Olympic Trials rolled around, I was falling apart. I had such a bad case of Achilles tendonitis in my right ankle from running to keep my weight down that doctors wanted to put me in a cast. It was so brittle and grinding that they worried it might snap. I was also peeing blood. I was an absolute mess, a wreck. I was so sucked up from dehydration that I looked like an anatomical chart for muscles.

In 2007, I ran into an old teammate who pulled out some pictures from a Salvation Army costume party we'd attended in 1988. I didn't even recognise myself. I was decked out in a silky shirt and slacks with a mismatched tie, and I looked like a psychedelic scarecrow.

My voluntary hunger strikes did pay off. I qualified for the Olympic Trials in 1988. I was unable to rise any higher than my third-place win at the Nationals, though, settling as the second alternate for the 1988 Olympic Games in Seoul, Korea, behind the number-one seed, John Morgan. Being a second alternate brought little privilege. I didn't travel with the team to the Games because there was another alternate ahead of me. I didn't really mind, though. I don't think anyone at that time expected me to win a spot on the team, because I was an army wrestler with no previous training. In the back of my mind, I knew I might get another chance at the Olympics.

My family was going through some changes of its own. In Germany, I'd been told that my mom had married Marco, the tavern owner who had ordered the hit on my stepdad Don all those years before. They had waited until my younger sister Traci left for college, and then Marco moved in. In college, Traci met Vince, my high school friend who had thrown all those crazy parties at his house and played in his band Reign. Traci and Vince decided to get married in August of 1988. I was in Kentucky at the time and able to attend her wedding. Traci expected our father, Ed, to walk her down the aisle, but our mother sat her down and revealed something she'd kept from all of us for more than twenty years.

"Ed's not your father," she told Traci. "Your father is Marco and he'll be more than happy to walk you down the aisle."

We were all shocked. Traci almost called the wedding off altogether. It created an identity crisis for her and she didn't know where she fit in the family. Though she looked like our mom, she had always felt she didn't resemble Yolanda or me, and now she knew why. We reassured her that sister or half-sister, she was our blood. It didn't change a damn thing. In the end, Traci allowed Marco to walk her down the aisle, but it took her a long time to come to terms with everything.

I'd never understood why my father had hit my mom in Marco's tavern when I was a little boy. The tensions obviously ran a lot deeper than what she had shared with me, and I saw there was an emotional disconnect because she wouldn't go into detail. I started to doubt my mother's reasons for their divorce: the lack of affection or that we'd moved around too much for her liking. I realised that it had a lot more to do with my mother's affair. I had only been getting one side of the story. I stopped looking at my father as a drunken deadbeat and began to understand him as a man who had been very hurt.

IN THE SUMMER of 1988, I decided not to re-enlist, but I had one final trip wrestling for the army. I had qualified for the team travelling to the World Military Games in Italy. The team also included wrestlers from the marines, the air force, and the navy. We trained for about six weeks in Pensacola, Florida. From there, we flew to Palermo, Sicily. Our team leader was my army supervisor from the sports complex. He coordinated our travel and oversaw the trip. He was my boss back on the base, so I had to watch what I said and did around him. Still, I got a kick out of watching the other wrestlers give him a hard time.

When we landed in Rome, we were told that an Iranian jetliner had been shot down while we were in transit. It was a big international incident. Both the Iranian and Iraqi teams were supposed to come to this event and our superiors were very concerned that we were on an island in the middle of the Mediterranean with the possibility of retaliation. They considered sending us back home but let us vote.

The rest of the athletes and I looked around at each other. Some of us hardly knew each another, but at that moment, it was as if we were the closest of comrades.

"Screw that," we said. "We're this far. We want to wrestle."

The overseeing committee agreed, but took precautions, ordering two armoured cars to meet us at the airport. We travelled to Città del Mar, or "City by the Sea," a spacious resort on the cliffs where all the wealthy Europeans vacationed. Palermo was one of the prettiest places I'd ever seen, and our resort had a series of terraces snaking down the cliffs that connected with slides flowing into pools. The final slide fed right into the Mediterranean. There were tonnes of topless women lounging around the pools on each terrace. Us military guys couldn't ask for a better spot.

We were sequestered from the other teams in a secluded part of the hotel with armed guards stationed outside our rooms. We rode back and forth between the event in the armoured cars. But we never ran into trouble with the Iranians. And the event was a fruitful one for me—I became the military world champion at 180.5 pounds in Greco, the first world title I had ever won.

When I came back from that trip, I had a couple of months to kill in my unit before I left the service in August, so I hung around the gym. A teammate was taking steroids, and started talking me up on a particular type. I thought about it. I bought the steroids from him, but I gave them away to somebody else and never ended up taking them. In a moment of weakness, he had convinced me that they were thing to do, but I chickened out. To this day, I've never taken steroids, even after I entered the UFC.

After six years of serving my country, my final exit date had arrived. I was twenty-five years old. But I wasn't worried about the future. The year before, I had travelled down to Chattanooga with the army team and wrestled in the Southern Open tournament, where I'd won in the 190-pound division twice. The college coaches had taken notice and started asking questions. When they found out I was in the service, their eyes gleamed. Collegiate wrestling regulations state that once you enter the service, your eligibility clock stops until you leave. As a world-experienced wrestler, I still had four full years of promising competition to offer. The phone started ringing and didn't stop all summer. I received calls from a slew of schools, including Clemson University, Southern Illinois University, California State at Bakersfield, and Oklahoma State.

At home, Sharon and I never discussed me going back to school. She seemed happy with whatever I wanted to do and never gave me a hard time about it. Our finances were not a real worry. We figured I would likely get a scholarship, and we were getting money from the army on top of that. I also had a savings plan through the Veterans Administration, and the kids were young enough to transfer schools with little fuss. It would just be another move, and we had been moving all over the place anyway. I think at that point, after living in Europe for three years and dealing with my crazy schedule, there wasn't too much that fazed Sharon.

I decided to tour a few of the colleges, starting with Oklahoma State. When I got off the bus, I was shocked to see Mike Sheets waiting for me. Sheets was an NCAA champion who placed second in the Olympic Trials in freestyle behind the great Mark Schultz, the 1984 Olympic freestyle gold medallist. It was quite a welcome wagon.

If they wanted to make a good first impression on me, they certainly hit the nail on the head. Instead of reporting directly to the wrestling offices or the gym, Mike took me straight out to the woods to go raccoon hunting. We ran around in the middle of the night wearing headlamps and shadowed the dogs as they chased raccoons around until three in the morning. My heart raced again like it did back in my childhood, with my father.

The next day, Mike took me to watch the team train. As a potential recruit, I wasn't allowed to wrestle, but I got to see some of the best wrestlers in the country, like 1988 Olympic gold medallists Kenny Monday and John Smith, sweating it out together in the same mat room.

Although all the college coaches put a lot of pressure on me and it was a tough decision, I enrolled at the storied Oklahoma State. Sharon and I packed up all our stuff and drove from Tennessee to Stillwater, right off campus. I knew the first week we arrived in Stillwater that I'd made the right choice. The people were so friendly. It was a quintessential college town, "Home to the Cowboys and Cowgirls." Oklahoma State was famous for college wrestling. Its athletes had won the first official NCAA Championship in 1929 and repeated the feat a whopping thirty-four more times. The National Wrestling Hall of Fame was on the campus, and it just had a feel to it that made me believe my wrestling career would be nurtured here. I felt like I belonged.

Amazingly, I wasn't the only married guy on the team. There were two others: Chris Barnes, a 170-pounder, and heavyweight Don Frye. Those were the guys I mostly hung out and trained with. I had already been to the Olympic Trials, and lived in Europe, and been around the world through the army. Compared to the freshmen who'd come straight from high school wrestling and knew nothing else, I was the old man of the group. I naturally drifted into a leadership role. It was a unique position to be in, and I quietly accepted the responsibility.

At home, I settled into married life for the first time. I didn't go to many campus parties. My friends took me out for special occasions like my birthday, but that was about it. Chris and Don were in the same boat. They weren't running around the frat houses either, which probably helped keep me on the straight and narrow. I decided to learn the two-step, and got into country music, and those were things I could do with Sharon.

On the road trips though, it was another story. We became crazy men, a team full of single guys out all the time. I was no exception. The team had a nickname for me that had rolled over from my army years. They called me "Bait."

"Put out the Bait and anything he doesn't want, we'll pick up," they'd say. I wasn't too keen on the moniker, but it wasn't enough for me to stop my straying ways.

I don't think all the married guys were out chasing around women. It wasn't like it was encouraged. Most of the guys on the team knew I was married and they certainly knew when I hooked up with a girl, but there was an unspoken pact—what happens on the road, stays on the road.

Back on campus, I stayed focused. It was all about wrestling.

I wanted to get into the Olympics and win a medal. As far as my education, I wasn't as sure. In Germany, I'd learned all the slang and swear words, but I didn't always know how to spell and speak the language. I gravitated toward German classes and liked it. I thought I could be a wrestling coach and teach, or maybe go into international business. I enjoyed it, and got A's and B's without applying myself. I eventually graduated with a major in foreign language and literature.

WRESTLING FOR OKLAHOMA State was a great honour. As a Greco man, I didn't fit the mould of what Oklahoma State usually looks for, which was a freestyle wrestler with slick single- and double-leg shots that would translate well into the collegiate style. The coaches saw something in me that they liked, though, and brought me on anyway.

It was a slow start. Come Christmas, when I had yet to score a takedown in the practise room, I thought I must be getting worse, but that was just the level of athlete I trained with on a daily basis.

The turnouts for meets were massive, and the competitions had an atmosphere all their own. The gymnasium was built to hold 5,000 spectators, but it was standing-room-only when O State came to wrestle. Sometimes there would be 7,000 to 8,000 people in the gym to cheer the Cowboys on—and I loved how the crowd was so loud and passionate. Sharon brought the kids to all of the home meets, and dressed Aimee up in a black-and-orange cheerleader's uniform to support her dad.

I wrestled at 190 pounds my first year and had to fend off senior Don Frye for my slot three days before the Big 8 Conference Tournament. Rugged and manly, with a gravelly voice and a thick, bushy moustache, Don looked like the Marlboro man on a health kick. Don had lost his heavyweight slot to Kirk Mammen, who had "redshirted" most of the year (meaning he trained but didn't compete to save his eligibility). Because Don was transferred in from Arizona State to compete with Oklahoma for his final year, he asked to challenge me for my spot. I didn't appreciate the extra pressure going into one of the final big meets of the season, but I wrestled off with Don and beat him handily on points.

Oklahoma had a top-tier Division I athletic programme, and my skills and dedication soared to the next level. I had just been breaking into the top three in the country when I left the army. My freshman year in college was a big step for me. I went to my first college Nationals tournament and wrestled against even more guys who had been to the Olympics or were competing internationally.

I did well that first year, and got within one match from making All-

American. I ended up losing to a kid from Iowa, Brooks Simpson, in a close match. Simpson went on to win the tournament, but the Oklahoma State team won a National title that year, which eased my disappointment.

Traditionally, Oklahoma State had a very strong wrestling programme, but they hadn't won a National title in seventeen years. Our win was credited to our new coaches, Joe Seay, and his assistant coach, Bruce Barnett. They steered our squad of young guns to National championships two years in a row. Barnett was probably the best coach I ever had. He had an uncanny understanding of the sport and how the athletes could make adjustments to come back and win. He was a super-positive man. You'd work your arse off for him and not think twice. Barnett was the nuts and bolts of the Oklahoma State programme and the driving force behind our success.

From October to March, I wrestled the NCAA collegiate schedule. In March, I went back to the Greco-Roman and freestyle wrestling, run by USA Wrestling, the national governing body of Olympic wrestling. Like all the other hopefuls, I aimed to make the World Team Trials in the non-Olympic years. During that sacred fourth year, the Nationals and Olympic Trials were my only goals.

My path was the same as the guys that were coaching me—many of them were graduate assistants who had taken their posts to train with the team until the next Olympics came around. The difference was that they were all trying to make the freestyle team. I was the lone Greco guy in the programme, and every spring I'd scramble to find Greco partners to wrestle with. I even convinced one of my freestyle teammates to switch over to Greco with me, and he placed.

I won the Nationals in Greco for the first time my sophomore year. That was the moment I realised I really excelled in that style, even though I still dabbled in freestyle in the off-season. I placed fifth that year as an All-American and I contributed points towards my team's National title win. I also became an academic All-American, earning a 4.0 grade-point average for three out of my four years at Oklahoma State.

Every year after the Nationals in April, many of us kept training together in summer camps across the country. I had travelled a lot as an All-Army wrestler, and my new travel schedule continued to wedge Sharon and I further apart. By the end of my sophomore year, Don and Chris were gone, and I was suddenly the only older, married guy on the team.

I FINALLY TRIED to approach Sharon. I hadn't done very well at an invitational in Las Vegas and had gone out and messed around with another woman. I came home feeling guilty and tried to talk to my wife about our lifeless marriage. I didn't tell her about my affairs because there was no one at that point that I thought was significant, but I did want to sort out what was going on in our relationship. I wanted to try and make things better.

I didn't feel good about it. I never felt good about what was going on. I knew that my affairs weren't right, or fair to Sharon. But it didn't make sense for me to drop my indiscretions on her now, simply for my own peace of mind. Instead, I asked her if she thought we would have made the same decisions if we had to do them over again. Sharon looked at me, her eyes flaring. She ran over to our dresser and flung her arm across the top, sending all of her make-up and perfume crashing to the floor. I never brought it up again.

At that stage, the relationship was what it was. We got married at eighteen and did what we had to do to survive. Sharon was pretty easy to get along with, an agreeable person and a good mother. I just wasn't in love with her anymore.

As my home life deteriorated, my athletic career soared, even through a scandal that hit Oklahoma State's wrestling programme my junior year. Our team had won two National titles in a row, and there was a lot of backstabbing and jealousy among the other college coaches in the NCAA. We suddenly found our programme under scrutiny for recruitment violation allegations, which launched an NCAA investigation. A wrestler that we later recruited told us that one of the Notre Dame coaches had turned us in.

The problem is that there are so many goddamn rules. The whole rule book for the NCAA looks like a phone book. I don't care how diligent you are—there's no way you can avoid breaking at least one of those rules, and some of them are so asinine and ridiculous. You couldn't loan one of your athletes your pickup truck if he was moving into a new apartment, or pick him up in the pouring rain and give him a ride. There isn't a programme in the country that hasn't incurred some kind of violation, and now it was O State's turn.

At the same time, our football department was under scrutiny as well, so the whole athletic division of the college was in the spotlight. Another wrestling violation would have probably resulted in a "death penalty," where the sport would be eliminated from the college altogether. I think that's why Coach Seay tried to cover up any violations that he had made. He didn't just say "Okay, we screwed this up" and make reparations. He made the officials dig up proof and go through a whole investigation process. And he eventually lost his job and was banned from coaching in the NCAA for some twenty years, until he was reinstated. Coach Burnett was also removed from the programme, although he wasn't banned from coaching elsewhere and was quickly picked up.

I was never questioned, but almost everybody else was under investigation. I don't think I had any violations, anyway. Up through Christmas of my junior year, only two other guys and I were eligible to compete. Most of the season was nixed and the dual meets, where we challenged another school, were cancelled. We all still practised, we just couldn't compete as a team. We managed to become eligible as a team for a handful of dual meets at the end of that year, and I was sent to some open tournaments alone. It had been a great strain on the team—we had number-one ranked guys, myself included, who had just won the Nationals twice, and were the top-ranked team in the country again for a third year.

When it was all said and done, we were reinstated right before the NCAA tournament that March. The NCAA tournament is its own event, and doesn't consider the season's team scores, so we went in fresh. My team ended up taking second to our rival, the University of Iowa.

In my senior year, I was the number-one ranked 190-pound wrestler in the country. I'd lost in the finals the year before but had gone undefeated since then. Now everyone expected me to win the college Nationals, and make the 1992 Olympic team.

I've often said that iron sharpens iron. One man sharpens another, and my teammates at Oklahoma State taught me how to take my athleticism and confidence to a whole new level. From junior high to the army to college, the wrestling skills I developed had a profound effect on the fighter I would eventually become.

Not all I learned was physical. With the help of our team psychologist, I acquired a fierce mental game that would eventually give me an edge in nearly all my fights. I learned to control that "little voice" inside, the one that chattered constantly a week before the big meet, telling me that I should have trained harder. I learned to frame my situations positively, to visualise every move I made until I raised my hand in victory.

I learned to respect my opponent, no matter what I thought of him. In wrestling, you shake your opponent's hand afterwards, win or lose. In army and international wrestling, you shake your opponent's hand afterward, win or lose. I did the same thing in college too. I would go even further and shake the coach's hand. It showed respect. It's what I thought was right.

There were lots of guys that threw fits or refused to acknowledge their opponent. I was embarrassed for the guys that would jerk away from the referee and stomp off the mat. It showed poor sportsmanship. That wasn't acceptable to my junior high coach, or my army coach, or my college coach. There was a reason they had all been so strict about demeanour and attitude and how I acted, win or lose. It taught me to stand up and take it either way.

I lost the NCAA finals to Mark Kerr, another wrestler who would later embark on a mixed martial arts career. In front of 70,000 people, he caught me out of the gate and scored. I never caught up. The loss was tortuous, but I reminded myself just how far I'd come and how much I'd accomplished. I was a three-time All-American, a member of two NCAA championship teams, and a two-time NCAA runner-up at Oklahoma State—all from a guy who never thought he'd step back onto a wrestling mat after high school. I had to pick myself back up. I still had the Olympic Trials ahead.

6 CHAPTER SIX:
DEVASTATION

ROLLING INTO THE 1992 OLYMPIC TRIALS IN CONCORD, California, I was ranked as the number-one 198-pounder in the country. There was a lot of expectation from both myself and my coaches, and this time I was confident. I felt like I was finally there, that this was real and what I was meant to do.

I tore my way through to the finals, and faced a wrestle-off with my nemesis, Mike Foy. Foy was a World silver medallist and a 1988 Olympian. He had wrestled for Minnesota in college and placed second in the 1989 World Championships, the best that anyone had placed for the United States in a long time.

On the mat, Foy and I wrestled a best-of-three series, and I lost. I was devastated. I had come so far, gotten so close, and lost to someone I knew I could beat. Foy represented our country in the 1992 Olympics in Barcelona, Spain and I followed behind as the alternate.

Being an alternate for the Olympic Games was an honour, although it was far less glamorous than I expected. Olympic wrestling is one of the few sports where the alternates don't get to suit up. I didn't get a uniform, or a pass to even enter the Olympic village, the housing compound where all the athletes stay. Once the weigh-ins took place, team members couldn't be substituted in any way because the tournament had officially started.

Alternates were brought over to support the team and act as

workout partners for the competitors. In the two weeks leading up to the Olympics, if a wrestler got injured, an alternate could be substituted in to make weight and fill the spot, but that never happened as far as I knew. The alternates were basically there to cater to the guys who made the team, which was hard. On the one hand, we felt pride in the team and wanted them to do well. On the other hand, we all wanted to be that guy stepping out into the big lights.

We called ourselves "the Scrub Club." We didn't get tickets to watch many of the competitions, and we didn't even get to attend the elaborate opening ceremonies and walk in with the team. We did get to watch the wrestling competition's opening ceremonies, and the international flavour of it all was spectacular. I distinctly remember how the Iranian section blew their horns and shook their rattles, which created a deafening noise each time one of their countrymen appeared on the mat. The Fins and Scandinavians travelled en masse and had a very strong presence as well.

The Olympics had an intense feel about it—it was clearly the best of the best. The athletes wrestled on the most pristine elevated mats, and there were fancy scoreboards and the best referees and elite officials from around the world to oversee the events. To be there firsthand, to see and experience all that, took away a bit of the bittersweet feeling of not being able to compete. At the same time, it created a burning desire. I knew next time it was going to be my turn, no matter what.

Spain afforded some pleasant sightseeing. On one of our days off, two of my Scrub Club buddies and I took a road trip to the small town of Sitges, a breathtaking beach community south of Barcelona. It was cheaper to buy beer than it was to buy bottles of water, so we drank beer the entire time. We stood atop a cement bulkhead, rating the topless women.

"Oh, look, those are silver-medal breasts right there," we said to one another, a little louder than normal. We assumed no one would understand us.

"Hey, assholes," a girl on a beach blanket yelled in our direction. "Not everyone here speaks Spanish."

"You're just pissed because we only gave you a bronze medal!" my buddy yelled back. We ended up having dinner with that feisty girl from New York.

It wasn't all play at the Olympics. During the wrestling competitions, our coaches put us to work in the stands, videotaping possible future opponents in our weight divisions. We filled out scouting reports for each round so our teammates had an idea of who they'd meet next, how their opponents' previous matches had gone, and what to expect. We had tonnes of video in the end, and I became an old pro with the camcorder.

I LEFT MY first Olympics feeling much more like a spectator than an athlete. It wasn't my last chance though. Like a lot of college graduates who had the twinkle of a gold medal in their eyes, I still had another Olympics to look forward to. I also had a job as the assistant wrestling coach at Oregon State University waiting for me when I returned. There had been a coaching change that summer, and Joe Wells had stepped in to the head position. Wells had been the assistant coach at Michigan, and I had challenged his student Fritz Lehrke in the NCAA semi-finals my junior year. Lehrke and I had gone back and forth in a tough barnburner match that went into overtime. Wells liked me as a wrestler. He also liked the fact I could juggle being an academic All-American, get through four years of college, and support my family.

I was still competing at a high level internationally in the hunt for my next Olympic bid, which meant I wouldn't just be a coach. I would be on the mats sweating it out with the athletes every day. Sharon and I packed up our belongings, traded in our old Ford Escort for a four-door Honda Accord, and drove from Stillwater, Oklahoma, to Corvallis, Oregon.

That fall was a time of new beginnings for me. After almost eleven years without a word, my father Ed called and asked if he could come by and say hello. He was visiting in Longview, just up the freeway from Corvallis, so he drove down to visit with his new wife, Carrie. It was one of the first times he had seen Ryan and Aimee since they were little babies.

It felt like I was meeting a stranger. I didn't know what to say, even though I knew it was my dad. I felt odd about it, but my dad and I weren't ones to express ourselves out loud. We just sat around the living room and got through the awkward moments in silence. I saw my father sporadically after that. He was still living in Alaska, but he came down to visit Carrie's family on holidays and special occasions. He started sending the kids Christmas presents. It was a start, at least.

I made another new beginning. When we moved to Corvallis, Sharon, the kids and I stayed at Joe Wells' house for the first few weeks until we could find our own place. That was the first time I laid eyes on Trish. She was babysitting the Wells' two small children one night when we all came back from dinner. Trish was tall and in good shape with dirty blonde hair. Wells introduced her as one of the coaches on staff. She had just graduated and was in her fifth year as an assistant volleyball coach.

Trish and I had offices right next to each other at the Gill Sports Coliseum where the wrestling team practised. Volleyball and wrestling are both Olympic sports in the same season, so our paths crossed daily. We saw each other in the office, in the hallway, in the coffee room, in the copy room, and at weekly coaches meetings. We struck up a few minor conversations and then ended up going to lunch together. And so began our relationship.

As a talented athlete, Trish was confident and independent. Even though she was only twenty-two and I had just turned thirty, we had a lot in common. I found Trish in my company more and more.

In my first few months as an assistant coach, I stayed late at night after work to finish correspondence courses I still had to complete to graduate from Oklahoma State. I was supposed to come back from the Olympics and finish my last twelve hours of coursework and my student teaching in the fall of 1992, but I had gotten hired by Oregon State that summer and didn't want to miss the opportunity. It was hard to go home and focus on the courses with the kids there. On one particular night, I ended up hanging out with Trish. We started playfully roughhousing and wrestling around in her office, and the next moment we were kissing.

This was the first relationship I'd ever started with another woman that was close to home. All the other times I had been on the road, somewhere far away from my everyday life. Because of that, those encounters never felt real to me. When I finished camps or competition trips, I said my good-byes and I never spoke to any of those other women again. Trish lived a half mile from my house. Our relationship grew quickly. Of course, we thought we were being secretive and sneaky, but everybody around us knew what was going on, including the guys on my team. I realised I had been playing with fire, but I was finally feeling the passion that had been missing from my marriage for so long.

Trish and I managed to keep our affair secret for a few months. One clear, sunny day in June, Sharon brought the kids to an outdoor fair being held on campus. They stopped by to see me, but I wasn't in my office. Suddenly, I heard the knock on my secretary's door. I'll never forget how it made me jump. I stood there, shirtless, while Trish dodged under the desk. I ran to the door to block Sharon from opening it, but she saw me through the adjacent window and began to cry. I don't think the kids saw me. I couldn't face her, so slipped out another door and ran.

I rode my bike home, playing out what had just happened in my head the whole way. When I got there, the kids had already been put to bed. Sharon was sitting in the living room in a chair. I sat down next to her and did something completely against my nature. I started talking. I told her everything from the very beginning, everything that I'd done, every woman I had seen behind her back for the last eleven years. She was obviously very upset. I felt terrible, but it was also an incredible release, like I had just become a thousand pounds lighter.

We decided to go see counsellors separately, mostly for the kids. I think in my heart I knew I was done with Sharon. I went with her to see her counsellor twice, but it didn't make a difference. We'd lost whatever it was that had originally brought us together.

Sharon wanted to know who Trish was, as I suppose most women would, but I wouldn't tell her. In my mind, it didn't really matter. It wasn't about somebody else. It was about the last eleven years we'd been married and all these other issues that led us to this place. I realised that we had married too young to really know what we were doing. I thought Sharon was a good person, and on some level, I loved her a lot. We had always gotten along, but there was always something lacking, even when we were high school kids. I finally told Sharon I cared about her, but I was no longer in love with her. I was in love with Trish.

AFTER COMING CLEAN to Sharon, I stopped seeing Trish while I tried to salvage my marriage. With the volleyball season and school semester over, Trish went home to her family in Corbett, Oregon. In July, I qualified for the Polish Grand Prix in Wrorcalv, the last major international event of the season. I was a zombie on that trip. My mind constantly drifted back to Oregon and my troubles there. Needless to say, I didn't wrestle well.

When I returned in August, Sharon filed for divorce, packed up the kids, and moved back to Seattle. I moved out of the house we had been renting and into a small apartment of my own, alone for the first time in eleven years. It was a difficult thing to get used to and I felt a tremendous sense of failure. I thought everyone looked at me differently.

Ryan was ten now and Aimee was eight, and I began seeing them every other weekend when they came down on the train. I missed my kids terribly, but I felt that Seattle was the best place for them. I didn't care about myself at that point. I knew that they would get the support they needed if they moved back to where both of their extended families lived. I knew Sharon's brothers were going to talk shit about me, but I wasn't worried about Sharon talking badly about me to the kids. She was never a vindictive person—on the contrary, she was very kind and a great mother.

There was a coaching change at Oregon State that fall in the volleyball department, so Trish left her position and started graduate courses. She studied for her MCATS to try and get into medical school. I continued with my assistant coaching position and tried to immerse myself back into wrestling. My apartment was across town from Trish's, but our romance rekindled quickly, and I found myself constantly at her place.

By the spring, my divorce had finalised. I was staying at Trish's place so much, we decided to move in together. I started paying the rent and taking care of some of the bills, while Trish worked at a local Hewlett-Packard plant and attended her graduate classes. The competition clock had started again—it was now two years until the Olympic Trials for the 1996 Atlanta Games.

That next February, Oregon State sent me on a recruiting trip to the high school state tournament in Portland. I brought along my friends Dave Millburn, an Oregon State alumni, and Rick Smith, to celebrate his birthday. We went to a local Benihana for dinner, then watched the wrestling finals at the University of Portland.

Afterwards, we went to a country-western bar to shoot some pool and throw back a couple of beers. It was about 12:30 a.m. when we crossed the street to pile back into Trish's car. A man in a Honda Civic suddenly swerved past us and hit the truck parked behind our car. He spun around and came tearing back up the street, so we jumped in our car and followed him, honking and flashing our lights to try and get him to stop. He finally pulled over and I parked in front of him so he couldn't drive off. I climbed out and approached the driver's side, asking him what his problem was. He was so drunk he couldn't even roll his window down, so I yanked his door open and tried to pry him out.

I didn't realise that he was still wearing his seatbelt, which gave him enough time to put his car in reverse and take off, with me in tow. I was stuck between the open door and the car, running down the street trying to keep up. He picked up enough speed where I couldn't run fast enough, so I jumped on the door's runner and grabbed tightly to the roof. He swerved up onto the sidewalk, hit a telephone pole, and the impact ripped the door right off the car. I was thrown into the street. A climbing spike from the utility pole punctured my chest on impact. I lay there, fully conscious, with blood trickling into my eyes.

The crash caused a lot of noise and the police and an ambulance were on the scene in minutes. The drunken man was arrested, and I was sent to the hospital, my chest aching the whole ride there. In the emergency room, they slid me off the gurney onto a table and started testing and evaluating me. The doctors were worried that my lung might collapse.

A nurse took off my boots and started to cut my pants off, but I fought with her to stop. I was wearing tight Wrangler jeans that were pretty common back then, but I also had on red thong underwear and didn't want anyone to see them. I hated the way boxers and briefs bunched up, so I thought I might as well wear thongs. The nurse finally got my jeans off, and I lay there, mortified. That was the last time I wore thongs. (Now, I know moms say to wear clean underwear because you never know. I'd like to amend that to "appropriate" underwear.)

My human cannonball impression earned me a big laceration on my forehead, a couple of broken ribs, and a punctured lung on my left side. I spent the next few days in the hospital until my lung stabilised. I didn't need stitches for the puncture, but I can still feel a knot in the muscle where it poked me.

★　★　★

FOR THE FIRST time, I missed Nationals because I wasn't healthy enough to train. Later that year, I petitioned into the Trials mini-tournament and won all my matches. In the finals, I picked up my opponent to throw him and he landed on my chest, refracturing my rib. I won the match, but I didn't recover in time to wrestle the number-one guy to make the World team. I was forced to take the rest of 1994 off.

I returned to competition in 1995 with a vengeance—I won Nationals and a spot on the World team. However, USA Wrestling decided there wasn't enough time to hold a wrestle-off for the Pan American Games team, so they went ahead and sent the National champions from the year before. It was a big deal because the Pan Am Games were the hemispheric championship and one of the qualifiers for the Olympics. But I had won the World Team Trials the year before and won the 1996 West Regional Olympic Trials, so I was still in excellent position.

My third try for a slot on the Olympics team was here. I was once again the number-one ranked 198-pounder heading into the National finals. If I won, I was only one more match away from making the Olympics. Mike Foy and I met again on the mats, and I was beating the dogsnot out of him. The score was 9-1, with about forty-five seconds left in the match. I could have stalled and coasted out the last few seconds, but I wanted to "tech-fall" him, or catch him in a throw to score past the ten-point maximum and immediately end the match. If I had just played it safe, I would have won on points, but that just wasn't the kind of wrestler I was. I tried to take him down one more time, but in the middle of it, I ended up on my back. I got pinned in the last twenty seconds and lost.

It just wasn't in my nature to sit back on a lead and play it conservatively. I always wanted to dominate and break my opponents and win matches by as much as I could. I never let up, sometimes to my detriment. My coaches wanted me to win too, but there was a fine line between being aggressive and being smart.

Okay, this means I just have to wrestle back, I said to myself. I still had the chance to enter the mini-tournament and win that, so I could challenge Foy for his spot.

In the mini-tournament, I wrestled one of my teammates from the army, the explosive Derek Waldroup. Waldroup and I had a phenomenal match. He took me down and turned me early, then went into stall mode. I came storming back and was within one point of winning the match, but time ran out. Waldroup went on to beat Foy in a controversial match and made the Olympic team. I was the second alternate for the 1996 Olympic Games in Atlanta, Georgia.

Missing the Olympics didn't get any easier, and the third time brought on three times the hurt and feelings of inadequacy. I felt like I had been the guy to beat in 1992, but I was still fairly new and hadn't experienced much international competition. By 1996, I'd already been to the World Championships three times. I'd been the number-one guy for some time, and had more or less dominated my weight class. I was at the right age. I'd done everything within my control, from training to diet. I'd made all the sacrifices. Everything pointed to it being my time, but it just slipped away again and I couldn't understand why.

Trish and I had talked about getting married after the Olympics. When I didn't make the team, we decided to go ahead and tie the knot. On July 16, 1996, we exchanged our vows against the backdrop of Multnomah Falls, a picturesque 620-foot waterfall cascading down Larch Mountain, just up the Columbia River gorge from Corbett, where Trish had grown up. It was a small gathering with about fifty people, including my mom and my two sisters, Yolanda and Traci. My father, Ed, arrived a couple of nights early and stayed for the ceremony too. He had just moved from Alaska and bought a place in Pe Ell, about an hour and a half from Portland.

Because Trish loved sports just as much as I did, we included the

Atlanta Olympics as part of our honeymoon, then went on to Florida and Aruba. As the second alternate, with Olympic experience under my belt already, I was invited to be a part of the Scrub Club again, but I passed. I decided to enjoy the Olympics from the stands without a camcorder in my hands. Trish and I took in the other sports as well, including boxing, volleyball, and basketball. We hung out with the wrestling team and joined them out on the town when they were finished competing.

Once we returned home, Trish and I both thought I was going to retire from wrestling. I had hoped to make the team, win the medal, and then call it quits. I'd been wrestling for nearly thirteen years. Trish was excited about the prospect of settling down and starting a family. She was finishing up her master's degree in nursing and had a job lined up when we got back. I think in her mind, the whole wrestling business would be over.

However, I couldn't silence the voice inside. I was certainly still capable of competing. *I'm thirty-three*, I thought. *So what? I can still wrestle and beat these guys*. I wasn't ready to let go. I told Trish I didn't want to retire. I hadn't achieved my goal yet. I think she understood how disappointed I was, and she agreed to hang in there for one more go.

Round Two

IT WAS ALWAYS
ABOUT THE
COMPETITION

7 CHAPTER SEVEN:
YOU NEED TO GET INTO THAT

MISERY LOVES COMPANY, AND SO DOES AMBITION. MY friend Danny Henderson had already made the 1992 and 1996 Olympic teams and was going to retire, but when he found out I was going to go another four years to try and make the 2000 Olympics, he decided he would too.

I had met Danny when we roomed together at the 1992 World Championships. He had competed in the 1992 Barcelona Olympics, where he'd placed tenth in the 180.5-pound division, the weight class below mine. We spent time together on a few tours overseas and developed a friendship attending wrestling camps and competitions together. We were both laid-back and quiet, but Danny had a wild side just like me, so we had a good time together. Danny would also become a big supporter of my future fighting career.

We started training together in the off-season. Danny lived down in Huntington Beach, California, so I would go down there for a month or two to train and hang out with him. Then he would come up to Oregon and stay with me. I also picked up his coach Bob Anderson, one of the first ten coaches to become Gold Coach certified, the highest certification in USA Wrestling. Bob had also been a world calibre wrestler himself.

In the summer of 1996, Trish and I moved into an apartment complex not far from campus, and I got my first glimpse of the

Ultimate Fighting Championship. It was August and training hadn't quite geared up again when one of my Oregon State guys came over and excitedly handed me a black VHS tape.

"You gotta check this out," he said. I threw the tape in my VCR. I saw two men circling each other inside a round, chain-link cage. Low and behold, there was Don Frye—the teammate from Oklahoma State who had challenged me for my slot on the team freshman year. I couldn't mistake his *Magnum PI* moustache.

"Oh, my God, I know that guy," I said. I watched Frye charge his opponent like a pit bull with a slew of left and right haymakers that crumbled him to the canvas.

Then, I recognised Paul Herrera, another wrestler from Nebraska, getting his arse kicked by a mean-looking black guy named Gary Goodridge. As the tape played on, the winners would reemerge from backstage and go at it again with the winner from another match. It was a wacky elimination tournament. Frye met Goodridge in the finals, took him down and pounded him into the mat until he gave up. I was immediately intrigued by what I was seeing, but I thought it was crazy.

I didn't think that much about it until five months later, when I took my Oregon State team to an invitational tournament in Las Vegas. I ran into one of my old wrestling buddies, Jim Townsend, who had come up from Malibu to check out the event. Jim was in the entertainment business running a production company called Titan Entertainment. We threw back a few too many beers at the hotel bar after the finals when he brought up the UFC.

"You see Mark Coleman? You see Frye?" he yelled excitedly over his beer bottle. "You need to get into that."

"Oh, nah," I shrugged, my lips curling up into a smile. But Jim was persistent.

"I know how to get the application and we can send in a wrestling tape," he said. I agreed, thinking maybe the beer was doing more of the talking than anything else. I figured it wouldn't go much farther than the barstools we were sitting on. Turns out, Jim did send in a tape and a got a quick response from Semaphore Entertainment Group, who owned and ran the UFC.

"We don't want any more wrestlers right now. We're looking for more exotic martial artists," SEG told Jim. "We'll put him on the alternates list."

At the time, Mark Coleman was the UFC's heavyweight champion, so I guess it made sense not to clutter the division with more wrestlers. I didn't give it too much thought. It wasn't that big of a deal to me. I had a good job, enjoyed wrestling and doing all the things I wanted to do. I won my third U.S. Nationals title that year in Florida and was voted the event's "Outstanding Greco-Roman Wrestler." Mark Coleman was there, walking around with his UFC belt, which caught my eye. I'd wrestled Coleman in freestyle at the 1989 Olympic Festival at Oklahoma State, but lost to him by a point. He went on to the World Championships that year and won a silver medal.

I also ran into Rico Chiapparelli, a former NCAA champion from the University of Iowa. We'd wrestled together in the off-seasons. Rico was a visionary. He knew there was something to the emerging sport that everyone was just starting to call mixed martial arts. Rico had the idea of building a fight team out of wrestlers to enter the competitions.

"We think we could do really well," Rico told me. "We think wrestlers are the best athletes out there, and you're one of the best." Rico had already been talking to a bunch of world-class wrestlers, including Danny Henderson, Matt Lindland, Sean Bormet, and Tom Erickson. I thought, *why not?*

In wrestling circles, the UFC was getting a lot of buzz, but the reviews were mixed. Some questioned its legitimacy, calling it nothing more than a sideshow. Others thought it might be a great place to showcase their skills and make some extra cash. Wrestling wasn't necessarily the most lucrative of endeavours. USA wrestling didn't want to take a stance on the UFC, and later, when a few of us tried to get them to co-brand and co-market it, they weren't willing to do it. But the whole idea was starting to sound cool to me, especially the idea of making some extra dough, so I signed a contract with Rico and his brother Lou to join the Real American Wrestling (RAW) team. Their motto was "Anyone. Anytime. Anywhere."

Rico started burning up the ear of SEG matchmaker Art Davie. He called him on a regular basis, and told him that his squad was ready to fight at any time, trying to get any of us into the UFC. Truthfully, I was still just wrestling and hadn't really done any other type of training to prepare myself. While Davie contemplated, Rico booked me for my first fight on June 15, 1997, in a promotion called the Brazilian Open.

I was also invited to the Pan Am Championships in Puerto Rico that May. The championships were different from the Pan Am Games— they ran every year and didn't have all the ceremonies, pageantry, or any of the other bullshit. It was essentially just the U.S. team competing against the Cubans, because most of the other countries had pretty small teams that weren't that talented. We had a long standing rivalry with the Cubans, and I had a personal grudge with one particular guy named Reynaldo Peña. I was one of his only opponents to beat him in the 1991 finals in Cuba, but I hadn't been able to duplicate my success with him since.

I was packing my bags for Puerto Rico when I got a call on May 13. It was Rico. "Somebody got hurt so they've got a spot for you in the UFC heavyweight tournament in two weeks. It's in two weeks," he repeated. "Do you want to take it?"

"Hell, yeah, let's do it," I said, without hesitation. "But I'll be in Puerto Rico for nine days. Where is this thing?"

"Augusta, Georgia."

"I'll meet you in Atlanta," I said.

Rico agreed and set up hotel accommodations in Atlanta for us when we arrived. Danny Henderson was already heading down to Brazil to participate in the middleweight tournament for the Brazilian Open on June 15, and Tom Erikson would be sent in my place in the heavyweight ranks. With logistics settled, I put down the phone and walked into the living room to tell Trish I'd be fighting in the UFC in two weeks. Then I called Coach Wells and told him the same. I could hear the astonishment in his voice. I had mentioned to him that I was filling out the application, but I guess he hadn't really believed I would actually go through with it.

Coach Wells expressed his reservations about the UFC, saying that it was bad for recruiting and bad for the university. He was probably also looking out for my safety as well, but the thought of getting hurt never entered my mind. I hadn't seen anyone else get hurt, and I certainly didn't think cagefighting was anything that would keep me out of wrestling.

"I don't think you should be fighting," Wells said. "I am not going to tell you no, but you need to call the athletic director and make sure it's okay with him, and if it's okay with him then I guess I have nothing more to say."

My conversation with Oregon State's athletic director, Dutch Baughman, went a lot smoother. I explained the situation, what the competition was about and he was immediately intrigued.

"Wow, that sounds really cool," Baughman said. He was just that kind of guy, a real cowboy. He gave his approval as long as it was all right with my head coach. I called Wells back and told him Baughman didn't have a problem with it, and asked if it would be okay for me to make a pit stop in Atlanta on my way back from Puerto Rico. Wells had no other choice but to agree.

I took a bronze medal in Puerto Rico, losing by a point to Peña in our match. I immediately flew to Atlanta and met Rico in the airport seven days before my UFC debut. We checked into a local hotel. God had made the earth in seven days. Could Rico make me into a fighter in the same amount of time?

THE NEXT DAY we began my MMA education. We visited a couple of jiu-jitsu places where I picked up some moves that were common in the UFC. Brazilian jiu-jitsu is waged on the ground, where you can catch and hold your opponent in locks and holds until he submits, by either tapping his hand three times or verbally calling it quits. Arms, legs, and the neck are prime targets, and you can latch on a choke or lock from the top or bottom position, depending on your experience. Wrestling utilises some holds that are similar to jiu-jitsu, but there was a lot I wasn't familiar with.

We kept it simple, focusing on the most fundamental positions. "This is what you have to watch out for here," Rico warned, standing over me as he pushed my body between my grounded partner's legs into what was called his guard. "This is the closed guard," Rico said, letting the guy underneath me wrap his legs around my torso. "This is how you pass the guard. This is 'knee on stomach.'"

Rico tried to show me what the guard was and what the jiu-jitsu fighters would do from the guard position to try to catch me, but it was basically a shot in the dark. We had no idea who my first opponent would be or what his background, strengths, or weaknesses were. I guess that was the excitement of it all.

The first few UFC events had been dominated by a Brazilian jiu-jitsu black belt named Royce Gracie, a skinny descendent of the discipline's first family. Gracie had toppled foe after foe in the UFC's earliest tournaments, beginning in 1993. He used jiu-jitsu's great manipulation of leverage and positioning to overcome much larger opponents.

Because jiu-jitsu had become such a fixture in the UFC very early on, there seemed to be a certain sense of entitlement with its masters. Rico and I felt that when we went to a particular school run by a Gracie Brazilian jiu-jitsu black belt named Jacare. A friendly man still in amazing shape for his mid-forties, Jacare invited us in, and we sat and watched his students roll around on his mats until the class was finished. After everyone had left, we asked Jacare for permission to work out ourselves. He shook his head immediately.

"You might end up fighting one of my students, so you can't train here," he explained without hesitation. Rico and I looked at each other incredulously. That was the most bizarre thing we had ever heard. There was nobody else there!

We found a little hole-in-the-wall gym that was more of a traditional martial arts place and continued to cram in as many lessons as we could. Rico and I also hit up the Georgia State University wrestling room, where I worked out with two huge pro wrestlers, Pat Aceloni and Tim Catalfo. Catalfo went on to fight in regional events like King of the Cage. Pat had studied shootfighting—a hybrid of martial arts not unlike MMA, but which only allowed open-handed strikes. Pat was a disciple of Bart Vale, an American who had done very well with the technique in Japan, where it was sometimes melded into pro wrestling matches. Pat was a New York motor mouth and thought he knew it all, but he was a friend of Rico's, so I didn't say a word.

In that first week, I discovered that this new sport had a lot of characters. After my UFC appearance, I heard that Catalfo was telling everybody that he had trained me for my fight and tapped me out regularly.

Right away I could sense a different mentality. From the Brazilian guys telling us we couldn't train at their school to the guys boasting feats that had never happened—it really made me question what I was getting into. What surprised me was that Catalfo was from the college wrestling world, where I never heard about athletes spinning tales of their mat conquests. I didn't understand why people would make stuff up like that, but it wouldn't be the last time.

The next five days passed quickly. I mostly grappled and wrestled, trying to learn the guard and a handful of submissions. We didn't box. We didn't even have a set of mitts to practise on, and certainly no gloves.

We rolled in to Augusta's Holiday Inn for the weigh-ins a day before the show, and I was introduced to Semaphore Entertainment Group, the company that owned and ran the UFC. They seemed disorganised. People ran back and forth between their makeshift offices with lots of paperwork and worried looks on their faces. The person that made everything go was Elaine McCarthy. With long, straight blonde hair that swayed fiercely as she bounced by at top speed, Elaine had coordinated events for SEG since *UFC 1*. She was married to "Big" John McCarthy, a six-foot-four, 250-pound lug of a man who refereed all of the events, and in theory, was there to make sure we didn't kill each other during the fights.

If Elaine hadn't been there, SEG would have been screwed, because no one else seemed to have any idea what was going on. She wore all the hats—ran the show, did the travel, issued the credentials, everything.

SEG had a table set up in the lobby where we signed in and filled out my information sheet. There were no medical tests or bloodwork required to compete. Then we filed into a tiny meeting room to take turns stepping onto a normal household scale so they could record our weights. There were no athletic commission officials present, which didn't really matter because there was no weight cap for my division. I weighed in around 225 pounds, which Rico and I reckoned would make me one of the lighter guys—if not the lightest—in the four-man heavyweight tournament. This didn't worry me. I thought I would have an advantage fighting bigger guys. I knew from my experience with wrestling that they didn't move as well. They weren't as fast or mobile, and I felt like that would give me a bit of an edge.

There was no audience at the weigh-ins, not even a single row of chairs set up in case anyone had shown up to watch. The fighters weren't announced, so I didn't get a look at who I'd be fighting first. It was just the SEG staff, the fighters, and whatever entourages they had brought, standing around in a room with cheap carpets that smelled of musty cigarettes.

A local promoter I'd never met named Brett Moses had picked Trish up at the Atlanta airport and drove her to Augusta. On the way, they'd stopped to pick up Dr. John Keating, who lent his name to the event for support and was working with Brett behind the scenes. Trish had joined me the day before the weigh-ins and followed me around in silence. She'd never made any objections, though I could see the look on her face as she watched all of the commotion going on to organise two guys into a cage to beat the crap out of one another. Just like me, she didn't know what to expect, but the prospect of her husband being one of those guys wasn't too appetising.

At the hotel, Brett handed me what looked like black, fingerless weightlifting gloves, but they had gel sewn inside the knuckles. They were prototypes that Dr. Keating had been working on.

"You're welcome to try them out if you want," Brett said.

I had no idea if they were good or bad. SEG hadn't told us whether or not we should wear gloves, and they weren't handing them out themselves, so I decided to wear them. To me, it didn't matter. In my mind, it wasn't a boxing match, so I wasn't going out there to throw punches with any of these guys. I was going out there to wrestle.

I never really thought about getting punched. *It's a fight*, I thought, *so we'll punch and kick each other and I won't be scared because I'll know it's coming*. I didn't want to think about the fact that the guy could punch me in the face. I framed the situation positively—*I'm a wrestler, so I'll just take him down before he can swing at me*. I didn't dwell on the punching on the ground either. I worried more about the submissions, but I knew once I took my guy down, I could punch him myself.

Rico found a kid with long red hair backstage, who had a pair of focus mitts in the warm-up area, so I practised pawing at him with sort of a ground-and-pound style, which was a term given to the guys that took their opponents down and started punching into their guard. This warm-up was the closest thing I'd had to a mitt workout the entire time.

We shared a dressing room with Royce Alger, another wrestler who represented Hammer House, Coleman's Ohio team. Alger was in a bout separate from the tournament and was a former college teammate of Rico's, so Rico helped him get prepared too. About twenty minutes before my fight, Rico accompanied Alger out for his fight and left me to warm up alone. Of course, I did what I'd done for the last twenty-two years. I ran sprints and pummelled and I did all my usual exercises.

★   ★   ★

I STEPPED OUT into the coloured lights with theme music blaring behind me. The Augusta Civic Centre was filled with two thousand screaming people. It was surreal. There were fans hanging over the railings so close they could touch me, wailing at the top of their lungs as I walked confidently up the ramp and to a cage propped up about four feet on a platform in the centre of the room.

You wouldn't have seen it in my face, but there was a little fear mixed in with that tingly, adrenaline-pumping feeling when I walked out there and saw the cage and the people for the first time. I was walking into the unknown. I had never been a street fighter; I had never been in those types of fights. The few times in my life I had been in an altercation I remember what my frame of mind was like, and this was nothing like that. My fears of getting hit crept in quietly. I had no idea what was going to happen, and that was the most intimidating feeling of all. I thought, *what the hell am I doing?*

I have to admit in that moment, I was very, very nervous. But then I saw Tony Halme standing across from me, snarling. Halme was a bald, bulky guy who seemed to be 300 pounds of pure muscle, like he spent his days and nights in the gym lifting. I found out later that Halme was a Finnish boxer who went on to pro wrestling under the name Ludvig Borga. I concentrated on Halme and I focused.

I didn't see any of the on-camera interviews Halme shot before the fight until later, in which he claimed that he was going to rip my arms off and that it was "kill or be killed" time, and I'm thankful for that. My mom started crying immediately as she watched on pay-per-view with my sisters and the rest of my family. My brother-in-law was sitting close to the TV on a footstool when they zoomed in on Halme, and said he nearly fell off his seat. Trish saw it on the big screen as the promo played for the audience. She freaked out and threw up in the garbage can outside the arena. She was so nervous sitting with all the bloodthirsty fans around her, yelling and betting with one another that I was going to get my arse kicked.

"Look, this guy is going to charge you," Rico had coached me backstage. "He's a great big guy, but he's a boxer, so he's just going to come right at you. Take him down with a double-leg and once you get him on the ground, punch him a couple times. Then he's going to turn over—just take his back and choke him."

And that's what happened, almost word for word. It was over in 56 seconds and I had not a single scratch on me.

Shit, that wasn't so bad, I thought.

I calmly walked back to the dressing rooms and did a TV interview with commentator Joe Rogan to set up my next fight. Rico told me I'd done it perfectly and to get some water and rest up for my next fight. I shut my eyes and replayed the other elimination bout I'd watched a few minutes before on the TV monitor—Steven Graham versus a Russian, Dmitri Stepanov. I'd be facing one of these guys in twenty minutes.

I actually thought the Russian was going to win, but Graham took him down and caught him in a keylock, or an Americana submission, that torqued his bended arm into the air to strain his shoulder joint. We'd gone over keylocks that week in the dojo, so I tried to remember what I'd been taught. It's an illegal hold in wrestling, and I kind of knew what it was, but I wasn't quite sure I knew how to get out of it. I tend not to worry too much about these types of things though.

My second walk to the Octagon was a little more comfortable because I knew what to expect. It didn't feel so overwhelming.

I got head-butted in the second fight. I took Graham down right away, but he scrambled back to his feet. I held onto him with a front headlock, then spun around and took his back. I had secured a double-wrist ride, with my arms slid in under his armpits, grabbing his wrist and forearm, when he reared up and head-butted me with the back of his head. That kind of pissed me off, so I head-butted him back and just started punching him until the referee jumped in between us to stop the fight.

The punching seemed natural. I didn't really think about it. I just went out there and hit him. I kneed Graham a bunch of times too, and it wasn't anything that I practised either. I had just done it. I ended up cutting his head with my knee and pulled him back down to the ground and spun around behind him to go for the finish. I won the entire tournament in a little over four minutes. It felt just as good as winning a wrestling title.

I met the UFC's owner Bob Meyrowitz as I walked out of the cage, in front of the live pay-per-view cameras rolling. Bob placed the tournament's gold medal around my neck and told me he thought I would have a bright future in the UFC. That was all he said to me that night.

My new trophy proudly displayed on my chest, I walked backstage and found Trish. She was excited, and we laughed together in relief now that the whole experience was over. That night, we went to the post-fight party at the hotel. There was music and talk with all the fighters who were there to collect the night's pay from SEG. I earned a straight $20,000 to compete, a price negotiated by Rico, whether I had won or lost the tournament. Royce Gracie and others had been paid $60,000 for their sixteen-man tournaments a few years earlier, but it seemed the UFC was heading toward leaner days.

I WENT BACK to Oregon State. My team had watched the show, and they were all going nuts. The guys thought it was cool as hell that I had tried it, so they had thrown a big party and watched the pay-per-view together. The rest of the staff thought it was a one-time deal.

I fell back into my normal schedule for the next few months. I went on to the World Team Trials, then trained all summer and dove into the World Championships in late August. I placed ninth, breaking into the top ten for the first time. I felt like I was really getting the competition routine down.

SEG had called Rico a week or two after my UFC win and offered me $25,000 to fight a young Brazilian knockout artist named Vitor Belfort in October. We were told the winner of that bout would then challenge UFC heavyweight champion Maurice Smith for his title. I hadn't really advertised this to anyone, and I returned home from the World Championships in early September not focused on fighting at all. Rico was in a panic.

"Dude, you need to come down and train here for at least three weeks with this boxing coach I have, and study tape," he urged.

I didn't know who Belfort was, although I'd seen him fight against David "Tank" Abbott, a potbellied street brawler. At *UFC 13*, Belfort had annihilated Abbott in just under a minute with rapid-fire punches. He was a fresh nineteen-year-old who looked pretty explosive with his hand work. Belfort was also a Brazilian jiu-jitsu black belt, though not a single one of his previous UFC bouts had needed to go to the ground.

The UFC was building Belfort up as their poster boy and had dubbed him "the Phenom." He won his fights quickly and decisively, so I didn't blame them. Belfort seemed to have a bright future ahead of him. I knew UFC owner Bob Meyrowitz thought he was throwing me to the wolves.

Rico and I sat down to strategise how we'd tackle Belfort, fourteen years my junior and quite a striker. Rico thought Belfort was juiced up on steroids and wouldn't be able to take a fast-paced fight past his usual couple of minutes.

Rico and I discussed trying not to stand and box with Belfort, but rather to make it a Greco match. I thought it was a solid plan. I hired a boxing coach down in Hermosa Beach to expose myself to oncoming punches and rolled up my sleeves for my next training schedule. I was already in great shape from the Worlds, but would need this time away to begin cross-training. I asked Coach Wells for three weeks off, but his attitude towards fighting had dramatically shifted in a few short months, and he threw a fit. He didn't like my timing—just as our college wrestlers were coming back to school to begin their season, I'd be away—so he gave me an ultimatum.

"What are you going to be?" Wells asked. "Are you going to be a fighter? Or are you going to be a coach?"

I went home and thought about it, but I didn't have to think too hard. The UFC would pay me more for the one fight than I would get the whole year as a coach at Oregon State. I also felt the time was right to leave the nest and free myself up to train full-time for the next Olympics. I no longer needed a college team to get the right training. It wasn't the same as the Greco training I was now getting on the outside with Danny Henderson, at the National camps, and during my time with Bob Anderson, Danny's coach.

I headed to California for three weeks and trained in Hermosa Beach. I worked with Eric Paulson, John Donehue, a jiu-jitsu black belt under Gene LeBell, and the famous Machado brothers on submissions and grappling—a term used to describe any activity a fighter waged on the ground. I boxed everyday with Scott, an Irish guy who owned the Boxing Works gym on the scenic Pacific Coast Highway. I also trained with Tony, who was visiting from Holland and was a trainer there.

I couldn't understand how I could be in such good shape and still get so tired during boxing workouts. I couldn't hold my arms up hitting the mitts, and I hadn't even gotten to much sparring yet. At first, I focused on footwork and mitt work and just trying to learn mechanics. The one benefit of starting from a clean slate was that I could train to box a southpaw (or left-handed boxer) without much fuss. Boxers usually train first for right-handed opponents, and the switch can be challenging later on.

Belfort had won four straight fights in the UFC, so it was easy to find tape on him and study his patterns. Everything he did was straight ahead: jab, cross, jab, cross. He didn't throw a lot of hooks or anything fancy. He was just very explosive. If you stood in front of him at all, he was going to try and blow through you. So, I wanted to circle a lot in the fight, especially away from his left hand, where he started all his combinations. As soon as I got the chance, I wanted to tie him up to clinch with him, so we drilled that over and over.

Coach Wells had given me the three weeks to train in California but had asked me to make a decision about my career. When I told Wells I was giving mixed martial arts a try, he told me he was going to hire a new assistant coach, but that the university would keep me on as a strength and conditioning coach. The season had already started, and it would take some time to replace me. My pay was reduced, but I kept my benefits, which was an amicable solution for all. Coaching had been a full-time job. Now all I'd have to focus on was fighting and the 2000 Olympic Games.

UFC 15: COLLISION COURSE was held on October 17, 1997, at Casino Magic in Bay St. Louis, Mississippi. Casino Magic was a gambling hall propped up on a river boat anchored in the great waterway to avoid state gambling laws. The event wasn't even going to be held inside the casino, but in a tent erected on the river's bank, as sure a sign as ever that the UFC was heading toward a low point. It wasn't gaining mainstream acceptance. At that time, Senator John McCain had even personally launched a campaign to see "Ultimate Fighting" banned in every state.

If the Augusta Civic Centre venue seemed shoddy, the tent was even more second-rate, although about two thousand diehard fans turned out for the show. That was fine with me. If the UFC had drawn bigger audiences before at nicer arenas, I didn't know the difference. We were given our own little RV to wait in, so Rico, his brother Lou, and I piled in.

The UFC format at that time allowed for the previous show's tournament winner to return in a headlining "Superfight" against a suitable opponent. There would also be a main event pitting UFC heavyweight champion Maurice Smith against *UFC 5* winner Dan Severn. However, Severn had fought another UFC vet, Kimo Leopoldo, to a thirty-minute draw the week before in a new Japanese promotion called PRIDE Fighting Championships, and somebody objected to him fighting again so soon. Tank Abbott was brought in to fight Smith, a hardnosed striker, who kicked him around like a windmill for eight straight minutes until Abbott gave up.

I had no illusions that SEG had an agenda for my fight with Belfort. I was viewed as the hopeless underdog to the dangerous Brazilian jiu-jitsu black belt with lightning-fast hands and pinpoint accuracy. I was a sheep to their surefire wolf, but that's the way I liked it. I'd spent my wrestling career rising far above what was expected of me. As the underdog, the pressure and attention wasn't on me, which left me alone to prepare.

The UFC's theme song roared as they brought me out to the Octagon first, amid the cheers inside the tent along the river. I climbed into the cage and let my body's weight adjust to the soft canvas. Rico stood behind me on the other side of the fence, talking and keeping me focused until Belfort made his entrance. A minute passed. And then another. And then maybe eight more. Something wasn't right. Rico started asking questions, but nobody on the floor had any idea why Belfort had yet to appear on the ramp.

On pay-per-view, the commentators described it as the old boxing tactic of "freezing him out," or making your opponent wait so he starts to think and get nervous. It had the exact opposite effect on me. I thought, *this guy is scared. He doesn't want to come out here. He's nervous, and that's what's taking him so long.* It gave me confidence and made me that much more relaxed. I put my shirt back on to keep my muscles warmed up, bounced around the cage, and smiled.

Ten minutes later, Belfort was on the ramp, nervousness washed all over his face. He just had that look in his eyes. As he got in the cage, I got a really good look at him. He was fidgeting with his hands, and he had a deer-in-headlights expression. It only fed the fire of my belief that

I was going to win the fight.

When the bell finally sounded, I popped Belfort out of the gate with a jab to his cheek. Although hitting was new to me, I felt that I could land some shots, even though that hadn't been the original strategy. I stayed tight with Belfort wherever the fight went, and grabbed him when the moment was right. I landed an uppercut in the clinch and could feel him "break." It was something I'd learned and executed many times in wrestling, where you mentally pushed your opponent until he quit struggling. When somebody breaks, you can almost hear it; you can feel it. They don't quit or tap out, but they give up the will to fight back.

When Belfort broke, I knew it was only a matter of time. Seven minutes and forty-three seconds into the fight, I took Belfort down and began to tee off punches. Belfort flipped over onto his knees with me in pursuit. The fight was stopped by referee McCarthy at 8:16.

I was told later that UFC owner Bob Meyrowitz screamed, "No, no!" in the production trailer because I had ruined his plans. But the audience chanted "USA! USA!" with such passion that I instinctually raised my arms. I went backstage, and Joe Rogan asked me when I was going to Japan to challenge for the title. In all my travels, I had never been to Japan, though I had always wanted to go. That's when it sunk in.

A short time later, a man named Joel Gold called me at home. He was owner of *Full Contact Fighter*, the first U.S. publication to ever cover the fights exclusively. Joel asked me if it would be all right if he nicknamed me "the Natural," because he said he'd never seen anyone adapt to fighting so quickly.

"Sure," I said. "I've been called much worse."

I had found my calling.

8 CHAPTER EIGHT: FINALLY NUMBER ONE

I HAD EXACTLY TWO MONTHS AND FIVE DAYS TO prepare for my showdown with UFC heavyweight champion Maurice Smith in Japan. SEG began negotiations with Rico and Lou right away to sign me to a three-fight contract, my first multi-bout agreement with the organisation. I'd be fighting for the title, and they didn't want me to go anywhere. Rico and Lou went back and forth with SEG's lawyer, David Isaacs, and UFC owner Bob Meyrowitz over what I should get paid. They were trying to put all this crazy shit in my contract, most of which I didn't pay much attention to. They finally settled after three weeks of long-distance phone calls between California and New York City, where SEG's headquarters were housed, and Maurice Smith became a reality.

Maurice "Mo" Smith was a world champion kickboxer in the 1980s and had gone undefeated for nearly ten years after he won the WKA heavyweight title at the age of twenty. Mo had slowly cut his teeth in MMA over the last four years touring through Japanese promotions like Pancrase and RINGS, which allowed open-palmed strikes, among other rule variations, that made for a slightly less dangerous experience.

At *Battlecade Extreme Fighting 3* in October 1996, Mo knocked out a monstrous Brazilian heavyweight named Marcus "Conan" Silveira with a head kick in the third round under full-on MMA rules, proving he was ready to join the UFC's ranks. SEG paired Mo up against UFC heavyweight champion Mark Coleman at *UFC 14: Showdown* on July 27, 1997, in Birmingham, Alabama. Keeping enough distance to avoid the takedown and utilising a heavy right outside kick, Smith punished Coleman's thighs and pushed him to exhaustion for twenty-one minutes, eventually winning by unanimous decision to take the title. Because Coleman had gone undefeated in the Octagon a whopping six times, the victory was seen as a turning point in the UFC, a changing of the guard from the dominant wrestler to the deadly striker. I assume SEG believed I would be the next wrestler to fall to the kickboxer. Of course, Rico had a plan.

I went back to training in sunny California with the guys at Hermosa Beach Boxing Works, and particularly with Tony, who was a kickboxer. It made no sense for me to stand with Smith—he'd pulverise my legs like he did to Coleman. The strategy was to take Mo down, so I began to learn about the timing of kicks and that split second when he would be most vulnerable to a takedown. I continued my ground education with John Donehue and Eric Paulson, and built up my cardio on the Aerodyne bike and by running on the beach.

Danny Henderson had won the Brazilian tournament that June, much to the disapproval of its raucous audience. They stormed the cage afterwards and nearly started a riot, while Danny waited inside for things to calm down. Danny was a few months off from his own UFC debut and wanted to learn the fight game as well. Together we floated around to California's local gyms like Neutral Grounds, which had a cage, and Brazilian jiu-jitsu black belt and two-time UFC veteran Joe Moreira's place in Irvine. We even dabbled a bit at the Inosanto Academy in Marina Del Rey, which catered to a lot of the traditional martial arts like jeet kune do and Filipino martial arts. Ten-time Greco-Roman Nationals champion and 1996 Olympic silver medallist Dennis Hall joined us at Boxing Works as well, which made for some eclectic training.

Even after ten years of world-class competition under my belt, I'd never been to Japan before. I'd flown east towards Europe countless times, but for the UFC fight I flew west to Tokyo for seventeen straight hours, which was a little different. It was actually easier for me. Jet lag is a concern for any athlete—including fighters.

Though I'd opened myself up to even more types of combat, I hadn't really adapted much past my wrestling training. I was still in the mindset of using just my wrestling to win, which wasn't necessarily a bad choice for this matchup. Danny came with Rico and me on this trip to be my workout partner. We found a little Japanese dojo in Yokohama where we could wrestle every day up until the fight. In the heavyweight division, I could top off at 265 pounds, so making weight was not an issue—I tipped at the scales at a whopping 226 pounds.

I noticed immediately that there were some major differences in the way mixed martial arts was viewed in the United Sates and in Japan. In the States, the sport simply wasn't mainstream—we were hoisting up tents on river banks to hold shows that drew a thousand people. In Japan, MMA was beyond mainstream—it was revered. The Asian culture celebrates the "budo" lifestyle, which translates to "the way of war," and fighters are seen as modern-day warriors. MMA was covered daily by the mainstream papers. I'd only fought in the Octagon three times, but the Japanese already knew who I was.

After weigh-ins that Friday, referee John McCarthy, the UFC's new commentator Mike Goldberg, and I attended a Pancrase event in the Yokohama Gymnasium. Though mostly a local event that featured Japanese fighters, we watched foreigners like Guy Mezger and Bas Rutten submit their opponents in the ring in front of a crowd of 6,000— three times the size of the crowd at *UFC 15*. Afterward, John and I walked outside and were immediately surrounded by a sea of people looking for autographs and pictures. It was pure comedy—I'm six-foot-one and John is even taller, so we stood there towering over all the eager faces.

The next night, the crowds followed us into the Yokohama Arena in the Kanagawa district, filling it with 17,000 people, the largest UFC attendance to date. It was certainly the largest crowd I'd ever fought in front of.

American audiences will let you know when they don't like something—especially if a match-up is light in leather throwing. The Japanese were polite observers. They understood all facets of the game, including the submission work on the mat. To say you could hear a pin drop in the Yokohama Arena when I stepped into the cage would have been an understatement. They "ooed" and "awed" and clapped at what they liked, but it was a controlled, respectful gesture at all times.

Some fighters need the crowd's energy to feed off of, but the silence didn't affect my game at all. It was kind of nice because I could hear the guys in my corner, and I could hear Trish throughout the whole fight. She wasn't sitting cageside, but I could hear her voice plain as day coming from somewhere.

Rico and I had put a lot of thought into the Mo Smith fight and how his kicks could be used against me, not just from a damage standpoint. I had seen the bruising inflicted on Coleman and Tank Abbott in Mo's last two fights, and I knew that had an effect on the judges and how they viewed who was ahead on the cards. They'd see the damage accumulate over the course of the fight and they wouldn't always rationally evaluate what they were looking at. To take that out of their hands, I decided to wear long bicycle leggings in case Mo managed to land some of his paddle-like shins on my thighs. Then nobody would see the damage, including Mo himself.

It was a nice plan in theory, though it ended up working against me. Mo never really landed any kicks. He kicked me two or three times the entire fight and every other time I managed to take him down. From his back, Mo used the half guard, where he laced his legs in between mine. With the leggings and my wrestling shoes, it created enough grip and friction that allowed him to tie me up pretty well. He was stuck there, but so was I. I was still winning the fight, but it was a little frustrating that I couldn't move to a better position or pass his guard to mount, which was the best position to be in. I couldn't do a whole lot to him in that position, and I remember lying there thinking I'd never wear long pants again.

The fight went the full twenty-one minutes without breaks, and I scored with a heap of takedowns for style supremacy. Two of the judges named me the winner, with the third judge ruling it a draw. They called it a majority decision, enough for me to become the new UFC heavyweight champion.

It was December 21, and probably the best Christmas present I could have asked for. The Japanese fans were very gracious to me and seemed enamoured with my sizable skills in a package somewhat smaller than the normal heavyweights. They had me take pictures with national Sumo hero Akebono and one of his colleagues after the fight. It was like standing between two Volkswagens.

Our bus ride back to Tokyo was only supposed to take two hours, but it ended up lasting five. We missed our flights home, and Trish and I spent an extra night in Tokyo. We flew out on Christmas Eve, at the end of an eventful year.

I RETURNED HOME in January with the 1998 Nationals looming and started training at camp with Danny in the Oregon State wrestling room. In practise, he tried to gut-wrench me, a Greco manoeuvre where you lock your arms around your opponent's midsection, squeeze, and roll with your opponent to expose his back to the mat for points. Danny squeezed me hard enough to pop cartilage in my rib cage.

Sitting out Nationals was disappointing, as I had been named the favourite going in because I had won the year before. SEG had also slated for me to fight former heavyweight champion Mark Coleman at their next event, but the injury kept me on the sidelines.

It took me a few months to recover, and I slowly stepped back into practise as Danny prepared for his Octagon debut at *UFC 17: Redemption* in Mobile, Alabama, on May 15, 1998. It was the first time

SEG introduced a middleweight tournament for guys under 205 pounds, and Danny ended up fighting twice in that one night against Brazilian Allan Goes and Canadian Carlos Newton to take the title. After I worked Danny's corner, I sat down cageside to watch Coleman face young up-and-comer Pete Williams. Williams shocked the world with a kick out of nowhere, right to Coleman's kisser, which sent him sailing to the canvas with his eyes rolled up in the back of his head. I wouldn't face Coleman now.

I had a difficult time staying away from the action. My first-place finish the year before allowed me to petition myself into the World Team Trials, held down in New Orleans. Honestly, I just wasn't ready to come back, but I'd never been one to wait when competition was right in front of me. I wrestled like absolute dog crap and took fifth in the Trials, losing to Dave Surovchek, a wrestler I'd never lost to before and had beaten on numerous occasions.

That spring, Oregon State found a full-time assistant coach to fill my position, so I left the university. Trish was still commuting to Portland to finish her master's in nursing. I was also driving up to Portland to train with the guys from the Straight Blast gym, so it didn't make sense for us to stay in Corvallis and have Trish driving ninety miles each way for school a few days a week. Her family lived in Corbett, a suburb of Portland, and I liked the area, so we decided to move to Gresham, about eleven miles east of Portland.

We ended up staying at her folks' house for three months while we house-hunted, which was a challenge. It's stressful for anyone to move back in with their parents, but we made it work. We finally found our own place, made an offer, and moved into a nice house on Paloma Avenue by summer.

I had always enjoyed coaching, so I was very happy to get a call from Vern Olsen, the head wrestling coach for the Centennial High School team, not long after we moved there. Olsen asked me if I'd like to assist him with coaching, and I gladly accepted. It was not a very lucrative position—I made $3,500 for the season—but that didn't matter. It was one small way I could stay involved with wrestling and give back.

That summer, SEG came back to me and asked if I was healthy enough to compete again. I told them I was back in training and would be raring to go. The UFC had recruited an athletic Dutchman named Bas Rutten, who they wanted me to meet at their *Ultimate Brazil* event in São Paulo on October 16, 1998. A champion in Japan's Pancrase organisation, Rutten was aggressive and acrobatic, and seemed a worthy opponent for my first title defence.

I should have known something was wrong when Rico got a phone call shortly after from John Perretti, who'd recently taken over the UFC matchmaking duties from Art Davie.

A part-time stuntman and lifelong martial arts enthusiast, Perretti's reputation preceded him. I'd seen Perretti on a grappling pay-per-view programme called *The Contenders* that pitted wrestlers against jiu-jitsu practitioners. Danny had grappled Frank Shamrock in the event and lost with an ankle lock in fifty-six seconds. Perretti was the colour commentator, along with 1972 Olympic freestyle wrestling gold medallist and University of Iowa coaching legend Dan Gable. They debated back and forth on the telecast. I thought that Perretti was a moron, especially the way he treated Gable and how he'd handled himself in front of the camera. In Japan, I met Perretti the week of training before the UFC with Mo and shook hands with him at the after-party. Later Rico told me that Perretti was telling everybody that he'd trained with me.

"Oh, yeah, I rolled with Couture," is what Rico said he'd heard.

I had just met the guy and shook his hand. It was another instance when someone made up some bull crap about me. This gave me a good sense of what Perretti was about and that I probably couldn't trust him. I figured he was the type of guy that was going to play both sides against each other, and he didn't prove me wrong. When SEG tried to pair me up with Coleman before my injury, Perretti told Rico that Coleman had been mouthing off about me. We knew he was calling

Coleman too, and telling him the same thing to stir up animosity for the fight. I guess Perretti didn't stop to think that we all knew each other from wrestling—Rico was talking to Coleman on the phone and knew the whole thing was bullshit.

So, when Rico got a phone call from Perretti, I wasn't optimistic. Perretti told Rico that they wanted me to fight Rutten, but that they couldn't pay me what my contract promised. Instead of my negotiated $80,000 purse, the UFC was willing to pay me $25,000.

At that point, Rico had spent a lot of time and effort setting up my pay scale. I had gotten $60,000 to fight Mo, then it was supposed to rise to $80,000, and then finally to $100,000 for my final fight under that contract. SEG was also paying me a training stipend of $4,500 a month, which was pretty good money for the time.

"I think they can pay," Rico said, and I couldn't help but agree. An executed contract was on the table that both parties had agreed to. I didn't buy all the "we don't have any money" crap anyway. I knew they were still making money off the pay-per-views and live gates, especially the meaty ones in Japan.

We decided to hold out and only fight if they honoured the contract. A few days later, SEG came back with their reply. They said that I'd chosen not to defend my title, so they would strip me of it. To crown a new heavyweight champion, SEG announced that they'd hold an elimination tournament over two events that would include Rutten, Brazilian Pedro Rizzo, Coleman, and Japan's Tsuyoshi "TK" Kohsaka.

Of course, I understood this wasn't just Perretti's directive. From the start, I knew it wasn't going to work out with Bob Meyrowitz, the absentee owner of the UFC. He was real pompous and not very personable. He'd kept himself at a distance from me at events, and I'd found him to be proper and stiff, like he felt he was better than everyone else. Behind the scenes, he'd become a standoffish tyrant.

Bob didn't think much of me and I knew it. He cared to pamper the sensational, exotic, flashy, or controversial fighters like Tank Abbott. I didn't fit any of those moulds, so I guess I was expendable in his eyes.

Full Contact Fighter had named me its "Fighter of the Year," and I was featured on the covers of *Black Belt* and *Grappling* that year, which should have indicated my level of accomplishment. But that didn't seem to matter.

I wasn't sad about SEG's reaction. I was pissed off. I felt like these jerks had wasted my time and if that was the way it going to be, then screw them. I had other things I could do.

I walked away. I wasn't going to try and take them to court because it wasn't worth it. They still owed me $9,000 for my November and December stipends. I had enough money in the bank then, so I thought I'd just turn back to training for the 2000 Olympics.

SEG might have been willing to write me off, but there were others that still wanted to see me fight. Shortly after SEG announced that I'd been stripped of the title, the Shooto organisation called and offered me a fight at their *Vale Tudo '98* event, scheduled for October 25 at the Tokyo Bay NK Hall in Chiba, Japan.

Shooto wasn't a terribly rich organisation, but they offered me $35,000 and gave us North American ownership and broadcasting rights for nine Shooto events to distribute on our own. The events included a few of the fights that would take place that night, including my own, and a few others from some rare events. A few years later, Rico and director John Myers collected these fights, as well as a few others, like Danny's MMA debut down in Brazil, onto DVDs and offered them on MMAClassics.com, of which I own twenty percent. (I don't know how much these fights have actually paid us back in the last few years, but I've enjoyed the idea of owning a little piece of the sport's history.)

For the first time ever in my young mixed martial arts career, I was being brought into a fight as the favourite. My opponent Enson Inoue, had made his UFC debut the same night as me, tapping out Royce Alger, Rico's former college teammate, who we'd shared a locker room with. A Japanese-American born in Honolulu, Hawaii, Enson was touted for his ability to bend his opponents' limbs into pretzels until they tapped out. As Shooto's heavyweight champion, Enson was pretty cocky, so I felt there was an expectation for me to come in and humble him. For the first time ever, I was overconfident.

Enson and I met in the ring in front of 7,000 anxious Japanese fans. He'd fought here many times before; this was only my second time in front of a quiet, tense Japanese crowd. I closed in on Enson into a tight clinch and didn't struggle much taking him down to the mat. He was used to being on his back though, and flowed right into an armbar, wrapping his legs around my arm. I felt like I was caught in a bear trap. Impulsively, I did exactly what you're not supposed to do—pull away. Enson was a technician, and flipped to his stomach to arch his hips into my arm until I had no choice but to tap out with my free hand. I lost in a minute and thirty-nine seconds.

I shook Inoue's hand with the arm that he had just tapped me out with, suddenly humbled by the sting of defeat and the realisation that I had a lot more to learn if I wanted to continue in MMA. But even though I lost, Shooto named it their fight of the year and mailed me a trophy that was over a foot tall.

Afterward, I felt like I hadn't given Enson enough credit. It wasn't that I didn't train hard. I trained as hard as I had for any fight. I just didn't think that he could beat me. As an athlete, I think you have to have a fleeting thought in the back of your head that reminds you, "Today this guy could beat me." It's not exactly fear—maybe more concern—but I think that is what motivates you that extra little bit. On any given day anybody can beat you, it doesn't matter who it is. That was a valuable lesson to me.

That day I made friends with the fact that I could lose any competition and it wouldn't be the end of the world. I began to figure out ways to ease the pressures of winning, and it made me a better fighter right away.

I TOOK A few months' break from fighting until March 1999, when I returned to Japan. The organisation was called RINGS, and after years of hosting fights with their own set of rules, they decided to hold an event using the standard MMA regulations. I wouldn't have agreed to fight in their organisation if they used their stupid rules anyway, with the rope escapes and hokey time limits. I was used to the political decisions in wrestling—the grey areas where the referee could affect the outcome of the match. I thought MMA was immune to that because there was no way an official could intervene beyond stopping the match. I thought I could get a fair shake.

I fought a Russian kid named Mikhail Iloukhine. I was pummelling him in the clinch in one of the corners when he tried to reach over my arm for a Kimura, twisting my bent arm backwards to put strain on my shoulder joint. He really didn't have the hold, and he couldn't pull me to the floor to finish the move because we were tangled in the ropes. I was standing there whacking away at his ribs, trying to get him to release my arm and change position, when the referee stepped in to call a stop and pulled us to the centre of the ring for a restart.

Though it wasn't physically possible, he tried to put us in the same position and actually gave Iloukhine the Kimura behind my back before restarting the fight. Out of the ropes, Iloukhine was able to finish the Kimura. I struggled to scramble out and wouldn't tap, but the referee stopped the fight anyway. I think this was the first time I really got screwed in the sport. I lost to a guy I should have never lost to, but this time I had some perspective.

This is bullshit, I thought to myself, *but what am I going to do? Write to my congressman?*

The Japanese media was especially sympathetic to me in the days following. I think it was because I hadn't made a big deal out of it. I guess they had been used to Americans throwing fits over calls like this, but I decided to take this one in stride.

It was April 1999. I didn't know it at the time, but I wouldn't step into a ring or cage again for another nineteen months. That's the way

God usually plans it, though. He gives you just what you can handle, and now, it seemed, my personal life needed tending to.

I had been seeing my kids Aimee and Ryan since the divorce every other weekend or when I could, visiting them in Seattle or having them come down on the train to visit me. Aimee was now fifteen years old and getting into trouble up in Seattle. She wasn't getting along with her mom, Sharon, who was having trouble controlling her. She was sneaking out to hang out with the wilder crowd and definitely walking a fine line.

Sharon was kind of straitlaced. She had the ability to guilt Ryan into toeing the line (plus Ryan was smart enough to get away with what he wanted without getting caught). But Aimee was a little more defiant. Sharon's guilt trips didn't work with her. I also think that females tend to bang heads a little bit more in the teenage years.

So Sharon sent Aimee down to stay with me and Trish. I thought it would be great. I was getting a second chance with my daughter. I had lost my kids through the divorce, and this was my opportunity to reconnect. First and foremost, we now got to spend a lot of time together, which made me happy. I took Aimee to a horse auction and bought her a dog.

However, it was a big change for all of us. Trish had to adjust to having a teenager in the house, and we struggled to set up rules and boundaries. Aimee was still in an adolescent tunnel-vision mode. She wasn't used to doing a lot of chores and had trouble keeping motivated. We encouraged her to get a job, and she picked blueberries that summer on Trish's mom's farm to earn money. I realised it would take time to get through to Aimee, but she wasn't going anywhere, at least for now.

THAT FALL, I also made a decision to leave my management under Rico and Lou. I had been a UFC champion for a year and hadn't gotten a single endorsement deal for it. The brothers weren't terribly organised, and they weren't on the same page. Lou had his ideas and Rico had his, but there was no coordination or communication, and it became frustrating. It felt like we weren't getting anywhere and I didn't really have anything going on, when I thought we should be taking advantage of me being the champion. I decided from that point on that I would leave Real American Wrestling and manage myself. Danny Henderson's split from RAW wasn't as amicable.

Danny and I were both supposed to re-sign around the same time, and he did so not knowing I had turned down the extension to stay with RAW. Danny's contract had expired before mine, so they had pressured him to sign before they'd secured him an October fight with RINGS. When he found out that I hadn't re-signed, he didn't want to be with the RAW team anymore either. Rico and Lou verbally agreed that they would allow him to get out of his contract, but Danny had to write a letter and fill out other paperwork. He was a bit of a procrastinator, though, and with his active wrestling schedule, it took him a long time to get that done.

Danny's October fight in Japan was the opening rounds of a tournament called *RINGS: King of Kings*, and he swept through two bouts in one night to earn a slot in its conclusion that next February. Danny returned to Japan for the finals and won the whole damn thing, earning a split decision over Antonio Rodrigo Nogueira and a couple of hundred thousand dollars. But because Danny hadn't yet filed the paperwork they'd asked for, Rico and Lou told Danny he owed them commission for the tournament's finals. Danny refused, arguing that he had gotten to the finals on his own.

It ended up going to arbitration, and I was asked to testify, which made me feel horrible. Danny lost the arbitration but later appealed because RAW hadn't registered as an agent with the state of California under its Miller-Ayala Athlete Agents Act. The ruling was eventually overturned.

To this day, there is still a lot of bad blood between all of them. Over the years, I've gotten along with Lou and Rico and even grappled in

Rico's Professional Submission League venture in 2006. We also launched MMAClassics.com together to distribute the fights that Shooto had given us in 1998. However, their relationship with Danny never seemed to recover. In 2006, Rico invited Danny to compete in the PSL alongside me, but he vehemently declined the invitation. He didn't want anything to do with them.

With the 2000 Olympics getting closer, Danny and his wife Allison moved to Oregon just a few blocks away from Trish, Aimee, and I, so he could train full-time. We trained together at the Straight Blast gym and a few other places for both our wrestling and our fighting. We went on all the wrestling tours together and went camping and hiking in our free time. I had cornered Danny in both his RINGS appearances, and we went to the Nationals and the World Team Trials together. After Danny won the tournament in February 2000, RINGS asked me if I wanted to compete in a heavyweight tournament. It would happen after the Olympics, and I figured I would come back in shape, then go off to fight. Sitting around one day with all this going on between us, Danny and I had a simultaneous thought.

"Man, we should open our own gym," we said to each other.

Just as we started looking for a space, a lawyer friend of ours named Rick Franklin came to us with a perfectly timed proposition.

"We have this fitness centre that my friend just foreclosed on," Rick said. "You interested? It's called the Third Street Gym. It's a turnkey with a big aerobics room in the back where you can lay wrestling mats. Then you have the full fitness centre around it."

We looked the place over and it seemed perfect. It was only a few minutes from both of our homes, and we could both train there together. Danny, Rick, and I each put $10,000 upfront to get it going, hired staff, and called it Performance Quest.

The wrestling centre grew fast—all of the local high school kids and other guys we knew started coming to practise. But that didn't pay the bills. The health club was supposed to earn the money, but no one was using it. You could hear crickets in there. And our small gym quickly got big competition. A brand new Bally's, as well as a 30,000-plus square foot Gold's, had opened up down the street, with a pool and racquetball courts and all those extras. We were just a little mom-and-pop fitness centre with a hot tub.

We were losing money hand over fist, but we didn't know what the heck we were doing. We had no clue how to run a fitness centre.

Despite our sinking business, my wrestling career had to keep moving to ensure I made it to the Olympic Trials in 2000. I won my fourth and final National title in 1999, placed second at the World Team Trials in Tampa, Florida, then went to the World Championships in Poland. I qualified for the Pan American Championships in Canada and had my old Cuban rival, Reynaldo Peña, nearly beat in the finals, but ended up getting taken down with thirty seconds left and lost by a point. Regardless, I was having a very good wrestling year going into 2000.

At the 2000 Nationals, my train derailed when I got beat by a new kid named Garrett Lowney, who seemed to come out of nowhere. Lowney caught me with an arm throw in the first minute of the match for three points. I came back and scored two points on him for passivities, or advantage points. I couldn't tie it up in time though. I ended up taking third, which meant I had to enter the mini-tournament and wrestle my way back to meet Lowney again in the Trials. But Lowney beat me again, handing me my fourth Olympic alternate slot in four tries. Lowney went on to win the bronze medal at the 2000 Olympic Games in Sydney, Australia, that summer.

Seventeen years had passed since that lieutenant had picked me out in the army barracks gym back in Germany. I was now thirty-six years old, watching a young kid come up on the international circuit at the open level—and it hit home. *I think it's time to focus on something else*, I thought. I couldn't see myself going another four years and I certainly wasn't making the kind of headway I needed to that late in the game.

I wrestled my very last match at those trials. I did travel to Sydney that summer, not as part of the team but just to enjoy the competition, this time as a retiree.

BECAUSE IT WAS only a five-hour flight from Australia to Japan, I decided to train for my first round of the RINGS heavyweight tournament in the land down under for thirty days. I headed to the Boxing Works there with Australian fighter Larry Papadopoulos. John Donehue, the Brazilian jiu-jitsu black belt I had trained with in Hermosa Beach for my fight with Mo Smith, had since moved back to Melbourne and opened his Extreme Jiu Jitsu and Grappling gym there. We met up at the Olympics and headed back to his gym to get to work.

In the second week of October, I flew to Japan to compete in the *RINGS: King of Kings Block A* tournament. I fought Jeremy Horn in my first bout of the night. Horn was in his twenties, but was already vastly experienced under the tutelage of UFC lightweight champion Pat Miletich. Both Horn and I exhausted ourselves in a fast-paced fight, and after the first two five-minute rounds, two of the judges couldn't make up their minds and called it a draw. They announced that we'd go into overtime for one more five-minute round. I heard Jeremy turn to his corner and say, "I think I am going to puke." I realised then that I could step it up here and win, and that's what I did. Though drained and fatigued, I won my second bout of the evening against a huge Japanese fighter named Ryushi Yanagisawa by majority decision. I'd secured my spot in the finals, which would take place in February 2001.

Returning to Oregon in the fall of 2000, Danny and I knew we'd have to close Performance Quest. It wasn't making any money and we didn't know how to save it. We decided we'd just auction off all of the equipment and move the mats, although we weren't sure where. And that's when Matt Lindland entered the picture.

Matt was fresh off an Olympic silver-medal win in Sydney and had trained with us at Performance Quest right when it had opened its doors in early 2000. At the time, Matt had been living in Colorado Springs with his wife and kids, training for the Trials at the Olympic training centre. He'd attended the University of Nebraska and had stayed on as their club coach after graduation in a special position they'd created for the wrestling programme.

We were all longtime friends from the National team. I'd first met Matt back in college. He was Nebraska's 158-pounder and wrestled Pat Smith, from Oklahoma State. Back then, I thought Matt had a tough grittiness to his wrestling that made him one of the top guys in the country. I met him later through the Greco circuit, when we started qualifying for the National teams together. I think the first time I ever spent time with him was at the Concord Cup in California. Matt wore Birkenstocks and black socks and was a bit goofy, but he was funny and he was always fun to be around. He was also a great wrestler, a hard worker, and tough as hell.

Matt offered for us to move our gym equipment to a car dealership he'd just opened. There was a warehouse space behind the lot, a metal structure that looked like a pole barn. We swept and cleaned it all up and laid down some really old wrestling mats that we'd bought from Bob Anderson, our old coach. Danny drove them up in a Ryder truck from Southern California to Oregon and slept on them a couple of times along the way. This was the beginning of Team Quest.

When I returned from Japan in October, I was surprised by a phone call from UFC matchmaker John Perretti. Our conversation was short and simple: SEG wanted me to come back and fight for the UFC heavyweight title they'd stripped me of some three years before. I quickly threw out a number I thought they'd never go for.

"I'll do it for $85,000," I said.

Perretti was silent for a moment, then said he'd call me back tomorrow. The next day, he called again and agreed to the straight purse without a bonus. The fight was in November, so I knew they were desperate. I told him that win or lose, I'd have to return to Japan in

February to honour my commitment to RINGS in the tournament I had already started. Perretti hastily agreed.

On November 17, 2000, after a three-year absence, I stepped back into the UFC's Octagon.

CHAPTER NINE:
9 ZUFFA MEANS 'FIGHT' IN ITALIAN

OF ALL THE QUESTIONS I GET ASKED, THE ONE I GET the most is, "Do you get nervous before a fight?"

Nervous? Why would I get nervous? How can nervousness help me? Do you think nervousness implies that something bad might happen? Think about the physical symptoms you associate with nervousness: sweaty palms, butterflies in the stomach, dry mouth, and feeling like you're going to pee. Now tell me what the physical sensations are when you're excited about something. By simply changing one word in your head, already you're smiling. You're not thinking that something bad is going to happen. Approach is key and well within your control. You have the power to keep it positive.

I love what I do. I don't sit backstage fearing what's going happen once I step into the cage. I get keyed up about it. I get so eager about fighting that I lean on the back legs of my chair watching the clock and counting the minutes until I can peel out of the locker room and climb in there.

Fear is certainly not something I felt before my fight against heavyweight champion Kevin Randleman at *UFC 28: High Stakes* the evening of November 17, 2000. I was coming back to the Octagon after a three-year absence, and my mindset was very different than my other fights. I expected to be there and felt that I deserved to win the title. I think it was the first time where I'd actually set goals in MMA. In the past, I had entered on a whim and thought, *Oh, yeah, I'll try that. It looks like fun.* The sport had paid me well so far and I'd always had one-fight deals with my past contracts, so it never felt like a full-time commitment. After not fighting for eighteen months and then retiring from wrestling, I set some standards for myself. I was going to put my mind to training and winning the title back and see what I could do with this sport at 100 percent. There would be no more juggling and no other distractions.

I think it would have been a shock to my system if I had just retired from wrestling and not gone back to any kind of competition. There would have been a big void in my life. A lot of athletes who retire feel estranged from their sport, but I never gave myself the opportunity to have second thoughts. I never considered wrestling again and I never thought about coming out of retirement for it. I didn't miss it at all. I was having a blast fighting, and the title shot afforded me the chance to get right back in the mix while still making a great living. If I had made the Olympic team, I probably wouldn't have continued fighting because I would have been satisfied. Disappointment is a funny thing that way.

The greatest advantage I had heading into my ninth professional fight was Team Quest. Though we didn't know it, the union of three laid-back wrestlers was the seed for what would become one of the most recognised teams in the sport. At the time, we didn't know that. Danny, Matt, and I were simply joining forces with the common goal of parlaying our talents into a relatively new sport. That was our motivation.

Our surroundings were humble, but Olympic wrestlers tend not to fuss after spending years bunking in grimy dorms and competing in dusty gymnasiums in the heart of impoverished Hungary or sweltering Cuba. Our trio of world-class athletes met inside the metal-framed warehouse behind Matt's USA Auto Wholesale dealership. The walls were drywalled but had no insulation, which made for nippy workouts during Oregon's bitter winters and sweaty sessions in the summer months.

It was a rough house. Holes created by two bodies slamming into the walls were treated as artwork and autographed. When only one piece of untouched drywall remained, we took bets to see who would fly through it first. Mats were pulled up to the wall and served as makeshift surfaces to simulate one of the cage's eight sides. We made do with what we had, which wasn't much.

A wrestler's mentality is to work hard and barrel through the pain, which directly influenced our training. In the wrestling circuit all our lives, we had a wealth of knowledge between us to shape a programme. I had been a college coach, and Matt had been one as well, so we knew how to run a practise. Team Quest mimicked a wrestling programme at the start, and we taught the guys that trained under us how to condition, how to run sprints, how to do the morning workouts, eat, rest, then return for the afternoon regimens. The back of our Team Quest T-shirts, soaked through with sweat and clinging to our bodies, summed up our training style. They read: "Pain is merely weakness leaving the body."

The best part about our team was that I didn't have to travel anymore for my training. I was still with the same guys I had been working out with all along, but I wasn't hopping planes to Hermosa Beach, California, or Melbourne, Australia, to meet them. I was doing it all right in my own backyard.

I ALWAYS FIGURED fighting another wrestler would probably be the toughest. I had done well against strikers and fighters that didn't have a wrestling background, but going up against another guy who had my same strength and background would be a test. Kevin Randleman was a two-time NCAA champion for Ohio State University with the fastest shot in MMA. With bleached blonde hair contrasting against his black skin, Randleman had tree trunks for thighs, which made him as explosive as any athlete I'd ever seen. Randleman was a true athlete, with incredible reflexes and a vertical jump that would put Kobe Bryant to shame.

In my three years away, the UFC had adopted five-minute rounds—three for regular bouts and five for championship matches—because of a controversial match between Kevin Randleman and Bas Rutten at *UFC 20: Battle for the Gold* on May 7, 1999. After watching the fight go twenty-one minutes straight, the judges and audience were split down the middle as to who had controlled the action longer. Randleman had led the first ten minutes or so, but Rutten had come on strong in the remaining ten. Randleman walked away the loser, but public uproar earned him a second shot at the heavyweight title in Tokyo, Japan, that November at *UFC 23: Ultimate Japan 2.* Randleman faced Pete Williams, the Lion's Den fighter that had knocked out Mark Coleman with a head kick, and controlled him for five rounds for the decision and the belt.

Like he'd done with Williams, Randleman knocked me around and held me down for the first two rounds, but I almost armbarred him from my back, which showed that other parts of my game were developing. In the third round, I finally got to take Randleman down and get on top, where I was more comfortable and dominant. As he squirmed underneath me, it was obvious he hadn't learned many skills from that position. He wasn't able to defend himself or tie me up to prevent the flurry of strikes I poured on him. The rules say if your opponent can't intelligently defend himself, the fight will be stopped. Referee John McCarthy acknowledged this by stepping in between us 4:13 into the third round. It wasn't the wrestling that made the difference in this fight, but my mixed martial arts experience.

Winning in Atlantic City felt particularly good, and I was surprised to see that some of the fans hadn't forgotten about me. Though the UFC had difficulty filling even an intimate 4,000-seat arena like the Trump Taj Mahal, the fans that showed up were die-hard followers. As they wrapped the belt around my waist, red and blue confetti fell from the sky, and fans huddled outside the cage for almost half an hour, waiting for me to emerge. I finished taking pictures with the photographers and stepped down into the crowd. It was quite a homecoming.

I felt like I was back, but I wasn't sure where that was going to lead me with SEG. I was concerned about our relationship after all the contract problems and the stripping of my title, but that would become a moot point soon enough. It was no secret that SEG was having financial problems and was struggling just to pump out five events a year. Behind the scenes, the show was a mess. Elaine McCarthy had left, so any sense of organisation was gone. Everyone associated with the event felt like they were walking on eggshells, never knowing if that next show would be our last. There had been rumours that Bob Meyrowitz was looking to sell the UFC and get out. John Perretti, the matchmaker, kept hinting that something big was on the horizon—I'd even heard that he was trying to buy the UFC himself.

In December, I flew with Danny and Matt to Japan for fights they had booked. Matt was making his UFC debut on December 16 at *UFC 29: Defence of the Belts* against a pro wrestler named Yoji Anjo at the Differ Ariake arena in Tokyo. While American pro wrestling is kept separate from real sports, the line between pro wrestling and MMA blurred in Asian culture. In Japan, MMA fights weren't predetermined like pro wrestling, at least not the ones I was around, but pro wrestlers often got into the cage with fighters to test themselves, sometimes with gruesome results. In this case, Matt manhandled Anjo with his wrestling and punches, and the bout was stopped three minutes into the first round.

In the lobby of Matt's hotel, I met Dana White, a manager who represented two light heavyweight fighters, Chuck Liddell and Tito Ortiz. Dana had called me up back in the States and we'd agreed to talk in Japan about him possibly representing me. In his early thirties with an excitable personality, Dana told me he was a fighter himself, and he understood the game. He said he liked my fighting style and thought he could do something with me. He seemed like an okay guy, but I really hadn't had any experience with managers outside Rico and Lou so I stayed noncommittal. I wanted a chance to think about it.

The week before, we stayed at Danny's hotel in Saitama. Danny's big win in the RINGS tournament had drawn the attention of another promotion called PRIDE Fighting Championships, and they'd brought Danny in to fight their 205-pound Brazilian champion, Wanderlei Silva, in the biggest show of the year, which broadcasted on national television. We'd find out later it was the stiffest first fight Danny could have ever been offered by the promotion, because Silva was a killer. Danny actually fared very well, taking the brutal Muay thai fighter down and pummelling his right eye until it swelled shut to the size of a ping-pong ball. But Silva was the champion for a reason—he was a vicious scrapper who tagged Danny real good with punches and knees in their clinches. Danny took Silva the distance for the first time in the champion's career, but the Brazilian walked away with the belt.

Bouncing between the two events in two weeks, it became abundantly clear that the UFC was on its last legs. While a little over a thousand people showed up to watch *UFC 29* at a relatively tiny indoor arena in Japan, 27,000 fans had shown up to Danny's *PRIDE 12* event. Granted, PRIDE was a homegrown promotion, but UFC's *Ultimate Japan* had drawn 17,000 spectators only three years before, when I'd fought Mo Smith. The drop in numbers was just too discouraging.

Everyone's fears were well founded, but there was a light at the end of the tunnel. In January, word spread that the UFC had indeed been purchased, not by Perretti, but by Lorenzo and Frank Fertitta, two wealthy brothers that owned a chain of casinos in Las Vegas. Dana White, the ambitious fighter manager who had met me in that hotel lobby in Japan, would be running the company from here on out. Dana was a close childhood friend of Lorenzo and Frank, and had brought the UFC to their attention.

It was a good thing I hadn't signed with Dana. Before taking the helm of the UFC as its president, he had pawned off his clients, Tito Ortiz and Chuck Liddell, to a lawyer friend because it would have been a conflict of interest for him to promote and manage fighters at the same time. I had also begun talking to a firm in California called Battle Management, which was lead by Jeremy Lappen and Peter Levin. Lappen, an entertainment lawyer and producer, and Levin, a longtime agent, had also approached Mark Coleman, Pat Miletich, and UFC lightweight champion Jens Pulver.

I took a meeting with them in Hollywood and was impressed by the way they saw fighters as professional athletes who were due all the sponsorships and opportunities that came with it. I also liked how they were connected. Not only could they manage my fighting and get the endorsements I'd missed out on my first time as champion; they could also open a lot of doors in Hollywood.

BY 2001, I'D already had a few brushes with acting. The U.S. Olympics Committee had selected me to appear in a commercial for NationsBank, which was one of their sponsors. I didn't get paid, but I got experience, and the whole process intrigued me.

I had also been in the right place at the right time to get cast in a Nike commercial. It featured athletes physically affected by their sports, competitors who had athletic "scars." A Portland advertising agency handled the campaign, and had a wrestler from Portland State University working in their casting office. They were auditioning actors with cauliflower ears—the trademark bloated, bumpy appearance of a wrestler's ear, caused by the cartilage breaking and resetting inside after hours and hours rolling over them on the mats.

The wrestler took one look at the auditioners and said, "Dude, those aren't cauliflower ears. I'll give you cauliflower ears."

He called several wrestlers in the area, including me. I came in and he took a Polaroid of my left ear. They called me back later that night to ask if I was doing anything that Monday, and if I'd like to fly out to California to do the commercial. I said, "Hell, yeah!"

They paid me $7,500 to stand around and show off my ear. I didn't have any lines. It was the first time I'd been on any type of big set, and watching a group of twenty people put together a thirty-second commercial was fascinating.

In sixth grade, I played Tiny Tim in *A Christmas Carol*, but that was the closest I'd ever gotten to acting. I was always into movies and the process of making one. Watching a movie, it seems like there are two people just sitting there, having a conversation. But watching them actually shoot a scene on a set, I realised that there's a lot more to it. It was exciting, like I was being let in on a secret.

After the Nike commercial, fate intervened again. One of the three men who judged my fight against Kevin Randleman at *UFC 28* was Douglas Crosby, who happened to be one of the industry's most experienced and consistently working stunt coordinators. Doug has worked on *Men in Black*, *Spiderman*, and practically any big-time movie you could think of, with all of the major directors.

Following my fight with Randleman, Doug sent me a book on ancient Pankration and a note telling me how he was impressed with my fighting. The note came on letterhead that showed a stick figure getting hit by a car. That was Doug's sense of humour. Doug and I began talking, and he told me he was contemplating using fighters for some of his stunt jobs because he thought it might be a natural transition. He wanted athletes who could take direction and follow his lead. He'd already been trying it out with Igor Zinoviev, a Russian fighter who had fought at *UFC 16*, and it was going well.

At the time, Doug was coordinating the stunts for the HBO prison series *OZ*, so he brought me and Frank Shamrock in. I flew to New York and played a prison guard during a huge melee that started after one of the inmates got shanked in his wheelchair. Doug's generosity helped me and a few other fighters get some interesting gigs over the next few years. I was able to pay the $1,200 dues and join the Screen Actors Guild (which my manager Jeremy really appreciated). I also made the earnings cutoff and got free healthcare through the union that year, which was a nice bonus for a fighter with none at all. Acting was something I really wanted to explore, but I had to start out like the rest, from the bottom.

Back in Oregon, word had spread quickly about Team Quest. I had just won back the UFC heavyweight title a second time, and Matt and Danny were making names for themselves as well. The classes grew by a guy or two each day, until we looked around one afternoon and counted thirty bodies getting thrown around on the mats. We weren't just attracting wrestlers either. There were all different kinds of guys wanting to train to be fighters or straight jiu-jitsu guys or wrestlers. The gym had even attracted a few women. Danny, Matt, and I looked at each other and said, "Damn, we should run this as a business."

We put up plywood over the demolished drywall, painted the walls, fixed the lights, and started transforming the warehouse into a gym. We put in a small amount of weight equipment, including a treadmill and a bike—just the rudimentary stuff we needed for training. We'd learned our lesson with the health club. Over the years, we eventually padded the walls, fenced in one side of the mats with chain link, and built a reception area with a front desk. We hired Robert Follis, who had worked at the Straight Blast gym in Portland, to handle operations. Robert became our fourth partner.

Just as we got things rolling, Danny and Allison decided to move back to their native California. They had two little children and didn't enjoy the rainy climate. Allison's dad had sold them a piece of property where they could build a house, so Danny agreed to run the team's web site from there and sell our merchandise to keep up his end. We all agreed with a handshake.

BY NOW, ZUFFA Sports Entertainment, the company that Lorenzo and Frank Fertitta had put in place to take over the UFC's reigns, was up and running. That February at *UFC 30*, I met the Fertittas, who also owned a chain of seven casinos in Las Vegas that catered to locals. They were both very cordial, as was Zuffa's new president Dana White, who told me they had big things planned. After feeling stifled by SEG the past few years, Zuffa seemed like a breath of fresh air.

Zuffa contacted my manager Jeremy, asking if I would defend my title at *UFC 31: Locked and Loaded* in Atlantic City on May 4, 2001, against Brazilian Pedro Rizzo. We accepted immediately.

I felt comfortable with the match-up. Rizzo was a kickboxer who had been plucked from the streets of Brazil by Vale Tudo legend Marco Ruas, who had won *UFC 7*. Vale Tudo, the Brazilian name for MMA, had been introduced there in the 1950s. Vale Tudo translates out to "anything goes," as the rules were much more open in those days and the fights were bare-knuckled. I knew Rizzo wasn't that good on the ground, so I didn't think I'd have to worry about submissions. I just had to be in shape and bide my time to close the distance and take him down.

I didn't do anything special to prepare for Rizzo. I watched his tapes, including his fights against TK Kohsaka and Kevin Randleman. In his mid-twenties, Rizzo wasn't an aggressive fighter. He waited and had trouble pulling the trigger, though he had obvious power behind his punches. I saw him knock out Josh Barnett at *UFC 30* and noticed it had all been off counterpunching, meaning Rizzo would only throw a punch once his opponent did. I thought I'd be able to go after him aggressively and avoid getting hit.

Though Rizzo was classified as a kickboxer, I hadn't really seen him use his leg arsenal on his opponents, especially kicking the head where a fighter could get knocked out. I had fought other kickboxers like Mo Smith, so I felt I'd be able to take him down if he kicked me. I did my conditioning and was ready to fight.

This was the first fight my mom decided to come see live. She sat in the stands with Trish, having decided the stress of watching me on TV was just too unbearable. She figured as long as she was there with me, it would save her the dreaded phone call to find out if I was okay afterwards. Having her in the stands again gave me an instant boost, like it always had when I was a kid.

The fight was a five-round back-and-forth brawl from the start. I thought the fight was going to end in the first round—I'd taken Rizzo down and pounded on him for well over a minute. Referee John McCarthy was giving the verbal indications that the fight was going to be stopped.

"You gotta get out of there, Pedro. You gotta do something. You gotta change position," he said to Rizzo, who was in a fetal position against the cage.

I continued to punch him with all my might. McCarthy was ready to step in and stop the fight, I could feel it. My corner told me there was twenty seconds left, and McCarthy still hadn't stepped in. I realised he wasn't going to stop this. Rizzo was trying to use his legs to push me away. Even though I cut him and was pounding on him, he was still in it. I slowed down and waited for the end of the round. I went back to my corner so tired, I was cross-eyed. I had punched myself out. It was the first time I'd gotten tired in a fight.

Rizzo came out fresh for round two and kicked the shit out of my lead left leg. He kicked me, and I blocked his leg with my arm and punched myself in the nose. My nose bled everywhere for the rest of the fight. He kicked me again and I buckled, just as I shot in. I spent a long time holding onto a single-leg, catching my breath. He definitely controlled the second round. It was a complete reversal of fortune.

I went back to my corner. The doctor came into the cage and checked my nose. The ten-second warning came, and McCarthy yelled, "Seconds out, seconds out," to signal my cornermen to leave. I just sat on the stool.

Bleary-eyed and gasping for breath, I gazed over at Danny Henderson and he asked, "What are you looking at me for?" I had to make a decision. Could I get off the stool and finish this fight or not? It was gut-check time.

I got up and finished the fight. In my mind, I felt I had clinched the third and fourth rounds by taking Rizzo down and controlling him. I didn't damage him much though. At that point, we were both tired and had spent a lot of energy. He came back and stole the fifth round from me. He battered my leg the entire fight.

When they announced that I'd won the unanimous decision, I made a funny face. It had been a very close fight, and some people thought that Rizzo had won. When they saw my expression, they assumed I agreed with them. It wasn't that I didn't think I'd won. I was surprised that it was a unanimous decision, when I thought it easily could have been a split decision. It had just been a good, close fight, and the toughest I've ever had.

Zuffa had added a pyrotechnics display to the fighter entrances, so there was still a trace of smoke clouding the air. By the time they raised my hand and the confetti fell, everything got foggy. My leg stiffened and tightened up immediately. I had to lean on Brad Anderson, my second cornerman and a buddy from the All-Army wrestling team, to get down the Octagon steps and back to my dressing room. On the way, I sat down to take a picture for *Flaunt* magazine. I saw the picture later and it looked like I was about to die.

That night, I couldn't walk. I hung on to my corner guys and hobbled back to my hotel room. I sat on the couch with my leg elevated for the rest of the night, just so I could get on the plane the next day. My leg started turning black. My thigh swelled so much I had problems putting my pants on. There were pockets of blood under my skin I could chase around with my finger. It was like I had an alien stuck in there. I had to get physical therapy and ultrasounds to break all that down. A therapist massaged my leg, and I wanted to punch her, it hurt so badly. I still have a dent in my quadriceps where my muscle died from the damage. It took three weeks for me to walk normally.

Evaluating the fight afterwards, I couldn't figure out why I had gotten so tired. I thought that maybe the smoke from the pyrotechnics had aggravated my asthma and caused my lungs to tighten up. From then on, I carried out a wash rag to breathe through until I got to the cage. I didn't want to take any chances.

★　★　★

WITH ONE FIGHT left on my contract, my Battle Management agents, Jeremy and Peter, started negotiations with UFC president Dana White and were discouraged when a new contract was presented for me to sign. It was a standard contract that Zuffa was issuing to all their fighters. They took one look at it and said, "No way." "Zuffa" means "fight" in Italian, which we were about to find out the hard way.

The new contract included a clause that handed over the ancillary rights for both my name and likeness to Zuffa "in perpetuity." These rights included pictures, video, or any other medium containing my face and name for advertising and merchandising, from posters to T-shirts to DVDs. "In perpetuity" means forever. Jeremy explained to me that this was exactly where I would make my money in the future. Jeremy and Peter had come from the Hollywood industry and knew what all those terms meant and what that stuff was worth. It definitely wasn't something they would sign away for nothing.

"We've never heard of anyone in any business meeting acting the way this guy acts," they told me, after dealing with Dana White. "He is so irrational and emotional, screaming and yelling and cussing."

Dana started to call me directly to go around my managers. "You know what that fucker said?" he'd ask me. Dana called my managers the "hair fags," because Jeremy had curly hair. I told Jeremy and Peter that Dana was talking to me, and we all agreed to play along.

I never doubted my management, even when Dana badmouthed them. But I had to be careful what I said, because he was my boss and could make things difficult for me or get rid of me all together. I listened to his interpretation of the conversations with Jeremy and Peter, keeping in mind what they had told me.

I thought it was sneaky for him to play both sides, but that is how Dana did business. He said he loved the fighters and would rather deal with them directly, but that wasn't in my best interest. Any promoter is going to try and get as much as he can for as little as possible. All I wanted to do was fight. I didn't understand the seventeen pages of rhetoric Zuffa put in front of me. That was what I was paying my manager for, but Dana didn't see it that way. He got real emotional about it and seemed to take it personally.

The negotiations reached a total gridlock, to the point where Dana couldn't take it anymore. He got way too worked up and had Jeremy and Peter talk to his matchmaker Joe Silva instead. I thought, *if Dana's that pissed off, my management must be doing the right thing.*

Not only wouldn't Jeremy and Peter sign over my rights, they asked for concessions to protect me. They asked for an automatic rematch if I lost by decision. We started negotiating for guaranteed fights. The UFC had cut clauses in all their contracts. If you lost a fight, they could just cut you. Jeremy and Peter made Zuffa guarantee me at least two of the three fights on the contract. I'd have to lose twice before they could get rid of me.

It was an ongoing negotiation for first-class airline tickets, hotel rooms, and most-favoured-nation status, where if anyone in the organisation got paid more, they'd have to match that amount with me. I'd never heard of or thought of most of these things, but as the heavyweight champion, Jeremy and Peter thought I deserved it.

Declining to sign the original contract had an adverse affect immediately. No other fighter had resisted this new paperwork, at least not to my knowledge, so Zuffa set out to make me an example. Part of Zuffa's initial campaign to clean up Ultimate Fighting's image was to market it to the mainstream as a trendy, new sport. In this vein, Zuffa hired pop culture siren Carmen Electra to pose in a provocative UFC ad that would appear in all the men's magazines, like *Maxim* and *FHM*. I had been one of the fighters selected to pose with her, along with Pedro Rizzo, UFC lightweight champion Jens Pulver, and welterweight champ Carlos Newton. The photo shoot took place in Los Angeles.

When the contract negotiations stalled, Zuffa paid a hefty sum to have me airbrushed out of the ads before they went to print. I was also excluded from the latest UFC home video game *Tapout*, which hit stores a short time later.

I never got off on the right foot with Zuffa, and now they were punishing me for not falling in line. I thought it was stupid and an irrational, knee-jerk response. We weren't asking for any money up front. I felt like they wanted to get rid of me for causing trouble. My suspicions were confirmed when they stipulated that my new four-fight contract would be contingent on giving Pedro Rizzo an immediate rematch. I signed it.

ZUFFA ANNOUNCED THAT I'd fight Rizzo at *UFC 34: High Voltage* on November 2, 2001, its second event in Las Vegas. Our first fight had been as close as they come, and Zuffa was so sure he was going to beat me this next time. I knew this because they had just signed Rizzo to a whopping six-fight deal, unheard of in the business at that time. It was obvious they had big plans for the young Brazilian and were betting on him to become the next heavyweight champion. His rematch with me would be his third consecutive attempt at the belt. I was thirty-seven years old—considered unequivocally over the hill— and Rizzo was ten years my junior. Ten years was a lifetime in MMA.

Zuffa's lack of faith in me felt like so many other times in my life. I wasn't pissed off. I was insulted, and that never feels good. It made me want to go out there and perform even more.

We were all hopeful that Zuffa's purchase of the UFC would bring big change, and it did. There were little things that remained the same, but they had a lot more sense of how to run the promotion like a business. They had a lot more vision. They wanted to change the perception of the sport and had the means to do that, which was crucial. I think the sport would have died if somebody hadn't stepped in.

Zuffa hired a full-time staff. SEG had crews come to run the events, but there was never an office to call with questions and concerns. Requests were now handled in a timely matter. Medical paperwork was filled out and filed ahead of schedule. Everything seemed to run smoother. People would pick you up at the airport with signs. The fact that Zuffa had flown us out to do an ad campaign was big. SEG had never done anything like that.

The venues changed dramatically. I went from fighting in a tent next to a parking lot to fighting in a sports arena in the boxing capital of the world. I saw a billboard with my picture on it for the first time. At the Taj Mahal, SEG had given us a pass to go down and eat with all the casino employees in the basement. With Zuffa, we got meal money to use at a restaurant of our choice. They put me up in a suite, and my corner guys had their own rooms. They didn't have to bunk with me anymore.

But the positive changes were selective. Guys like Frank Shamrock and Mo Smith couldn't get into events without having to pay for their own tickets. These were guys that had won UFC belts and had helped perpetuate the sport. It didn't make sense to me. Why didn't Zuffa take care of them? They were champions.

Preparing for my second fight with Rizzo, I realised that I didn't have anyone in my camp that could help me with kickboxing. Rizzo had found a glaring weakness in me. I'd never been kicked like that before. I had to learn something different to deal with that, or he was going to expose me again. There was no way I wanted to go back in there and get kicked again. It hurt way too much. Luckily, I knew who to ask.

Mo Smith and I had always gotten along. I gave him a call.

"Look, I don't know if you saw my last fight," I said, "but I have to fight this kickboxer again. I would love to be able to come up and train with you and try and refine some of my techniques to get ready."

Mo welcomed me up to Seattle. I took one of our Team Quest students Nate Quarry, with me, and we stayed at my mom's house. Nate was a solid guy with a good head on his shoulders. It would be the first of many trips to the AMC Pankration gym to visit Mo and Matt Hume, one of the best trainers in the sport.

Mo took me to the Washington Institute of Sport, a big sports complex and rehab centre where he had done a lot of his previous conditioning. They had a lot of plyometric drills, which incorporated short, explosive movements similar to what I needed in MMA. They had industrial treadmills, and I learned some new running routines. Mo revamped my stance, and taught me how to punch better and to check kicks and defend.

In my first fight with Rizzo, I'd realised that I'd put myself in harm's way every time I stepped in to be offensive; Rizzo countered with a kick or a punch. I knew if I kept my distance and was a little more patient and diligent about when I chose to attack, it would be harder for him to change his angles and counter. I couldn't take any open shots. I was going to have to fight my way into the clinch, and attempt all my takedowns from there with trips and body locks. Mo taught me a little shuffle-left inside kick combination that was quick, and I felt comfortable with it. I brought Mo back with me to Las Vegas, along with Danny and Matt.

I was a completely different fighter for the rematch. The changes in tactics, footwork, stance, timing, my approach, and how and when I attacked made all the difference. I was in Rizzo's head. He couldn't get into his groove, and I ended up punching him into a bloody pulp. I caught him with an elbow that opened his cheek wide open. The blood stained his white trunks pink. I simply overwhelmed him, and referee John McCarthy stopped the fight in the third round. It wasn't even a contest. I hadn't gotten kicked once.

This was the first fight my father, Ed, came to see me live, and I was just as happy to have him there as he was to see me compete. I walked back to my hotel room that night on my own accord, my UFC heavyweight belt tucked underneath my arm.

10 CHAPTER TEN:
HANGING UP
THE GLOVES

THEY CALL IT MIXED MARTIAL ARTS FOR A REASON,
and that was never clearer to me until my two fights with Pedro Rizzo.
When I returned from my trip to Seattle after training with world-class
kickboxer Mo Smith, I took a good look at the way we were doing
things at Team Quest. We were all in great shape and beat each other
up every day, but there wasn't a lot of technique going on. We were not
improving our game.

At Mo's gym, it was almost the opposite. It was all technique and
drills with hardly any "live goes" at sparring. I thought, *how the hell do
you get in shape for fights when you don't spar and get after it?* But I
learned a lot about stance and the mechanics of throwing a punch, and
my striking improved by leaps and bounds.

Nate Quarry and I brought that knowledge back with us to Quest
and set out to find a happy medium. We brought in Brazilian jiu-jitsu
instructors like John Lewis and Pedro Sauer to teach us. Later, we
opened our doors to striking greats like Bas Rutten and conditioning
guru Frank Shamrock. I also visited Seattle many more times to train
with Mo and Matt Hume. We studied techniques certain nights of the
week and ran drills over and over to get them down pat.

There was still a couple of nights a week where we would come in
and strap the gloves on and just throw down, but our training began to
evolve much the way the sport had, by taking what works best, and

dropping the rest. We even began to develop our own techniques that were recognised as specialties of our team, like "dirty boxing," which involved short, packed punches from the head clinch.

Coming off my second victory against Pedro Rizzo, I wasn't originally scheduled to fight Josh Barnett at *UFC 36*, which took place on March 22, 2002, at the MGM Grand Garden Arena in Las Vegas. The event had been tagged *Worlds Collide*, as Zuffa had planned to match up light heavyweight champion Tito Ortiz, an American, against Brazilian Vitor Belfort, a bout they had tried to make happen a year before at *UFC 33*. Unfortunately, Belfort punched his arm through a window next to the ring and sliced his bicep a few weeks before the fight. A year later, Ortiz tore the anterior crucial ligament (ACL) in his knee and required surgery. Seven weeks out from *UFC 36*, they asked Barnett and me if we'd step in.

Barnett was a bigger guy for the heavyweights: six-foot-three, 250 pounds, and only twenty-four years old. He had decent wrestling skills, but I wasn't impressed with his stand-up. I watched him from cageside get knocked out by Pedro Rizzo at *UFC 30*. For a big guy that didn't look all that athletic, Barnett did move well, though, especially on the ground. I had trained a few times with Barnett, Mo, and Matt Hume up at their AMC Pankration gym. I knew leg locks and kneebars were his strength, holds where he could grab your ankle and twist your legs and knees to make you tap out. When I trained with him, he was constantly going for them. That was the one thing on the ground that I wanted to watch out for.

I thought Barnett was cocky and full of himself. He was a nice, personable guy, but at the same time he had this arrogant edge to him that I found abrasive. I didn't like the motion he made at the end of his fights, where he pretended to slash his own neck with his thumb. Barnett had a passion and flare for pro wrestling antics, which was something I felt went against my amateur wrestling grain. He had even licked his own blood off his hand once after a fight. We had enough people thinking we were maniacs. I just thought it was over the top.

Seven weeks old and already dreaming

Smiling in the cage at an early age

My father, Ed, and me

I rode my yellow bike
everywhere, even in the
living room

One tooth shy in kindergarten

Even at the 1980 Washington 3A high school wrestling regionals, my eyes were on the prize

Sharon and me at our senior prom

I asked Donnie to be Ryan's godfather and he inspired both of us

A proud papa at the age of eighteen

The night before boot camp, shaving my head on my own terms

My 1987 promotion to E5 (Enlisted Rank)
Sergeant at Fort Campbell, Kentucky

Wrestling my way through the 1985 World Championships—I didn't place

Old man on campus: with Ryan and Aimee after a dual meet at Oklahoma State University

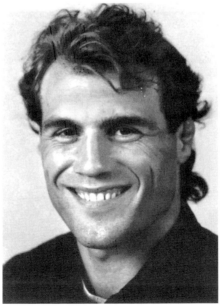

My 1990 headshot for Nationals—
mullets were all the rage back then

I made the national team for the first time in 1990. Can you find the other future fighter?

With my sisters, Yolanda and Traci, and my mother, Sharan, at my second wedding, in Multnomah Falls, Oregon

My first walk to the Octagon at *UFC 13* (May 30, 1997). Do I look scared to you?

Danny and me hiking the Oregon trails—we dove into cagefighting together

After three years away from the UFC, I was happy the fans hadn't forgotton me at *UFC 28* in Atlantic City, New Jersey (November 17, 2000)

With Aimee, sixteen, and Ryan, eighteen, at out Gresham, Oregon, home

A time for new beginnings at *UFC 31*, with owners Frank Fertitta, Dana White, and Lorenzo Fertitta

Rub a dub dub: "Charlie Brown" and me

PHOTO BY PETER LOCKLEY

UFC 43: Nobody expected me to stand and trade with Chuck Liddell—least of all "the Iceman" himself

PHOTO BY JOEL GOLD WWW.FCFIGHTER.COM

On the set of HBO's *Oz*, manhandling fellow UFC champ Frank Shamrock

UFC 49: After getting battered for three rounds, Vitor
Belfort couldn't stand up and return to his corner

My father, Ed, came to lend his support at *UFC 52* (April 16, 2005)

Entering the arena for *UFC 52*, the only time I wasn't ready to face the crowd; I was knocked out for the first time ever that night

It took me the entire first round to get Chuck Liddell down during our third and final fight at *UFC 57*, but I got her done

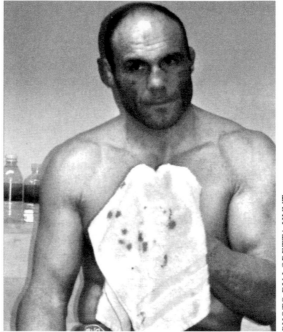

Backstage after *UFC 57:* the weight of my loss hit me harder than my retirement

Sharing a moment with Kim

PHOTO BY SSG DAVE WHERLEY "GOLDEN KNIGHTS"

Choked out at 13,000 feet by the U.S. Army Parachute Team

SPORTS ARTIST EDGAR J BROWN WWW.EDGARBROWN.COM

The punch heard 'round the world: an artist's rendition of the overhand right that toppled Tim Sylvia at *UFC 68* (March 3, 2007)

My first lead role, in *The Scorpion King: Rise of a Warrior*. For once I got to play the bad guy

A couple of old warriors on game day: meeting Green Bay Packers legend Brett Favre (December 9, 2007)

This was one of the few times when I had a personal agenda. There was no way I would let Barnett carry on like that at the end of our fight.

With our new open-door policy at Team Quest, I'd been working mostly on my jiu-jitsu skills, and I felt they'd paid off in the Randleman fight. I didn't think Barnett was going to submit me. My jiu-jitsu was pretty good, I thought.

In the fight, my confidence worked against me. Barnett used his girth to overwhelm me, and I couldn't find the takedown no matter which way I turned. In the scramble, I did something I never do—I pulled guard and put myself on my back. Instead of flowing into some brilliant submission like I thought I would, I found myself trying to deflect punches and elbows from all directions. Barnett pinned me against the cage and whacked away, gaining momentum with each shot.

I knew I was being hit and tried to move, protect myself and fight back. I needed to change something, to improve my position fast, but nothing came to me. In thirty seconds, you really don't have time to evaluate. You just have time to react. I hadn't trained to react to get out of that situation. It felt like it was happening at an accelerated speed. I got hit once or twice, made a noise, and the fight was stopped with only twenty-five seconds left in the second round.

In the heat of the moment, I was disappointed, but I didn't argue the stoppage. The next day, I had very little damage to my body. Watching the tape later, I saw I had certainly been in a bad position, but I felt like I was still in it. When I found out there was only twenty-five seconds left on the clock, I thought I could have made it. The referee isn't watching the clock, though. He's evaluating what he sees in that moment and makes a decision from there. I wasn't out or dazed, but I was getting hit hard, and that was enough to stop it. It was my first loss in the UFC.

"It had to happen sometime," I told Trish backstage as we walked back to my locker room.

It was an important fight, not only because it was my first loss, but because it forced me to reevaluate what I was thinking during the fight. I thought about who I was as an athlete. I was a wrestler. Why was I pulling guard? What has been going through my head to make me put myself in position to lose the fight in the first place?

I went back to wrestling and the mentality I had about being on my back. I realised it didn't matter how good I thought I was at jiu-jitsu; I hadn't spent my whole life developing jiu-jitsu skills, so I couldn't really play that chess match. It was stupid of me to intentionally put myself in that position. I started thinking about scrambling, getting up, using my legs more, creating space, thinking about what a wrestler would do if he ended up on his back. Obviously that's the last place you want to be in a wrestling match. That's where you get pinned, and the match is over. I started training more with that in mind. Learning all of the disciplines wasn't enough. I had to balance them in just the right proportions.

Less than two weeks later, it was announced that Josh Barnett had tested positive for Boldenone metabolite, an anabolic steroid commonly used in bodybuilding circles. It was the first steroids case in the sport, and it ripped through the community. The Nevada State Athletic Commission had just begun formerly testing for steroids at the start of the year, and we all had been required to give urine samples after our fights before they divvied out our paycheques.

When I looked at Barnett, he didn't have the telltale signs of someone on steroids. He had a softer, athletic appearance, and I knew his body image was an issue for him. He always said, "Not bad for a fat kid." So I guess I wasn't too surprised that he'd tried to improve his appearance.

I didn't think of him as a cheater. I thought guys that used steroids created an advantage for me. They were thinking the wrong things. They didn't have confidence in themselves. They were more interested in having big, superficial muscles than having the technique and stamina to go the distance. As the fight wore on, the steroids would hamper their performance.

Zuffa contacted my management right away. They wanted to call the fight a no-contest and give me the title back. I said no. In my mind, I had still lost the fight and they weren't just going to simply hand the belt back over. Through my manager, I told them I would fight for the vacant heavyweight title.

I wouldn't fight for another six months, while Barnett appealed the test results and tried to contest a pending suspension. Barnett and his manager and coach, Matt Hume, took a different approach to the allegations than a lot of the athletes would that followed them. Barnett got in the face of Zuffa and the Nevada commission, telling them he didn't take the steroids, and consequently, I think, his eventual suspension was tougher.

From April through September, the UFC's heavyweight title was in limbo. I trained, travelled for seminars, and waited for everything to shake out.

AT HOME, THE tension between Trish and my daughter Aimee began to mount, and I was caught in the middle. When Aimee moved in with us in 1999, she had a typical teenage attitude toward staying in our home and what was expected of her. She didn't want to play sports or participate in any other after-school activities.

"Look, I don't care what you do—basketball, basket weaving—it doesn't matter, but you're going to do something," I told her. "You're not just going to come home and plant your arse on the couch after school every day."

Aimee decided to sign up for swimming. She also started taking water polo as well, and seemed to make friends pretty quickly. She also started taking jiu-jitsu with some of the other girls who trained at Team Quest and liked that. Then my wrestling buddy Brad Anderson suggested Aimee try judo. His wife competed in it, so Brad encouraged her to pursue it because there were so few women involved. In Aimee's age group, she could start going on tours and travel all over Europe. She wanted to travel, so she started training with the gi, the white uniform you see karate practitioners wear.

The next summer, I sent Aimee out to Colorado with Brad and his wife for a couple of weeks so she could prepare for her first Nationals, which you could just register for and enter. She was doing well and enjoying herself, until she broke her ankle a week before the competition. It was a pretty bad spiral fracture break that put her in a cast for three months. She watched the Nationals from the stands. There were only four girls in her weight class, so she knew she could have done well. I think seeing that broke her spirit.

Aimee returned to Oregon and decided that we had pushed her into doing judo when she hadn't really wanted to do it in the first place. She didn't like the pressure of competition. Aimee and Trish were now constantly banging heads.

It strained my relationship with Trish immensely. Trish was still going to nursing school and Aimee didn't have a driver's license, so Trish had to drive her around to swimming or judo practise. When Aimee didn't lend a hand around the house, Trish called her lazy. I was away a lot with training and competing, and Trish began to grow resentful.

It all came to head with the diary episode. Aimee was sharing her diary with her mom in Seattle—she'd write in it and mail it to Sharon, who would write back. Aimee wrote some spiteful entries about Trish and our life in Gresham, how we all weren't happy. Trish found the diary and read it, which caused a huge meltdown. Trish was very hard on Aimee. I didn't agree. This was my daughter. I wanted the best for her, but I also wanted her to be happy, and I wasn't going to torture her. I wasn't a drill sergeant, but I realised Trish saw things in black and white.

That's when my relationship with Trish started to change. I began to look at our relationship and our history differently. She had criticised how I had left the coaching position at Oregon State and how I'd let

Coach Wells "talk to me that way." She had badgered me about Performance Quest and how I had run the gym. She constantly nagged me, to the point where I told Trish I didn't want her around Performance Quest anymore unless she wanted to run the whole place herself. She just never seemed to be content with the way I handled anything.

Trish had a big gripe with how I kept in touch with my ex-wife, Sharon, through phone calls and letters. Sharon and I stayed amicable after the divorce and tried to work together to raise Ryan and Aimee. Trish didn't like that I paid Sharon alimony or sometimes split the costs of special expenses with her. Trish called Sharon a loser.

"Oh, poor me," Trish mocked. "She got a divorce and she's going to be a hairdresser, but she expects you to pay for alimony."

I realised Trish had always been like this; I just hadn't noticed in the beginning. Everything was fresh, new, and exciting, like a fairy tale. Trish was smart, athletic and we had fun together, but there were signs I overlooked.

Trish's ex-boyfriend was a third- or fourth-string quarterback for the Cincinnati Bengals. At the start of our affair, Trish had fooled around with her ex-boyfriend one weekend when he came back to town, and I was away on a road trip. We spent all night on the phone talking about it. I tried to walk away from her, but she convinced me not to.

I was a married man straying from my wife with a woman who initially cheated on me. The foundation of our relationship was shaky, to say the least.

Enough became enough. For the second time in my life, I checked out. Rather than deal with the issues at hand, I withdrew. Trish was always in my face. She had strong opinions about everything, and I just didn't want to hear it anymore. I started scheduling more dates just to be away from home. Trish saw through that, and it developed into an even bigger issue. It became a vicious cycle.

I wasn't surprised when Aimee decided to move out that summer.

She went back to live with her mom and graduated from Bothell High School in Washington. She decided not to go to Woodenville, the "preppy" school her brother Ryan had attended. Bothell was the other-side-of-the-tracks kind of school.

I admired Aimee for her bold choices and recognised that Aimee's rebelliousness actually comes from me. I realised that my two older kids reflected the two sides of me. My son, Ryan, is the intelligent, soft-spoken, very considerate side of me. He's got a similar fear of confrontation. Aimee is the artsy, bohemian, life-of-the-party side of me. She's not afraid to stick up for what she wants, even though it might be the harder road to navigate. I am proud of both of my children for being individuals.

★   ★   ★

WHILE I FOUGHT a battle in my own home, Josh Barnett challenged the Nevada State Athletic Commission's steroid allegations to clear his name. Unable to prove his innocence, Barnett was suspended from fighting in Nevada for one year and the UFC stripped him of the title that July. Zuffa offered me a fight against Ricco Rodriguez, another younger and larger heavyweight, for the vacant title at *UFC 39: The Warriors Return* on September 27, 2002, at the Mohegan Sun Arena in Uncasville, Connecticut.

Rodriguez was a Brazilian jiu-jitsu black belt, a rare accomplishment for a twenty-five-year-old, who also happened to be six-foot-three and 240 pounds. He'd also won four straight bouts in the UFC, all from referee stoppages due to strikes. Rodriguez wasn't particularly well-conditioned and was a little soft around the midsection. He didn't like to get into striking battles. I was confident that I could athletically outmanoeuvre him on my feet and keep him from taking me down. Then I'd take him down myself and beat him up. I thought the harder I pushed the pace, the closer I'd get to breaking him.

I knew I shouldn't go to my back if I could help it. In the early rounds, I was able to prevent the takedowns and take Rodriguez down myself. On top, I hurt him with fists and elbows and won the first three rounds pretty soundly. But Rodriguez was such a big guy that when he did finally knock me down in the fourth round and got on top of me, I couldn't find the strength to create enough scramble to get out from underneath him. I spent the whole round on the bottom.

He knocked me down again in the fifth round's final minutes and that's when his right elbow caught my left eye. A few people told me later that I let out a huge yelp. I knew instantly that something was very wrong. There was a huge flash, and a wave of pain ran across my entire face. I opened my eyes and everything went lopsided. It was very disorientating, and I got nauseous. I wasn't sure if I had gotten knocked out. Both my eyes were swollen.

"That's it. That's it. I'm done," I voiced to referee John McCarthy.

Rodriguez backed away and said, "He's tapping. He's tapping." McCarthy stepped in instantly.

My cornermen helped me up and out of the cage. I felt like I was drunk. I was staggering. Trish met me at the stairs, and I leaned on her to walk through the aisle to the tunnel entrance to get backstage. In the crowd, I saw Alex, one of the wrestlers I had taught when I volunteer coached the Junior Nationals team a year before. He was going to school on the East Coast, and had driven hours to see me fight. He was standing there, halfway between the tunnel and the cage, and despite the pain, I gave him a big hug.

My dressing room was total chaos. I sat on a stool and a doctor examined me as paramedics and medical staff ran in and out. They had me sign a form I couldn't see and told me I was going to the hospital immediately. The media was also trying to enter my locker room and Nate Quarry got pissed.

"Get the fuck out of here, all of you. Give the guy some space," yelled Quarry, chasing off a mass of cameras and microphones.

I felt like I was in the Joker's Playhouse. Everything tilted sideways. Trish didn't have time to cry. She went right into medical mode. They put me on a stretcher to transport me to the ambulance. They pushed me out into the hallway and wheeled me past a white curtain that partitioned off a section set up for the press conference. On the other side of the curtain, Rodriguez was at the podium giving his victory speech.

After X-rays and a few other evaluations, it was determined that my orbital bone had been fractured, and there was really nothing they could do about it. My doctor didn't want me to fly, so I stayed at the hotel an extra day in a daze of pain medication. Every time I stood up, I threw up.

I flew back Monday and made an appointment to see an eye specialist at the Oregon Health and Sciences University. I was admitted the next day and underwent surgery. They peeled my eyelid down, freed the medial muscle that was trapped in the crack of the fracture, and placed a Teflon patch over the fracture so the muscle wouldn't catch again. I wore a black eye patch for the next few weeks.

I had been scheduled to leave six days after the fight to compete in *The Eco-Challenge* that year in Fiji, an adventure race that had been made into a TV series by Mark Burnett, the producer of *Survivor. The Eco-Challenge* was a non-stop race consisting of hiking, running, swimming, kayaking, and mountain biking. I had raised most of the sponsorship funds for the team and felt bad letting them down, but they had to take the alternate with them instead.

My eye muscle had been stretched, and the nerve was damaged, so even after they had repaired it, I still had strabismus, or double vision. The doctors believed my brain would make the adjustments and correct itself over time. My vision improved in the next few weeks, but I had to tilt my head down and to the right to bring the two images I saw together.

During this time, I was invited to compete as a guest on the popular game show *The Weakest Link*, for an episode on the world's most dangerous occupations. I couldn't tilt my head down far enough to see the panel in front of me to write my answers.

When my vision didn't improve in the next two months, I became worried. I knew I couldn't fight again with double vision. My doctor told me they could perform another surgery or give me eyeglasses. Instead, I decided to go to experimental eye therapists that performed all kinds of crazy exercises with refracted lenses and balls. Working with the therapists made a huge difference right away. They retrained my damaged nerves and strengthened the muscle. I still have double vision below my sightline. I can't look down at a book in my lap—I have to tilt my head down to see it correctly. But it's in my lower field of vision, so it doesn't really affect my daily life or my fighting.

The therapy took six months. It was a difficult time because Trish, my mom, and my sisters were all putting pressure on me to quit fighting. They told me they didn't want to see me get hurt again. They told me I was old. I was thirty-nine, and Trish had been asking me to have a child for several years. I wanted to tell her that I didn't want another kid; I already had two. But I felt if I said no, I would have been selfish. I knew how much my kids meant to me. I made a compromise with Trish. I had one last fight left on my contract, so I agreed to fulfil that, and then hang up my gloves. Trish seemed satisfied with this resolution and got pregnant right away.

I'D ALWAYS BEEN light for the heavyweight division, and weighed around the same size as the 205-pounders more than the heavyweights. The light heavyweight fighters all cut down for the weigh-ins, but would be back up in the 220-pound range the next day for their fights. My wrestling buddies, who knew I could make the cut easily, encouraged me to fight Tito Ortiz, the UFC's light heavyweight champion. So I told UFC matchmaker Joe Silva I would be willing to move down to the light heavyweight division.

"Yeah, yeah, yeah," Silva said, "but we want you to fight Andrei Arlovski."

I don't think they really took my suggestion seriously, but it didn't bother me. I could still fight at heavyweight if that's what they wanted.

Zuffa scheduled my next fight against Arlovski, an incredibly athletic twenty-four-year-old sambo fighter, who had immigrated to America from Belarus. With a penchant for boxing, the six-foot-four, 240-pound Arlovski would be as dangerous on his feet as Rizzo had been, except Arlovski enjoyed attacking first. The bout was scheduled for *UFC 42: Sudden Impact* on April 25, 2003, the promotion's first trip to Miami.

About five weeks out from the fight, my manager Jeremy got word that Arlovski had broken his hand back in his native homeland of Minsk and had bowed out of the fight. UFC matchmaker Joe Silva felt he couldn't find an adequate replacement in time, so I was scrapped from the roster all together.

It turned out to be a blessing in disguise. While sixteen fighters entertained the crowd at the American Airlines Arena in Miami on April 25, my second son, Caden, was born in an Oregon hospital. He was perfect. When they placed him on the table in the delivery room, I walked over to see him and welled up. It was overwhelming.

Having a child at forty was a new experience entirely. I was at a completely different stage in my life. Ryan was born when I was nineteen, and we had Aimee when I was twenty-one. I was now much more aware and able to take in what was happening before my eyes. Over the next few years, I was in a better position to appreciate the smiling, the walking, the talking and all those little things that make being a parent so special.

My suggestion to matchmaker Joe Silva a few months earlier must have gotten back to UFC president Dana White. After months of contract disputes with light heavyweight champion Tito Ortiz, the UFC was on their last nerve. White cooked up a scenario where I'd fight Chuck Liddell for an interim light heavyweight title that June.

The Ortiz-UFC feud had gone on for months. First, Ortiz got injured and couldn't fight. Then, he'd taken on a movie role that prevented him from defending his title when the UFC asked him to. Zuffa was getting frustrated, and speculation mounted that Ortiz didn't want to fight Liddell, who was rumoured to have knocked him around in practise. I felt like the UFC was looking for a way to legitimise Liddell and strip Ortiz. It was a shot at a title, so I didn't really care what their reasons were. I signed a new three-fight deal, which would start with a five-round title bout for the UFC interim light heavyweight championship at *UFC 43: Meltdown* on June 6, 2003, at the Thomas & Mack Centre in Las Vegas.

My preparation for the Chuck Liddell fight was a seven-year culmination of all that I had learned in the mixed martial arts game.

Liddell had been a Division I wrestler at California Polytechnic State University. In 1994, Cal Poly had hosted the Pac-10 tournament and I took the Oregon State team there. I met Liddell in a local bar. He was a quiet, good-natured guy, despite his trademark mohawk and *Kanji*-character tattoos on either side of his head.

Liddell was a decent wrestler, but used those skills to keep himself on his feet. In recent years, he'd taken up kickboxing and discovered he had a stiff hook not many could debate. Liddell could be taken down, but had an uncanny ability to pop back up to his feet like a jack-in-the-box. That's why Liddell was more dangerous than any other striker I'd faced. I would have to take him down multiple times. The others strikers I only had to take down once and that was it. They never got back up. Liddell would. That was a guarantee.

"Look how he does that," I'd say to my teammates as we watched Liddell scramble to his feet, "he does that easy enough." Then I'd go out and try to mimic it in practise.

From the loss to Barnett, I learned that I had to have answers for the worst-case scenario, those horrible positions my opponent could trap me in.

Training for Liddell was different because my worst-case scenario with him was getting knocked out. I had to make friends with the fact that this guy could, in fact, knock me out and if that's what happened, that's what happened.

Dropping the weight was a cinch. I was walking around at 225 pounds, so I just eliminated dairy products from my diet and started eating raw foods and greens. I still ate red meat but tried to eat more frequently during the day. I also started drinking a concoction of wheat grass, barley grass, and different types of greens. I thought it made a big difference in how I felt, energy-wise. I seemed to recover from the same workouts, the same sprint routines, and the same lifting circuit without any muscle soreness. I recovered faster without losing my strength. Ten pounds fell off just like that.

Losing the weight seemed like a big deal to everybody but me. No fighter had ever attempted to drop down to a lower weight class in the UFC before, so it was something new to talk about. A majority of people still weren't aware of my wrestling past, so they questioned if I could even do it or if the cut would make me too weak to fight the next day. I cut about nine to ten pounds of water weight to make the weigh-ins, which wasn't painful or uncomfortable. When I got back to my hotel room, I had a doctor hook me up to an IV so I could rehydrate.

That was the first time I have ever rehydrated from the IV, and I did it for every light heavyweight fight after that. I'd known wrestlers that had cut a lot of weight for the World Championships or the Olympics, then used the IV to rehydrate. It's a pretty simple procedure, and I think it's the most efficient, much more so than actually drinking your way back, which takes much longer.

I don't think anybody gave me much of a chance of winning against Liddell. Everyone thought I was going to get knocked out. Nobody really says that sort of thing to your face, but when the betting boards have you as a 3-to-1 underdog, it doesn't get much more blatant. But it never bothered me. I had been there before, and it just solidified in my mind that I was going to go out there and win.

Zuffa made a big pomp and circumstance about the fight. After ushering me in under the bright lights of the Thomas & Mack Centre on the University of Las Vegas campus, the lights dimmed to pitch-black for Liddell. This long, elaborate introduction played out on the Jumbotron screens and Liddell entered to a remix of "Ice Ice Baby" by Vanilla Ice. Was Zuffa counting on Liddell to pull this one out, or what?

My plan seemed to work right from the opening bell. I knew he wanted to throw, so the second he stopped moving, I threw first. I never allowed him to find his range and get into his rhythm. I kept coming forward and connected with punches as he tried to swat me away like a yellow jacket. By the end of the first round, I could see a slight hint of frustration overcome Liddell. I watched the tape later and noticed that he'd paused and looked around before he turned to his corner with an expression that said, *what the hell just happened?*

The second round was much of the same. I cut Liddell off before he could find his punch, but now I started to incorporate takedowns. As expected, Liddell was slippery, but I kept chipping away at him. By the third round, I had him flustered and on the run. During my very last takedown along the fence, I let out a growl like we used to do in wrestling to release all our power into the move. This time, Liddell didn't get up and I forced the stoppage at 2:39. The audience was in awe. I wasn't supposed to win.

As the interim belt was being strapped around my waist, UFC president Dana White whispered in my ear to egg Tito Ortiz on for our pending match. "Tito, if you want this belt, you're gonna have to come in here and take it," I told the audience decisively.

By winning the interim light heavyweight title, I became the first UFC competitor ever to hold belts in two weight divisions. During the pay-per-view broadcast, commentator Joe Rogan began to call me "Captain America." Dana White picked that up and stared to call me Captain America too, which I didn't mind. People seemed to like the name, and it took on a life of its own, as fans began mailing me drawings, cartoons, and other artwork. I appreciated the support and thought it was all funny. I didn't take myself too seriously.

Within a week or two we got the phone call that Ortiz wanted to fight me, and he would start pushing for that fight to happen. The timing was a little suspect. Ortiz had gone to great lengths to avoid Liddell, but now that I'd taken him out, the champ seemed ready to defend his title. Ortiz was a big showman, who tried to use a war of words to get into his opponent's head. Almost immediately, Ortiz began telling the press that I wasn't the real champion. Zuffa scheduled the fight for September 26, 2003, at *UFC 44: Undisputed* at the Mandalay Bay Events Centre in Las Vegas.

★ ★ ★

I HAD MADE my deal with Trish, but now I had a title to defend. She never said anything about me continuing on, but her attitude spoke for itself. The more standoffish she became, the more it drove me away to other fight events, training camps, and seminars. My home became a pit stop between fight appearances. We had several disagreements about it, and she expressed that she was unhappy that I was gone all the time.

"Do you want me to just quit?" I asked her. "Do you want me to stay at home? I'm not a nine-to-five guy."

I didn't want to be around her, as much as I loved my son and spending time with him. Instead, I turned my attention to Ortiz—a brash, Division I wrestler who'd held onto his UFC title for three years but had only fought six times in that period.

My strategy for Ortiz was the opposite of the one I'd followed with Liddell. I had to work on my footwork so I could change the angles as Ortiz pressed me. I would need to create openings more from moving back than moving forward. That would make it harder for him to take me down, and later in the fight, I would be able to switch gears and go back into that hunting mode.

It was a more conservative approach for me, which I might not have been able to stick to in the past. But I framed it for myself in a positive way. Just because I would be giving ground at times didn't mean I wasn't being aggressive. In training, I focused on that. It was a learning experience, one more skill that I was able to add to my game.

The biggest mistake I could make in this fight would be to allow Ortiz to stay on top if he took me down. I had to be able to scramble and make it hard for him to hold me down. I had to get back up to my feet or reverse him. I went back to my Liddell tapes to learn that from the master.

Though he had dominated the Octagon with his wrestling, Ortiz's real strength was his aggressive nature. He fought on emotion, which was sometimes just as much a weakness for him as it was a strength. To work up that emotion and anger, Ortiz liked to trash-talk in the months and weeks leading up to his bout, like a ticking time bomb. It was very effective for him and had gained him a lot of followers. I didn't think there was anything necessarily wrong with it, either. Entertaining the fans was an important aspect of the sport. Still, I knew this was going to be a challenge for me. I am quiet by nature, and talking ill of my opponents just isn't my style.

Ortiz expected me not to react, so I decided to get in his head a little bit and give it back to him. I caught him off-guard when we both appeared on FOX Sports Channel's *Best Damn Sports Show Period* hyping the fight. He started with his usual put-downs, and instead of sitting there and taking it, I started dishing it back. I told him that he was just jealous of my ears and that his wife liked them as well. Ortiz stuttered, then paused, not knowing what to say, which was unusual for him. I took more well-timed jabs at him in the weeks leading up to the fight. I'll admit it made me uncomfortable, but I had an idea that it was working.

My suspicions were confirmed at the *UFC 44* weigh-ins. In our staredown, he couldn't look me in the eye, and he had sweat beading up on his upper lip. He looked really nervous, which wasn't really like him either.

I had told the press that this fight would boil down to wrestling, to who was going to be able to take who down, and I think this struck a chord with him. He said he wanted to be the first guy to knock me out, but I think that deep down, he knew that wasn't going to happen. He knew I was on the mark. It would come down to the wrestling.

Back at my hotel, my children Ryan and Aimee had joined Trish and me. Ryan had just turned 21, so after the weigh-ins, he went out with some of his buddies and got hammered. At 4:30 a.m. the day of the fight, there was a knock on my door. I opened it, and there was my son, slouched over in a wheelchair with four security guards surrounding him.

"Where do you want him?" one guard asked.

"Put him on the couch," I said.

Ryan was awake, but he couldn't even piece a sentence together. He didn't know if he'd gotten into a fight or what had happened. He couldn't explain to me why four security guards had escorted him to my room.

"I don't know, I don't know," was all he could mumble.

I called downstairs to the front desk and asked to speak with the head of security. I got dressed and went downstairs to meet him. He told me Ryan had passed out in the elevator lobby on our floor. How he made it to my floor, I don't know. Shy and soft-spoken like me, Ryan was embarrassed when he sobered up.

Down at the pool that same day, Ryan bought some drinks for Aimee, who was still underage, and she started to get bold with her words. This was one of the first times Aimee and Trish had been around each other since Aimee had moved out of our home, and it wasn't pleasant.

ONCE AGAIN, I was considered a heavy underdog in the Ortiz fight. I think people acknowledged Ortiz as a dominant wrestler who took everybody down, so I wasn't surprised that people thought I would lose. A lot of fans were unaware of my wrestling background, but I certainly didn't feel the need to clue them in. I kept it all behind a grin. Ortiz ran around with his flag and sprung up and down like a jumping bean. I stood at the other side of the cage, watching him bounce around.

Go ahead, expend that energy, I thought. *You're going to need that later.*

Ortiz spent incredible amounts of energy trying to take me down in the first three minutes, but I countered and countered some more. He hung on my legs and got me to my butt, but I bounced right back up. Ultimately, I took his back and took him down first, which I thought was the turning point of the fight. That's when he realised he was in trouble. That was the first blow that took him to the edge of breaking. Had he had any success putting me on my back, the momentum of the fight could have changed completely. But I'd convinced myself beforehand that there was no way I was conceding a takedown from him.

In the second round, I had him pinned to the ground in his half-guard when he started talking to me. "Is that the best you got?" he asked, between my punches and elbows.

I just smiled and punched him again. It was the first time anyone had ever talked to me in a fight. He said something as we broke apart and I got up to go back to my corner. I turned around and stuck my tongue out at him. It was all a part of his game, to try and get me upset and distracted, but I wouldn't bite.

Time was running out for Ortiz. By the fifth round, he was desperate and needed a knockout or a submission if he was going to pull off the win. On the mat underneath me, he tried to roll to a kneebar, but I ended up sitting on his thighs and turned my body at an angle so he couldn't finish the move. The only thing I could see was his butt staring up at me. I couldn't go anywhere else myself, and it just popped into my head to spank him on the arse.

I didn't think about it much at the time, and later people told me they had thought I had tapped out to the submission. Thank God referee John McCarthy knew what he was watching, and saw that Ortiz had nothing on me. We ended up scrambling for the remaining few seconds, but Ortiz had nothing to stop me. The bell rang.

I had to give Ortiz credit because he never did break. I felt him teetering in the fourth and fifth rounds. I felt him struggling, but then he'd get pissed off and fight back. He refused to go down and I respected that.

It was the second major upset I'd accomplished that year. At the podium for the post-fight press conference, Dana declared that he'd never bet against me again. I was going to hold him to that.

My celebrations were cut short that evening. Aimee had a few beers that night at the event. She wasn't belligerent or sloppy, but she swore in front of my manager and several other people at the post-fight press conference. Trish reprimanded Aimee for representing me in such a poor way. Aimee went into pout mode and was upset that she'd been chewed out. She went out that night with Trish's sister Tina, but was supposed to be back at the hotel at a certain time to meet Trish to catch a cab to the airport for an early flight.

At 5:00 a.m., Aimee had still not returned to the hotel, so Trish grabbed her bags and headed for the elevators when the doors opened. Aimee came out of the elevator and passed by Trish, not saying a word. Trish turned around and followed her back into the room. They began shouting at one another. Aimee lost control and called Trish "a fucking bitch," while Trish screamed back at her. I was in bed naked, so I couldn't really move with Aimee and Trish's sister in the room. Ryan got upset and pleaded for them to stop. Trish stormed out and headed to the airport on her own. I never even asked if they sat next to each other on the plane.

This was the first altercation they'd had since the diary episode. They each wanted me to choose sides, which was something I didn't want to do. I thought they were both right and wrong. It was a complicated issue. I couldn't take sides, and therefore neither felt supported by me. It was a lose-lose situation. Trish and Aimee exchanged letters afterwards and buried the hatchet to some extent, but it was never the way I would have liked it to be.

11 CHAPTER ELEVEN:
REALITY

HOW DO YOU KNOW IF FIGHTING IS FOR YOU? WITHOUT question, it boils down to a burning desire, a passion in your heart. Do you have faith that this is what you were put on earth to do? Only you can answer those questions. There are sacrifices. You sacrifice time away from your wife and kids. Trust me, finding a wife who will put up with a fighter's lifestyle is not an easy task. There is a give and take, and it's a very, very fine line.

In late 2003, coming off two of the biggest back-to-back wins of my career to Chuck Liddell and Tito Ortiz, I was teetering on that line. My success in fighting was growing, as were my paydays, which gave me a little more flexibility in my life. Trish and I had moved into a nicer home in Gresham right before Caden's birth. We had been looking around for the right place for about eight months. We wanted to get out of town and buy some acreage to spread out. I thought we would find either a great house and a crappy piece of land or a great piece of land and a crappy house.

We found a nice big house on a piece of decent property, already fenced in, with a fantastic view of the Clackamas River. It was an older house, but I saw that as our chance to remodel it, to gut it out and rebuild it to our own liking. There was a workman's shop on the property, which I liked, and I had a vision of how I wanted it to look finished. Heavyweight fighter Tim Sylvia stayed with us for part of the remodelling, and he helped tear out some of the old moulding with me. I had a bunch of the fighters from the gym come over in the next few months, and we did a lot of the renovation ourselves. Trish wasn't too crazy about the house at first, and like a lot of people, we had a lot trouble with contractors, but once it was done, the final product was beautiful.

I built an extension onto the shop and transformed it into a horse barn. We bought two steeds: a beautiful, sorrel quarter horse named Fritz, and Patches, a very mild-mannered paint horse.

I also began flying, something I had wanted to pursue since I was eighteen years old and joined the army. Our friend Rick Franklin, who had helped us open our first Performance Quest gym, owned his own airplane, and he invited me to fly with him many times. He never let me take off or land, which are the critical parts, but once we were up in the air, he'd let me grab the controls. I looked into starting the forty-hour requisite ground training at the community college in Gresham to get my license, though I never ended up finding the time to do it.

My greatest hobby of all was my son. Caden was a special kid. He was a very good baby and wasn't fussy at all. He was fun to be around. I called him "Charlie Brown" because he had a perfectly round noggin, just like his old man.

Caden brought me and my father closer together. When he was born, Ed seemed to suddenly have all of this regret, and he took greater pains to see Caden than he had Ryan and Aimee. He was now at the age when his own father had died, and he was having medical problems himself. He'd been a smoker all his life, and was diagnosed with emphysema. Though he never said it, I think a sense of mortality set in. He began to visit more and shower Caden with attention and gifts. This gave him the opportunity to be a part of my life again. On the one hand, I welcomed it. As Caden got older, he called him Grandpa Ed and really seemed to enjoy the time he spent with him. At the same time, I have to admit it still hurt—I'd never had the chance to experience a lot of that in my own childhood.

Around the same time Caden was born, Ed and his wife Carrie took in a teenage boy whose parents were having issues and couldn't care for him. I was a little jealous to hear that my dad had temporarily adopted this kid when he hadn't ever spent time with me. Combined with his affinity for Caden, I felt that envy a little more.

As a child's arrival can often do, Caden's birth relieved a bit of the tension between Trish and me. It took some of the focus off of our problems, and Trish became consumed with the baby. Suddenly, it didn't really matter what I was doing or where I was going, or that I'd gone back on our deal and would continue to fight. Trish was all about Caden, which was fine with me.

MY NEXT FIGHT offer came pretty quickly, within a month of the Ortiz fight. I would face Vitor Belfort for the second time in my career. After a strong start in the late 1990s, Belfort had had mediocre success in Japan's PRIDE Fighting Championships before returning to the UFC's Octagon in 2002. His performances there weren't as inspiring as his earlier fights. The once promising Brazilian "Phenom" that I had been fed to back at *UFC 15* in 1997 was fading into a shadow of his former self.

I didn't agree that Belfort should have been given the rematch, but after Liddell and Ortiz, there wasn't a whole lot of depth in the division. Belfort had savagely ripped open Marvin Eastman's forehead with a knee at *UFC 43*, the same card that hosted my fight with Liddell, so I wasn't surprised he'd been called up for a title shot. Eastman's head had looked like a pomegranate smashed open, and it instilled a bit of hope in the die-hard fans that the old Belfort might be resurrected.

Behind the scenes, I had the benefit of seeing where Belfort's head was really at. At *UFC 43*, I could sense that the memories from our first fight seven years before were still fresh. While I cut weight for the Liddell fight, Belfort followed me around like a puppy dog and asked me about everything, from what I ate to what times I worked out to what I did in my workouts. He attached himself to me the entire time for the whole week of the fight.

One of the greatest mental hurdles any fighter has to overcome is preparing to climb back into the cage with somebody who didn't just beat him, but beat him up. Belfort lost to me at a time when no one thought he could lose. He knew he'd quit. He knew he'd given up. It was obvious he was still carrying that burden around, and I knew that would make it easier for me to break him again this second time.

I thought Belfort was very personable, talented, and explosive and it was a shame that he didn't seem to be taken care of by the trainers and people he'd chosen to surround himself with. I didn't think he'd been supported very well in his career and put in the right fights or training situations to really flourish. At such a young age, he had been hyped up, and I think he started to believe that hype, instead of being realistic with himself to push his training and become a better fighter. Ultimately, he was his own captain, but if I'd been his trainer or manager, I would have handled him differently. He had great raw potential and talent, but it hadn't been nurtured properly.

For the first time ever, the UFC fashioned an event after me and dubbed *UFC 46: Supernatural*. It would also be the first UFC event to be held over Las Vegas' premium Super Bowl weekend. The show was scheduled for January 31, 2004, at the Mandalay Bay Events Centre, and there was a lot of enthusiasm that the show would take place on such an important weekend. Even though I'd originally felt like Zuffa had been trying to get rid of me, I thought they finally might be changing their tune.

I was fortunate enough to have Matt Lindland, Chael Sonnen, and Chris Leben—all left-handed—at the Team Quest gym to spar with, to help me train against a southpaw again. I also went down to Sacramento and held a camp with a bunch of fighters from that area. I'd taken some time to train there for my Ortiz fight as well, and it was beneficial to get away from the distractions of Oregon and isolate myself. I just ate, slept and trained.

The Sacramento camps earned a bit of notoriety for the mix of fighters they attracted. Around that time, there was a lot of cross-training occurring between camps, and the fans were always interested to see what unlikely couples were working together. Quinton "Rampage" Jackson and Joe Stevenson attended, along with James Irvin, Scott Smith, and Billy Miles. All of them would become UFC veterans down the road, and the local guys formed the Capital City Fighting Alliance fight team shortly after.

I worked with an Iranian kickboxer named Nasser Niavaroni, who'd helped train world kickboxing champion Dennis Alexio and was currently housing Eric Regan, a 170-pound boxing champion. Nasser had a slightly different approach for Belfort, something that went against what I'd heard from traditional boxing trainers. With left-handed opponents, you're always taught to circle away in your footwork from your opponent's power hand, which is what I'd really focused on in the 1997 fight. This time, Nasser wanted me to circle into Belfort's left hand.

"You know he's going to throw that," he told me, "so you bait him into throwing it while you're just out of range, and that's when you can slip the punch, move in, and close the distance."

I knew once I could trap Belfort in the clinch, I could steal his heart. I also continued with grappling and jiu-jitsu under black belt Cassio Werneck in his small gym located in the back of a big karate studio. It was great camp for me.

Just a few weeks before the bout, Belfort's sister Priscila, in her twenties, had disappeared in their Brazilian homeland. She was at work one moment, left for an errand, and then disappeared. Belfort was a celebrity in Brazil. He'd starred on a soap opera and had appeared in his country's version of *Big Brother*. He got a lot of attention on the show, flirting on-screen with Joana Prado, also a TV star and model, who Belfort eventually married. Because of Belfort's visibility in Brazil, the possibility that his sister had been kidnapped was probable.

However, the Belfort family hadn't heard a word from anyone yet. It was an emotional time for Belfort, and I felt bad for him. The preparation for a fight is enough without a personal tragedy pulling away your focus.

The Saturday night before Super Bowl XXXVIII, Belfort entered the Octagon wearing a shirt with Priscilla's picture on the front. His message was clear. He was fighting for her.

I sympathised with Belfort, but I had a job to do. Referee John McCarthy signalled the start of our rematch with his usual call of "Let's get it on!" and I came right out and went for a left kick to an overhand right like Nasser had shown me. Just like Nasser had explained, Belfort threw his left hand in response, and it just grazed me as I bobbed my head away. I didn't feel an impact at all, and we ended up in the clinch, exactly where I wanted to be. The only problem was that my left eye closed, and I couldn't open it. I touched my cheek, and there was no blood, so I couldn't figure out what was wrong. Getting poked in the eye is a very distinct feeling. You see a huge flash and you feel like your eyeball just got popped out of the socket. I hadn't gotten poked in the eye, but something wasn't right.

We stood against the fence chest to chest, and Belfort could feel me slow down and tense up, so he didn't try and break away. Referee McCarthy noticed that I was wincing, so he halted the bout. The clock was stopped and cageside physician Dr. Margaret Goodman was brought inside the Octagon to evaluate me. As soon as she pried my eye open, the blood started flowing. The outer seam of Belfort's glove had acted as a razor and sliced my eyelid. She immediately announced that I couldn't continue. In forty-nine seconds, I was no longer the UFC champion.

An apologetic Belfort half-heartedly took the belt around his waist, while a confused audience looked on. The cut had been caused by a legal punch, so it was treated just as if Belfort had broken a bone or cut me open. No-contests only came from illegal blows.

An ophthalmologist saw me that night in Las Vegas and stitched up my eyelid. The cut spanned both my top and bottom lid, something the doctors hadn't noticed in the arena. He stitched me up and told me to leave it alone for ten days.

I was upset. It was Super Bowl weekend in Las Vegas, and I knew everyone was expecting an epic fight. UFC president Dana White came backstage and told me they would give me a rematch right away, which was written into my contract. Since Belfort needed to focus on his family matters at home, I wouldn't get the rubber match for another seven months. I didn't mind. I truly wanted his sister to be okay, and I also didn't want the situation to be an issue for the next fight.

I HADN'T HAD much luck with my left eye. It seemed like I didn't have luck with the whole left side of my body. I'd sprained my left knee in college, torn up my left elbow wrestling, broke my left orbital bone during the Rodriguez fight, and now had this fluke accident. I started to wonder if I led too much with my left side, if I needed to change my stance.

Over the next few months, I travelled for a bunch of seminars. One of the seminars was in Sweden, which made Trish apprehensive. She worried about taking six-month-old Caden on such a long flight. But Caden was no trouble at all. He was a peach. I carried him around in front of me in one of those baby slings, and he was happy as a clam snuggled up in his snowsuit. Trish and I still bickered, although we had a pleasant time in Stockholm. There was plenty to see to keep us busy.

Back in Oregon, mixed martial arts was going through a renaissance. Our student Chael Sonnen had started his own local promotion called the Full Contact Fighting Federation in 2002, which utilised amateur fighters. When he ran into some issues with Oregon's athletic commission, Chael took them to court and Matt and I testified for him on three separate occasions. Oregon had a law banning "extreme fighting," but we were able to prove that we did not meet that definition because we had rules and moves and holds that were barred. The commission eventually started working with us instead of against us when they saw the potential for revenue. Chael started paying a 6 percent tax to them, even though it was an amateur show. We ended up becoming the commission's consultants when they decided to officially legalise the sport a couple of years later.

The success of the FCFF opened doors in Oregon, and we all saw opportunity. Under the Team Quest business, we had already formed four entities: Team Quest Productions, Team Quest Management, the Team Quest Training Centre, and the Team Quest website. Each of the owners had been designated one of these departments to run. The training centre was the first branch to take off like gangbusters, and membership shot through the roof. The management part was moving, but there wasn't much money to be made at the time because all of our fighters were young and only getting small purses. We hosted a couple of grappling events under the production helm in the past but knew the timing was right to shift our focus.

We were all surprised to find out that Matt Lindland had registered a separate entity called Sport Fight to begin promoting fights. It looked like he was going to try and do it on his own, so Robert, Danny, and I called him on it. He reassured us he wasn't trying to branch out without us and we all moved forward with Sport Fight. Our first event debuted on February 21, 2004, in Portland, just three weeks after my loss to Belfort. As the front men for the event, Matt and I wore tuxedos, and I had a matching black patch over my eye.

Sport Fight quickly became a local draw, and it also doubled as a place for Team Quest fighters to test their skills. Ed Herman, Nate Quarry, Chris Leben, Matt Horwich, Josh Burkman, Chris Wilson, and Ryan Schultz were but a handful of our guys that got their feet wet in Sport Fight, then went on to make names for themselves in the sport. Along with Team Quest, Sport Fight welcomed other local fight teams like Victory Athletics, Oregon Jiu-Jitsu, and Pearson's Black Belt Academy. To date, Sport Fight has held close to thirty events, with attendance reaching 6,000 spectators.

My third and final match with Belfort was decided for *UFC 49* on August 21, 2004, at the MGM Grand Garden Arena. It was fittingly entitled *Unfinished Business*. Belfort and I were one a piece on the scorecards, and he had something of mine that I wanted back.

I went back to Sacramento to train again. This time, Tito Ortiz joined us.

After our fight at *UFC 44,* Ortiz had contacted me and asked if he could come to Portland to train at Team Quest. I wasn't necessarily opposed to that, but I talked it over with Matt and Robert, and we all agreed it wasn't the best idea. We had a lot of younger fighters who were impressionable and looked up to Ortiz, and we weren't sure that he was the best influence. Ortiz was well known for partying and late nights out drinking. We could see our guys taking Ortiz out and not getting a lot of training done, which was something we were trying to steer them away from. So I stalled—but then Ortiz heard I was coming to Sacramento and asked if he could meet us there. I didn't object.

Ortiz turned out to be a great training partner. He trained in the southpaw stance for me and had a feel for Belfort's style. He was also a very skilled wrestling and grappling partner. His personal life never came into play during our time there at all.

The first day of camp, fifteen of us congregated in Sierra Junior College's wrestling room. There was a potent amount of testosterone in the room, with Quinton Jackson, Ortiz, and a slew of young, eager fighters, so I felt compelled to say a few words.

"You know we are here to train, so no bull crap," I said. "We are going to push each other to the limit, but let's take care of each other at the same time—no egos and no one trying to knock anybody out."

The guys nodded their heads and we began to pair off into training teams. I climbed into the ring with Scott Smith, a young, local fighter only about twenty years old with fast, powerful hands. I had been working on a triple-jab lead-in to close the distance and parry that I would follow with a high kick. Nobody would expect me to throw a high kick in my fight. I was a wrestler.

One minute into the first round of sparring, I threw the jab and whipped this high kick up that slapped Scotty right in the neck. He went all wide-eyed and fell to one knee. He was out of it. The entire room broke out into hysterics. The preacher had knocked the very first guy out! Scotty and I were beyond embarrassed.

The commotion of having a few notable fighters in town brought a steady flow of cameras and reporters in and out of the wrestling room. We decided to hold a public training session at a nightclub in downtown Sacramento owned by the guy Ortiz was staying with. We advertised it on the radio and wheeled mats onto the dance floor, so people could watch the fighters go at it for $5 a head. We had a huge response and donated all the money to the junior college that had graciously lent us their wrestling room the entire time. I left Sacramento on a high note.

Analysing our previous fight, I decided that kicking Belfort wasn't a good idea because it put me off balance. It was a lot smarter to keep my feet on the floor and get to Belfort as fast as I could. I looked at this fight not as a rubber match at all, but more of a continuation of our second fight.

The fight went exactly the way I had planned it the first time, if I hadn't gotten cut. I made Belfort work harder than he wanted to by staying in his face. Belfort had spent time training with some Cuban Greco wrestlers for this fight, and it showed. It took me three to four minutes to wear him down, take him out of position, and get him down to the mat in the first round. In that handful of minutes, Belfort had claimed there was an illegal head-butt, but I watched the tape over and over in slow motion later and saw that it was a punch that cut him first. There was a sizable gash on the corner of his right eye that bled onto my back and everywhere else. Once I got Belfort down, each time got easier, and he struggled to get back up. His will to fight had long gone.

In the third round, I stacked his body and postured up to throw more punches and elbows, making it difficult for him to launch any offensive from his back even though he was a jiu-jitsu black belt.

The end of the third round came, and I walked back to my corner wet and sticky from Belfort's blood. My white shorts were pink. Belfort propped his back up against the fence with the most miserable look on his face, rested his arms on his knees, then took a large pause before he stood. A doctor followed Belfort to his corner, took one look at him, and called the fight. I had won the UFC light heavyweight title a second time in my career.

IN THE SPAN of fourteen months, I had taken out three of the UFC's best light heavyweights, and they were all at least ten years younger. It was a pivotal moment in my career. Because of my age, I felt I'd always been pushed halfway out the UFC's revolving door. Tonight, I'd jammed my foot in it and brought it to a screeching halt.

You could say I was in the right place at the right time, and I wouldn't disagree with you. UFC events had become the best around, the measuring stick to which all other promotions were compared and judged in the United States. They were making the greatest strides in getting mixed martial arts TV and media exposure, driven by Dana White's ironclad will and insane ambition.

Since Zuffa had purchased the company in 2001, I'd known one of the UFC's goals had been to get a TV contract on a network to begin airing live fights. However, the stigma of the sport's earlier, disorderly years still resonated with the networks. After four years of knocking on doors and banging on boardroom tables, Dana was able to get a deal with the fledgling cable network, Spike TV. Spike had just changed its name, image, and focus to lure in the lucrative young male demographic. Cagefighting might fit the mould, the TV executives thought, but Spike wouldn't agree to air straight fight events. And so, in a late-night session at the Zuffa offices in Las Vegas, *The Ultimate Fighter* was born.

The pitch was simple. Sixteen fighters would live together, train together, and compete with one another for UFC contracts. Two teams would be led by two of the UFC's biggest stars, and each episode would culminate with an unedited elimination fight. It was reality TV's biggest gamble. Spike TV had the balls to say yes.

I don't think I was originally considered for one of the coaching slots for the first season. Charismatic UFC Hall of Famer Ken Shamrock was on the short list, as was the equally outgoing Tito Ortiz, who'd fought Shamrock at *UFC 40* in 2002 and given Zuffa its largest pay-per-view numbers to date. For some reason, Zuffa couldn't get Shamrock or Ortiz to the table, so more brainstorming led to me and Chuck Liddell.

Dana saw the show as a way to create build-up for the Couture-Liddell rematch, which was scheduled to coincide with the season's conclusion. After years on the outs with the organisation, I'd actually cultivated a bit of a rapport with Dana, which my manager, Jeremy Lappen was well aware of. Jeremy and Peter Levin had parted ways some time ago, and Jeremy continued to manage me under Triumph Entertainment. Dana had tried to steer me away from Jeremy by telling me he'd used his position with Zuffa to try to parlay tickets and airline flights for himself, which wasn't ethical. He called Jeremy "a leech" and "a bloodsucker." I never told Jeremy and I never questioned his integrity. Dana's backdoor antics with my contract negotiations had angered Jeremy enough to threaten Dana with a "tortious interference" lawsuit if he didn't stop. I didn't think that was necessary. Jeremy and I agreed it might be best to let Dana talk to me on the side anyway, so I could gain some footing on my own.

With the sport rapidly gaining attention, I think everybody thought the UFC was on the rise and making money. Zuffa was a professionally-run company that hosted high-quality events and promoted them through their own public relations department. They sold UFC merchandise and scheduled public appearances and autograph signings with their athletes. Compared to my first weigh-ins held at the dingy Holiday Inn in Georgia, the UFC weigh-ins became events unto themselves, sometimes attracting two to three thousand people a pop. The UFC's attendance numbers were steady too—around 10,000 per event and climbing.

All looked well, but it wasn't. Zuffa was spending more money than they were making, something both Dana and Lorenzo confirmed to me during the course of the TV show's shoot. The first season of *The Ultimate Fighter* was funded entirely by Zuffa, and the price tag was well in the millions. Lorenzo decided that this was the last money he was going to throw into his investment, and if the show didn't catch on, they were going to put the UFC up for sale. Later, Dana would publicly admit that the company's debt had reached into the eight figures. Some said it was as high as $40 million.

For the show's fifty-day shoot, Zuffa asked me to come live in Las Vegas, where the Ultimate Training Centre was located in an industrial area off the beaten track of the world-famous Strip. Trish didn't want to go, but softened a bit when we saw that Zuffa would put us up in a nice condominium with a pool. Little Caden started swimming there like a fish at six months old.

I was pleasantly surprised when the production staff asked me for input to get *The Ultimate Fighter* off the ground. It was the first season, so there was a lot to figure out. How would the teams be picked and how would they train separately? What would workouts focus on? How long should the workouts last?

I wrote out my ideas for the production team and they scheduled some of them into the show. I enjoyed getting the chance to help think through that initial phase.

A big question for Spike TV and Zuffa was how the chemistry between Liddell and I would play out, and ultimately how it would promote our April rematch. The hatred between Ken Shamrock and Tito Ortiz was palpable, but Liddell and I were very similar and actually fairly good friends. We were both relatively quiet, so I pushed myself to speak up a little more on the show and come out of my shell.

I wouldn't trash-talk—that was never my thing—but I tried to speak my mind when and where it was needed. Having cameras and microphones around me for hours on end was also a great experience and loosened me up.

During the tryout process, Liddell and I evaluated the crop of guys and jotted down our team selections on our clipboards. I tipped my hand a little bit with Forrest Griffin, a determined Georgia police officer who was about to quit the sport when he got the call from Spike. I was sure that Forrest and Stephan Bonnar, another promising light heavyweight from Illinois, were the top two guys in the gym. I saw Forrest as a little more reckless because he didn't exhibit a lot of control. It wasn't that I didn't like him—he had a funny personality, but he was going to hurt himself. He was going at it too damn hard for a training environment.

Earlier, Dana and I had argued about the fighters wearing headgear. Dana wanted them all to wear it during the sparring.

"Head gear is for pussies," I told Dana. "The guys can't grapple and do MMA with big-ass head gear on."

In the sparring tryouts, I yelled at Forrest to watch his intensity and told Liddell he needed to keep an eye on him. Sure enough, within five minutes, Forrest and Stephan collided and Stephan was rushed off the set to get stitches in his forehead. I was pissed that it happened when it could have been avoided. To make it worse, Dana said, "I told you so."

After that, I told Liddell I wasn't going to select Forrest for my team, thinking in the back of my mind that I could set it up to choose Forrest a little later in our draft so I could go after one or two other guys first. But Liddell picked Forrest before I could get to him. Overall, I got the guys I wanted, including two of my own Team Quest guys, Chris Leben and Nate Quarry.

It felt good to be coaching again, and I felt really comfortable in the environment. I think it showed throughout the course of the show. I was interested in the whole production process and was appreciative of the support I got from the on-set producer Andrea Richter, and Craig

Piligian, the producer who had helped the UFC bring the idea to Spike TV in the first place.

Over the course of the show, I think I also gained respect for UFC president Dana White. I saw that he had a genuine passion for the sport and the fighters. He invited me and Liddell to his house to watch a boxing match, and his office was plastered with UFC posters and memorabilia. The walls of his son's room were actually painted with UFC fighters. It was obvious that this was more than just a job for him. I think that was something that we both saw in each other that changed our relationship. We had been adversaries throughout years of contract negotiations, but this was the first time we were ever on the same side.

There were moments on the show that affected me. I had been working with Alex Schoenauer, who had just been transferred from Liddell's team to mine to rebalance the numbers. Alex needed some help with his takedowns and defence, so I was spending a little more time with him trying to get him up to speed. I moved to take him down, and he ran into Nate Quarry from behind, landing on his calf. The collision twisted Nate's ankle pretty badly, and the doctors said he would probably need surgery.

I felt awful. I was disturbed that one of my own guys from Oregon got hurt from a stupid situation and had lost his big opportunity. Liddell felt bad as well, so we both agreed to try and find a way to keep Nate involved in the show. We asked Dana if Nate could stay on as my assistant coach. Dana agreed. Luckily, Nate's injury wasn't as bad as they originally thought, and I was glad to be able to keep him around.

I saw the show as the perfect vehicle to expose the sport to new audiences. It was a behind-the-scenes look at who we were and what we did. I was happy with the athletes that were involved, though they sometimes got a little carried away at the house. Chris Leben was one of the most emotional fighters at Team Quest, a real loose cannon, so I was only half surprised when he pissed on a guy's bed, then kicked down a door and put his fist through a stained-glass door after a night of boozing.

As the coaches, Liddell and I didn't spend much time at the fighters' house, and we only got snippets of info through the gym's grapevine of things that had gone on there. When the show aired, I watched a lot of footage for the first time, and found myself a bit shocked at all the drama.

"Come on, guys!" I yelled, from my couch. "Would you put your shirts on and stop crying? What the hell are you guys doing?"

MY TIME IN Las Vegas was probably the closest I'd ever come to a nine-to-five routine. This didn't change anything between me and Trish, and we continued to fight. Trish was resentful when Dana and the Fertittas had invited me, Liddell and Willa Ford, a pop starlet who hosted *The Ultimate Fighter*, to the Oscar De La Hoya-Bernard Hopkins boxing match at the MGM Grand. She had to stay home with Caden. It was more of a publicity appearance, but Trish didn't understand that.

When my son Ryan came into town with six of his buddies for a bachelor party, I took them out to dinner and the Tangerine nightclub at Treasure Island. Again, Trish was irritated that she hadn't been asked to join us (even though it was a bachelor party) and was upset that I'd spent money on them.

The coup de grace came when I got an e-mail from John Donehue, my old training buddy from Australia. He invited me over to teach another seminar and bring some of the Team Quest fighters with me to compete in an event he was hosting. I ran the idea by Trish, telling her that John had offered to buy her a ticket to come out as well. But it seemed to be the last straw for her, because she flipped out.

A few days later, Trish and Caden left Las Vegas to be with her sister Trudy, who was in labour with her first child. A huge sense of relief washed over me. It was like a huge weight had been taken off my back. It was overwhelming. Sitting there alone, I suddenly realised that if I was having this reaction, then things were a lot worse with Trish than I wanted to admit. I wondered how I'd gotten here again.

I had two weeks left in Las Vegas until the show finished shooting. My friend and fellow fighter John Lewis had been continually sending me phone texts and inviting me to parties he was promoting at the different nightclubs in town. I'd told him I didn't really have any time, but sitting there with the show winding down and not much to do, I reconsidered. I grabbed Nate Quarry and we met John at Light, the trendy nightclub inside the Bellagio Hotel and Casino. I'd never been there before, but it was a typical Vegas nightclub, with a big dance floor surrounded by roped-off VIP booths with expensive bottle service. John had one of these VIP tables.

I wasn't really drinking or partying. I just sat there and people-watched. John introduced me to a woman named Kim, who had been sitting at the table with us all night. We struck up a conversation, although neither of us was having much fun. To break up the boredom, I talked Kim into getting up and dancing with me. Afterward, she gave me her business card and said that maybe she'd see me around again. I took the business card and threw it on the coffee table when I returned to my apartment alone. I didn't give it a lot more thought.

Over the next two weeks, it seemed like wherever I turned, I ran into Kim. I saw her at Simon's Restaurant inside the Hard Rock Hotel & Casino, where Spike TV had decided to take the cast for dinner before a Kid Rock concert. It was the first night out for the fighters after being locked up in the house for nine weeks, and they went wild, getting so drunk and obnoxious that we had to pack them into their van after the concert and send them home. A few of us continued on to Body English, the nightclub inside the Hard Rock Hotel, where I saw Kim again. Out on the dance floor, in the darkness, we kissed.

Two days later, Kim called me and invited me over to her house for dinner. That's when I told her I was married.

"I should have told you sooner," I said sheepishly. "I wasn't trying to act like a single guy and I didn't expect this to happen."

Kim told me she already knew. She had asked John Lewis after the night at Body English. John had told her, "Have fun or whatever, but don't get attached. After he leaves Vegas you are probably never going to see him again."

Hearing that, I felt the need to explain. I laid it all out on the table about Trish, our six years of unhappiness, and that I thought my marriage was over.

I wasn't sure if Kim was going to throw me out, which would have been perfectly understandable. Instead, she sat and listened.

We formed a bond that evening, and I didn't want to break it. Kim invited me to come with her to a friend's birthday party at Simon's Restaurant in the Hard Rock Hotel & Casino. I don't think she expected me to say yes, but I did. She had to leave me there for a couple of hours with her friends to go do some work for the Wynn Casino, where she was employed as a host to high rollers, so I waited for her. When she returned, I had had a few drinks and was wearing a goofy cap that one of her friends had given me—I looked like Robin Hood. We both laughed at the silliness of it all. It was one of the most enjoyable nights I'd had in a while. The next day, we went to lunch and talked for three hours.

I spent my final days in Las Vegas with Kim, away from Trish and the problems wedged between us. I left Sin City with my heart in turmoil for the second time.

Round Three

COMING AROUND AGAIN

3

12 CHAPTER TWELVE:
CONFRONTATION

MY GREATEST ENEMY IS CONFRONTATION. I DON'T have the stomach for it. I know that sounds odd for someone who fights in a cage for a living, but I'd rather take Chuck Liddell on any given day than have to communicate with someone when emotions are involved. My quiet and shy nature doesn't necessarily lend itself well to this cause.

Back in Oregon that November after *The Ultimate Fighter* had wrapped, I knew the problems in my marriage were waiting for me. I saw clearly now that Trish and I were going in opposite directions. I hadn't felt a connection with her for years, and we couldn't share our feelings on an intimate level anymore. The only thing holding us together was our two-and-a-half-year-old son, Caden, and Trish had already begun to box me out of parenting him with her. I had no intention of leaving my son, but my career was on the upswing, and I'll admit, I wanted it to move that way. I'd been lucky enough to get cast on a reality TV show, and I was still aiming to launch my acting career down the road once I couldn't fight anymore. I felt any success would only help provide for my son in the future.

I didn't have to gather the nerve to approach Trish. Things came to a head with her pretty quickly. Within a week, she had a sense that it was time to talk. Sitting on the couch downstairs watching TV after we'd put Caden to bed, she turned to me.

"Am I losing you?" she asked. I saw a mix of hurt and resentment in her eyes.

"Yes," I answered honestly.

The conversation turned ugly. She asked if I had met another woman, but I told her it wasn't about that. It was about us. I was just as much to blame for avoiding our problems for the last six years, but we had gotten ourselves here together.

We started to see a marriage counsellor, but I felt like I was going through the motions. In one of our sessions, I recalled that I'd had thoughts of leaving Trish a few years before. When Aimee had been living with us, I'd wanted to pack my daughter up and walk away. I didn't think there was anything left to salvage in the relationship, but I wouldn't say that out loud.

The tension around our home seeped into every room, so I sought refuge behind closed doors to call Kim in Las Vegas. Kim encouraged me to stay in counselling to sort things out with Trish, but that wasn't what I wanted. She told me I needed to be sure this was what I wanted and to exhaust all efforts to make it work for Caden's sake and my own. I tried to stop calling Kim, but she was the only person I could talk to besides my mom.

My mom knew what was happening. I told her the truth—that Trish and I had been arguing back and forth for nearly six years. I also revealed my relationship with Kim to my mom, and she listened patiently.

Trish and I took Caden to Seattle to visit our families for the holidays and everybody could tell that something wasn't right. After Christmas, Trish and I flew to Tokyo to watch Danny fight in PRIDE's New Year's Eve event. Danny brought his wife, Alison, and Matt Lindland's wife Angie came as well, so the men concentrated on the fighting while the wives spent time together. Matt and I cornered Danny, who came down with a raging fever and flu-like symptoms before the bout and eked out a split decision to Yuki Kondo. Rulon Gardner, a 2000 Olympic Greco-Roman wrestling gold medallist who had been training under Danny, also made his debut that night and won.

Other than our team's victories, the trip wasn't a pleasant one. Trish and I argued constantly about every little thing, whether we were in front of our friends or not. It only solidified in my heart what I already knew: Trish and I weren't meant to be together. That trip would be the last time Danny, Matt, and I—the core members of Team Quest— would spend time together with all our wives.

I hadn't told Danny or Matt about my sinking relationship with Trish, but I didn't have to. Matt had asked me point-blank if I was seeing anyone else when I returned from Las Vegas, and I had lied to his face. I didn't want to confide in Danny and Alison. Their marriage had been tested the year before, and they separated, but Matt and I encouraged them to get counselling and keep their family together. Nine months later, here I was with one foot out the door myself. But I felt Danny and Alison's marriage could be saved. I didn't believe mine held the same possibilities.

Promotion for *The Ultimate Fighter* was gearing up, and I was asked to go to both Las Vegas and then New York to shoot ads and conduct interviews for the series. Kim and I met for dinner in Las Vegas. Sitting across from her, I knew she was who I wanted to be with. In New York, I made an appearance on *The Carson Daly Show,* which was exciting—the UFC had struggled for four years to get fighters onto late-night talk shows.

I met a friend for dinner and he asked me if I was ready for my life to change. I hadn't really thought about it or placed any expectations on the show. I told my friend that God has a way of keeping us all humble. My mind was on what I had to do once I got back to Oregon.

THE ULTIMATE FIGHTER debuted on Spike TV on January 18, 2005. I watched it at home by myself with a little flutter in my stomach. Dana told me if the show debuted to a .8 rating it would be considered a success. The next day, *TUF* came in at a solid 1.2. Spike TV was ecstatic. I was relieved.

A few nights later, I told Trish I was moving out. She started taking down all my wrestling and UFC posters and pictures from the walls and stacked them in a spare room in the basement. Her gesture was so final.

I moved into a condominium on Robert Street in Gresham. The building was owned by my friend Rick Franklin. Ironically, these were the condos I had envisioned moving into with Aimee when I first thought about leaving Trish years before. I guess I ended up there eventually.

In late January, I flew to Los Angeles to take some meetings about movie work. Kim surprised me by driving out to California with a friend of hers to meet me. A couple of weeks later, I flew Kim out to Malibu to be with me. Since the credit card bills still went to my house, Trish found the receipts for the airline ticket with Kim's name on it. That's when all hell broke loose. Trish started to go through our phone records and tried to call Kim herself.

In hindsight, I should have been honest with Trish and told her about Kim upfront. I should have told her exactly how I felt. I didn't love her anymore, and I didn't want to be married to her. Instead, I tried to spare Trish's feelings and spare myself the embarrassment of having to admit that I'd gotten involved with another woman again.

I aggravated matters when I took Kim with me to *UFC 51* in Las Vegas that February.

I honestly didn't think it would be that big of a deal. I wasn't trying to flaunt my new relationship, I just wanted Kim there for support. But I underestimated what a circus it would become. We walked out of the tunnel into the Mandalay Bay Events Centre, and there we were on the Jumbotron screens. Twelve thousand fans went berserk. I grabbed Kim by the hand, and we made our way to our seats as fast as we could, to sit with the rest of the *TUF* cast. Kim looked like she was going to pass out.

The rest of the night, the TV cameras kept finding us. We weren't holding hands or hanging on each other, but we didn't have to. It was obvious to everyone there that we were together. I realise now this was a disastrous decision. I'd wanted to make a statement and prove my commitment to Kim. I paid for it, though.

I was still training at Team Quest, but my separation from Trish had a ripple effect on my relationships. My decision to reveal Kim to the world only intensified the friction at the gym. Robert, Matt, and some of the other Team Quest fighters were upset with me for disrespecting Trish in public. I didn't see it that way, and I felt more and more isolated from them.

The harshest criticism came from, of all people, my mother. The day I moved out of the house, she began calling me a couple of times a day and left me the most horrible voice-mail messages. She told me I had no balls, and if I was half the man I had once been I would take care of my responsibilities. She would call me at six in the morning, screaming and crying hysterically.

"If I can't sleep, you can't sleep either," she said. I had never had anyone talk to me that way, let alone my own mother. My relationship with my mom had been one of my pillars growing up, and now she was going after me more than anyone else. I didn't expect her to agree with what I was doing, but I'd hoped she'd at least find a way to support me and help guide me through difficult times. I got none of that from her.

I realised that if my mom was acting this way, then my whole family must be coming from the same place. I started to look around. I thought my friends must be harbouring similar feelings for me at this point too, and I suddenly felt estranged from everyone.

My youngest sister, Traci, didn't really say anything. She was very close to my mom and Trish, which put her in a tough spot. I talked to Traci's husband, Vince, who had strong Christian morals and tried to counsel me from a biblical perspective. He told me that once I jumped off the cliff, I couldn't come back. I didn't want to hear that. I knew how I felt. My sister Yolanda was the only one who didn't treat me differently. She was upset, confused, and worried, but she was willing to listen and didn't judge me.

I finally called Yolanda and said, "If this is the only shit that mom has to say to me, and that's the best she can do, then tell her to quit calling me. I don't want to hear from her." The phone calls stopped, but there was one more message after I took my relationship with Kim public at *UFC 51*.

"What kind of person are you?" she asked, then hung up.

Trish called me after *UFC 51* as well. It was the first time we had spoken in almost a month. She told me she was filing for a divorce.

After that, going back to Team Quest was like heading into enemy territory. I felt like anything I said or did made its way back to Trish. There were only a few team members that had been to my house and saw what Trish was like. They knew full well what I'd put up with, but they probably didn't know to what degree and for how long I'd endured it. I'm sure it was a surprise to everyone when I left Trish, because I didn't share a lot of personal feelings or my personal life with them.

Though I'm a team player and have thrived on camaraderie all my life, there are very few people that have gotten past my emotional wall. I think that's why Kim and I established such a strong connection early on, because for whatever reason, I shared all my thoughts and feelings with her.

Matt was disappointed—he concluded that we hadn't been good enough friends for me to tell him the truth about Kim when he'd asked, back in November. Honestly, I hadn't felt like I could have told anybody. I wasn't prepared to handle the criticism. In November, I was still trying to focus on my marriage and finding a way to make it work. I'd actually stopped calling Kim to try to sorts things out with Trish. I knew that people would assume it was all about the other woman and not acknowledge that my marriage had been failing for quite some time.

It is very difficult to train in a place where you know every whisper behind your back is about you. I was with a team in Oregon, but I wasn't sure it was mine anymore. I headed down to Sacramento for a couple of weeks to get in some more conditioning work and kickboxing training with Dave Miranoble and the Capital City Fighting Alliance team. I went back to Team Quest for a week or so, then left for Las Vegas.

I ARRIVED IN town a couple of weeks early to get ready for the live season finale of *The Ultimate Fighter*, which culminated in a fight night one week before my bout with Liddell on April 16, 2005. I would be cornering the fighters that had been on my team during the show, and I stayed with Kim in my downtime. That's when I first met Kim's friend Mike Pyle, a welterweight fighter from Tennessee with the wit and timing of a professional comedian. We trained together at my friend John Lewis' J-Sect gym, along with a boxing trainer named Ron Frazier. I felt welcomed right away.

Robert, Matt, Danny, and Nate met me in Las Vegas to corner me for the fight. Danny and Matt were my guys, and I wanted them there. We'd started this thing together, and I trusted what they saw in the cage that I couldn't see myself in the heat of battle. I can't tell you how important your corner can be for you in those final days before a fight. They set the mood of your entire experience. They make you laugh. They make the time go faster. They give you that last boost of confidence if you need it. I wanted so much for my team to give me all of that, but I couldn't stop the momentum of change between us all.

The last few days leading up to the fight were full of anxiety. There was a palpable tension between Robert, Nate, and Kim. Kim had loaned them her car and was doing anything she could to support the team, but they didn't cut her any slack.

I was stressed out; I weighed in at 201 pounds without cutting a single ounce. I'd lost 20 pounds in the last four months. The rift between my mom and me really bothered me. We still weren't talking, and she didn't attend the event. It was the first one she'd missed since my first fight with Pedro Rizzo four years earlier. That weighed heavily on me.

What else can we throw on the pile? I wondered.

Strategically, I thought I wouldn't have to change much in the fight because I assumed Liddell wouldn't adjust a lot of his game. You never know what adjustments somebody's going to make, and I always think the burden is on the winner in a rematch. It was harder for me to objectively say, "Okay, what do I need to do differently?" because what I'd done the first time had worked. It's always easier to correct mistakes.

I knew my hands had progressed and improved, and I felt comfortable out there. Our initial exchanges went well until I caught a thumb in the eye about a minute into the first round. I immediately stepped away and reached for my eye, which referee John McCarthy caught and responded to by temporarily stopping the bout. It was my left eye, of course. I immediately remembered that Liddell's last two opponents, Tito Ortiz and Vernon White, had complained about getting poked in the eye as well. I got upset.

I took a few seconds to recover, but I probably didn't take as much time as I should have. We restarted, and rather than continuing to be the methodical hunter, my overaggression kicked in, and I went after Liddell. I overcommitted on a left hook and missed. The momentum of the punch carried me into the cage, and I had to reach out my right hand to catch my balance. Liddell stepped to my left side and threw a straight right hand that hit me right on the button. The whole sequence lasted about two seconds.

I had been "flashed" once. Danny had hit me years ago during a training session and suddenly I was on my arse wondering how I got there. I'd never been knocked out before, though.

It's a strange sensation to get knocked out. You don't feel any pain. You don't really feel anything. One second you are the hunter, and the next you are looking up at a bunch of faces standing over you with lights shining in your eyes. You lose a little piece of time, and you know something's not right, but it's over so quickly it doesn't even matter.

I've seen fighters get knocked out, and it takes them a minute or even a whole night to get their wits back. I felt fine afterwards. I stood up and wasn't dizzy or wobbly. I gave a post-fight interview right there and I was able to understand what I was being asked and answered back.

"You stay in here long enough and it's bound to happen," I told the crowd. Honestly, I wasn't sure exactly what had happened. All I knew is that I'd been hit and wouldn't be leaving the Octagon with the belt.

When I got back to my dressing room, a Nevada State Athletic Commission representative told me I would have to go to the hospital for a CAT scan and that an ambulance was waiting for me outside. Our friend John Bardis always threw an after-party for me, but that would have to wait. I grabbed my bags, and we all made our way past the reporters to the back entrance of the arena. The emergency medical technician told me I could have only one person ride with me in the ambulance, so I brought Kim. I was cleared that night to return to the hotel, and we all made it to the party eventually.

Losing the title seemed the least of my worries. Back in Oregon, a rumour began to circulate around the gym that Kim was a Vegas stripper I'd met during my midlife crisis. In reality, Kim had a very prestigious position as an executive host at the brand-new Wynn Casino, where she designated the credit lines for the high rollers. I began to see that no matter what I did, Kim would never be accepted by the team.

The level of trust the members of Team Quest once had in each other was crumbling, and the business was affected. We'd taken over the lease of the whole property a year before, when the auto dealership had gone out of business, and started renovations that were now almost finished. We were expanding and set to make more money, but business issues bubbled to the surface.

Danny had been designated to develop and run the website when he moved to California, but the three of us felt it wasn't being properly managed. Matt, Robert, and I decided jointly to reduce Danny's partnership. He was still a member of Team Quest, but he wouldn't get any money from the training centre. Danny and I had been close, and it was a tough decision for me, but I agreed that it had to be done. It only added to our sense of awkwardness around one another. We spoke less and less until we barely spoke at all. Team Quest had never put anything down in writing, and now our handshakes weren't holding up.

The gym's renovation was nearly complete, but I was at a crossroads. I had helped build the Team Quest gym from scratch, and our Sport Fight promotion was thriving in the Portland area. The young fighters we had all nurtured were starting to make names for themselves, and the stock of our team had never been higher. Still, I felt like a black cloud was hanging over me. I was dealing with everyone in Oregon at the same time: Trish, my friends, my business partners, and my family. I decided to move to Las Vegas permanently to separate myself from all the madness and be with Kim full-time. There I could deal with one person at a time, which is basically what I did.

MY MANAGER JEREMY offered me the opportunity to open a gym in Los Angeles with him and fellow fighter Bas Rutten, who he also managed. I decided to take the offer, and we began scouting locations there. I started to split my time between Las Vegas and Los Angeles. I went back to a Portland courthouse a month later to meet Trish for a mandatory parent counselling class required by the state. This was the first step in our divorce. Trish and I had both been seeing our individual counsellors, and it seemed we were both getting a handle on the separation.

We were civil to each other throughout the hearing, so I asked her if she'd like to go get a cup of coffee afterwards. We sat at a local coffee shop, sipping our drinks and making small talk. Trish had brought a bunch of pictures that she'd found and thought I might want. I was grateful for the sentiment. Then she gave me her news.

"By the way, I'm hiring a private investigator to look into Kim," she told me. "There have been some red flags thrown up about her character and background."

My mouth dropped. I couldn't believe what I was hearing. Red flags? What red flags? I was furious, and demanded to know what she was referring to, but Trish wouldn't go into detail.

Over the next few weeks, it was like a domino effect. First, I was told that Kim was a hooker. Then I was told that John Bardis, my trusted friend, had corroborated the story. None of this made sense to me.

The private investigator provided Trish with the phone number of Kim's ex-husband and an ex-boyfriend, with whom she'd had two children. Kim's exes were bitter about her success and willing to feed Trish whatever she wanted to hear. Trish wanted to believe Kim was corrupt and a bad mother. But I knew Kim wasn't dangerous to anyone, including our son, Caden.

I was most disappointed in how my friend John Bardis handled the situation. The founder and CEO of a very successful medical supplies company, John had sponsored many of my fights and outside endeavours, including *The Eco-Challenge* race I never got to compete in. I first met John at the 1996 Summer Olympics in Atlanta, Georgia. I was scrambling outside for tickets when a professional-looking guy in a blazer approached me.

"I know you," he said. "What are you doing?"

"I'm looking for tickets to go watch the wrestling," I answered.

"I can't believe a four-time National champion doesn't have tickets to this event," he said, and introduced himself. He gave me a stack of tickets for the rest of the competitions and invited Trish and me to his home for an event he was hosting that day for FILA, wrestling's international sanctioning body, and USA Wrestling. It was a big to-do, with all the top FILA officials and USA Wrestling brass gathered for a big barbeque at his beautiful mansion. Later, John addressed the crowd.

He described meeting me that day and how he'd given me tickets to the event when I couldn't get any myself. He didn't directly call out USA Wrestling for not taking care of one of its athletes, but he didn't have to. His story painted the picture perfectly.

He announced right there that his company was going to sponsor me from now on and provide me with whatever I needed. I'd only met John a few hours earlier, so hearing this news in front of a group of strangers was a bit overwhelming. I was just happy to get the free tickets.

But John stayed true to his word. He started sending me a monthly stipend for my training, and I made appearances for him, and even spoke at one of his company's motivational seminars. John became a part of the team. He had wrestled for the University of Wisconsin, so we shared our war stories and our mutual affinity for the sport. I always felt John was someone I could count on. He was a very honest and straightforward guy, and probably one of the most giving individuals I'd ever met.

Now nine years later, my separation put John in a precarious position. He was also close friends with Trish, and he continued to advise both of us and even mediated a few conversations between us when things got volatile. I had spoken to him many times leading up to the second Liddell fight and he had remained supportive of me, which I felt was in short supply from the other people around me.

John was so much of a confidante that I felt comfortable having him meet Kim before anyone else. We joined him at one of his company's speaking engagements, and the three of us went out to dinner together. He told me afterwards that he'd thought Kim was sharp and very nice. Later, I found out that John had been upset that I'd asked Kim to ride with me to the hospital the night of the Liddell fight. He told both Trish and my mom that he thought Kim had only cared about getting to the post-fight party quickly, rather than about my health. He'd also said that Kim had gotten in the face of one of his female employees who had spoken to me at his company event, poked her in the chest and said, "He's with me, stay the fuck away from him."

Kim swore that she never said a word to anybody. I felt these were horrible rumours. When I spoke with John about it, he said that Kim wasn't somebody he wanted to spend time with. I didn't know how to reply.

Every summer, John rented houseboats out on Lake Mead to throw a big shindig for his employees. He invited me to come, and I brought Kim and my son Ryan. John acted cold and distant. It made Kim feel uncomfortable, so we decided to leave early. As we got on the small boat to take us towards shore, John came out onto the houseboat's deck. I rose to my feet and gave him a military salute. I'm not sure why I did it. But that was the last time I ever saw him.

WHEN I'D GOTTEN divorced from Sharon, I was a wrestling coach who only made $25,000 a year. None of my family and friends had given me a hard time about it. Now I was part of an up-and-coming sport, and there was considerably more fame and money involved. I couldn't help but think some of the reactions from my family and friends were based on that.

The Ultimate Fighter gained more viewers each week and ended its first season with a 1.9 rating, some of the best overall ratings Spike TV had ever earned for any of its programming. The show's success brought on more sponsors, and that green-lighted more opportunities for us to be featured outside the fighting niche. I posed for the cover of *American Health and Fitness* and was invited to do TV appearances with mainstream outlets that wouldn't have given MMA a second thought a few years earlier.

I never shied away from talking to the media. I knew the sport needed the exposure. I remembered the days when the UFC didn't even need to set up a press section because no one ever came to cover it. Talking to the media is something I've always enjoyed, so I did newspaper, magazine, radio, and TV appearances whenever I was asked. I was honoured that reporters wanted to speak with me. I loved talking about the sport and defending it when I could. I gave my personal cell phone number out to any reporter who asked and always tried to return every phone call I could. To me, that was, and still is, a part of the job.

UFC events began to attract even larger crowds. After my second fight with Pedro Rizzo, I made the mistake of walking down the Studio Walk at the MGM Grand Hotel and Casino with my family to get to the elevator bank. It took us three hours to get back to my hotel room. Now, it was even worse. I had to ask security to meet me at my room and bring me through the back service elevators and hallways to avoid the crowds. I wasn't trying to avoid the fans. I just had to get to where I was supposed to be on time.

I was suddenly getting recognised everywhere, at grocery stores and gas stations. At Costco, a guy bought an economy package of nine instant cameras just so he could take one picture of me. At a Sport Fight show, a young woman started crying and shaking, waiting to get an autograph. A guy even followed me into the bathroom at a UFC event so he could strike up a conversation. Things like that had never happened before, and I didn't know what to do. It was strange to see people react this way.

The public saw "Captain America," a perfect, patriotic hero who defied all the odds. But behind the scenes, my personal life was a mess. I felt defective, like I was more prone to unstable relationships because I had experienced them in my childhood. It wasn't exactly the same scenario, but there was a pattern in the way I'd left Sharon, and now Trish. I had helped to created these situations, and they kept repeating themselves, rooted in my inability to communicate. Having just lost the belt, and in the midst of a nasty divorce, I felt at odds with myself and for the first time, I had no clear plan for the future.

13 CHAPTER THIRTEEN: A REVELATION

YOU KNOW HOW SOME PEOPLE SAY THEY GET A PHONE call that changes their life? It sounds corny to even describe it that way, but it happened. It actually started as an e-mail from a woman named Lori. I'm not sure how she got my e-mail address. Lori wrote that she'd seen me on *The Ultimate Fighter* and that I looked a lot like her uncle. She said her mother had recently passed away, and her uncle Wally had opened up to her around the time of the funeral, admitting that had a son he'd never gotten to raise or meet.

Who's this wacko? I thought to myself.

But then she started mentioning names of members of my family. She wrote that her mom had been friends with my Aunt Yvonne—who had died during childbirth when I was young. There was no way she could have known any of that unless she really did know my family. My interest was piqued.

I am not one to rush into decisions. I'll always take a few days to think something over. So I waited a few days, then I e-mailed her back and asked for her phone number. When she sent it, I called her that day.

"His name is Wally Johnson," she told me. It could have been Bob Smith or Mike Jones, for all it mattered. I had never once heard of a Wally Johnson and I wasn't sure if I wanted to start right now. Still, Lori's account of things seemed feasible.

I got off the phone feeling confused. Was there a chance that Ed wasn't really my father? Had the man I'd idolised my entire childhood not been who I thought he was at all? I wanted answers, but I couldn't call my mom. We still weren't speaking to each other. I sat with this new information for a few days and stewed.

I called my dad, Ed, the next week. I wasn't on the greatest terms with my father, but we'd made headway over the last few years. After my divorce from Sharon, I had talked to a counsellor about my feelings towards him. The counsellor had asked if I was happy with myself and I said yes.

"Well, despite all the things your dad put you through, if you're content with who you are now, you don't need to be upset or feel anger toward other people," the counsellor said. "Instead, try thanking them for helping make you who you are. They contributed, whether it was good or bad."

Those words changed the way I thought about my life that day. Instead of being pissed off that my father was never around, I decided to change my attitude. I didn't have a breakthrough with my dad. It was a gradual process where we got more comfortable being around each other. I never called him first. I'd always left it up to him. If he wanted to see me, he had to let me know me he was in town.

When I called him that day, he knew right away something was wrong, but he played dumb at first.

"I don't remember anyone like that," he told me.

"This guy is claiming he is my dad," I said. "Is this true?"

My dad began to cry. Angry and upset all at once, Ed told me he had raised me like I was his son, then he stopped talking mid-sentence.

"Am I your son?" I asked, but my father wouldn't answer. He had basically already admitted it, but he said he didn't want to talk about it any further. I wasn't one to push, but I felt I was owed a straight answer.

I knew who I wanted to call next, and I didn't care if she didn't want to talk to me. My hands shook as my fingers dialled the number and it began to ring. My mom picked up the phone, and I just exploded.

"Where do you get off judging me and saying all these things about my divorce and treating me the way you have when you did the same thing?" I screamed. "You've never told me the truth!"

My mom hung up on me. I called her back, and we yelled at each other until she hung up the phone again. I wanted to know the truth, I told her. I wanted the real story. She told me I was crazy and that I wasn't living in reality. After a few more hang-ups, she stopped picking up her phone.

My world came crashing down around me. My mom had lied to me. She had called me a cheater when she had been there herself. I felt betrayed.

The only family member I could confide in was my sister Yolanda. Like me, Yolanda had constantly been seeking the approval and love of our father. She left home at the age of sixteen to go live with Ed and had developed a stronger relationship with him then I had over the years. Yolanda is more aggressive and strong-willed than me, and on my behalf, she went to Ed and asked him flat-out. I learned that my mom and Ed had separated at one point during their marriage, and she was already pregnant when they got back together. Ed believed I could be his son, but he wasn't sure. This was the first time Yolanda and I had heard any of this.

Ed didn't want Yolanda to tell me. "Don't screw this up," he told her. "I finally have a relationship with him."

Yolanda didn't like being threatened. At that point, she was the only one of us who was Ed's child without a doubt, and she felt he wasn't making any effort to maintain a relationship with her. She stopped speaking with him shortly after and hasn't seen him since.

IT WAS TOUGH not to let these new concerns consume me, especially when I was juggling so many balls in the air. I had recently moved in with Kim in Las Vegas, and my fight career was moving forward. I still loved to fight, though the personal conflicts with my family and friends were weighing me down.

Getting knocked out by Chuck Liddell made me look vulnerable again in front of the fans. I had just turned forty-two years old, which was well beyond the accepted expiration date for an athlete in the sport. There had been speculation that my age had finally caught up to me. How much longer can he keep on fighting? I was back in the role as underdog, which was oddly comforting.

My next opponent, Mike Van Arsdale, had a few things in common with me. At forty, he too was older, and was an accomplished amateur wrestler before he had delved into fighting. A three-time All-American for Iowa State University, Van Arsdale was a NCAA Division I champion in 1988 and had also served in the U.S. army.

Van Arsdale had made the transition from wrestling to MMA in 1998 but hadn't competed as many times as I had in those seven years. This was only his tenth fight, while it was my twenty-first bout. I believe when you match a wrestler against a wrestler, it always makes for a technical match-up. But I predicted this time, it would be the other pieces of the mixed martial arts puzzle that would make a difference. We were set to meet at *UFC 54: Boiling Point*, at the MGM Grand Garden Arena in Las Vegas on August 20, 2005.

This was the first fight I trained for away from Team Quest. In Las Vegas, I trained at the UFC Training Centre, where we'd shot *The Ultimate Fighter*. I worked with first-season winner Forrest Griffin and castmate Alex Schoenauer, along with Mike Pyle and Jay Hieron, a bright kid from Long Island. It felt rejuvenating to be surrounded by young, motivated athletes.

I also ventured out to Florence, Colorado, to train with Brad Anderson, my wrestling buddy from the All-Army team, at his Gunbare Judo Club. Brad had been an Interservice champion and an Olympic alternate, so he had the credentials to fine-tune my wrestling skills. Brad wasn't interested in the politics surrounding my divorce or my decision to take some time away from Team Quest. He was just there to train me without any obligations or strings attached, which was what I needed more than anything. I was determined to keep the negative feelings about my divorce at bay as I prepared for the fight.

Before I made it out to Brad's gym, about three weeks out from the bout, I felt my knee getting sore. At first, I wondered if I did something to it the day before in training. By the afternoon, my knee had swelled to twice its size, and I could feel an intense heat burning underneath my skin. I knew what it was right away, so I went to the local hospital's emergency room.

I had a staph infection in my knee, which had developed into cellulitis, an infection in the skin's deeper layers. It causes tenderness, swelling, and redness around the wound and will continue to spread if left untreated. Staph infections are fairly common among fighters, who are usually exposed to the bacteria on the mats. The doctor gave me a shot and some oral antibiotics to combat it. He also drew a circle around the swelling and told me if the redness reached outside of it, I would have to come back to the hospital to take antibiotics intravenously.

Kim and I flew to Colorado the next day to train with Brad, and by the time we landed, I had to go straight to the emergency room for the IV because the infection had spread. They fed me the IV for the next two days, as I tried to train through my leg's stiffness and soreness. I couldn't straighten my leg or put my body weight on it. But I wasn't going to drop out of my fight. I didn't tell anyone at Zuffa. I didn't tell a soul. News like this spreads like wildfire.

Instead, I went to another doctor when I got back to Las Vegas, who gave me a high-powered anti-inflammatory to get the swelling down. Three days before the fight, the medicine started to kick in. The tenderness subsided, and I got almost all my range of motion back.

The day before the fight I attended the weigh-ins as though everything was normal. Before stepping on the scale, I went through the usual final physical with the doctors, but they normally only check your face to make sure that your nose isn't broken and your hands to make sure they are intact. I think my blood pressure was a little high from the antibiotics I was taking, but it was certainly within the acceptable range, so I wasn't flagged. I wasn't limping, so no one noticed.

I weighed in at 206 pounds, technically one pound over the limit. In Nevada, however, they give a one-pound allowance in all bouts except title fights. I was officially cleared and ready to compete the next night. Van Arsdale weighed in at 205 pounds on the dot.

Amazingly, after eight years, I'd never fought in a three-round non-title bout in the Octagon. When I had started fighting in 1997, rounds hadn't been implemented into the sport yet, so we fought in long twenty-one-minute spells. When I returned to the UFC to face Kevin Randleman for the heavyweight championship, title bouts had been allotted to five rounds. And all seven of my UFC fights that followed had been in pursuit of or defending a title.

Like all of my opponents, I weighed Van Arsdale's strengths and weaknesses. He was only an inch taller than me, but had a lankier frame and long limbs, so I expected him to keep his distance and use his jab and reach to draw me in and try to find a way to take me down. Because he was a wrestler, I knew he'd go that extra mile. I mentally prepared myself for a longer, drawn-out fight. I would have to make him work real hard, and give him a reason to quit.

For my corner, I used Brad Anderson; Ron Frazier, the local boxing coach I had met at the J-Sect Academy; Mike Pyle, and Team Quest's Robert Follis, who flew in a couple of days before the fight. Robert had been my head corner guy for some time now, so I wanted him there, even though I hadn't trained with him in Oregon. Robert and I had our differences, but we buckled down together that night to get our jobs done.

I didn't expect an easy fight and I didn't get one. Freeze frames of the fight captured a wrestling match. You would have thought we were back out on the mats again in college somewhere in the Midwest, if not for the chain-link cage surrounding us. With our bodies hunched over, we touched heads like two rams butting horns as we tugged at each other's necks to keep close and compact. We got into some technical scrambles I think only two wrestlers could get into. In the first round, we took each other's back multiple times as we tried to establish control on the mat. Van Arsdale landed a beautiful hip toss I didn't see coming and my body flopped to the mat like a limp fish on a piece of newspaper. It was the only time I had been taken down like that in a fight, and I had to create space quickly to get out from underneath him.

In practise, I had been perfecting a submission called the gator roll, where you wrap your arms around your opponent's neck and trapped arm, then rotate your body much like an alligator spins through the water. What made this submission so unique for this fight was that you could apply it from the north-south position, where both fighters would be on their knees with their heads facing each other. Because both Van Arsdale and I were wrestlers, I knew we'd end up in this front headlock position often.

I tried to latch on the choke in the first round, but Van Arsdale was too fresh, so I kneed his shoulders to soften him up. This was something that hadn't been done in many fights before because it's illegal to knee a grounded opponent in the head. I didn't want to waste letting go of the position, though, and trusted my aim, though it didn't help my sore knee any.

By the top of the third round, Van Arsdale and I were spent. We'd kept up a noble pace, and I'd managed to cut him somewhere in the second round, I think, with an elbow on the ground. Before the final bell to begin the round, I saw Van Arsdale bent over across from me, his hands on his knees, gasping for breath. I had my hands on my knees as well, but I jumped up to attention and bounced around, throwing him a little smile. A look came over his face that said, *Oh, crap*, and I knew he was close to breaking. I was almost there.

We traded a handful of punches, and I shot right away, dumping Van Arsdale against the fence. I moved back to that front headlock position and applied the gator roll. I tried to flip to my back but I had no room against the cage, so I turned to the other side and cradled my body, squeezing my left hand on my right bicep to crank Van Arsdale's neck. He tapped out at fifty-two seconds into the round. The last time I'd tapped anyone out in the Octagon had been in my first fight against Tony Halme in 1997.

My obvious exhaustion caused a lot of people to doubt me. Fans said I looked slower and that retirement might be my best bet. To this day, not many people know I had a staph infection. My blood cells had been fighting the infection and couldn't efficiently carry oxygen to the rest of my body.

By now, my relationship with Team Quest had soured, and Robert Follis was the last guy I asked to work my corner from that group. I was the one that had initially brought Robert into Team Quest. I'd convinced Matt and Danny to make him a partner. He had worked hard to help build the team and brand, but he started complaining that he wasn't getting his due. He took on the air of a world-class trainer, and asked me why I never thanked him in my speeches. I had never intentionally not shown gratitude, but when he began to demand it, our dynamic changed. I started to feel like he didn't have my best interests at heart.

Robert and his wife Willow had also jumped on Trish's bandwagon throughout the divorce. I believe they were the ones who told Trish that Kim was a hooker. Then I heard they'd said, "I can't believe Randy doesn't want to stay here and raise his kid." I'd given them a shadow of a doubt, but now they were attacking my ability to be a father. I was paying Trish over $12,000 a month in child support and seeing my son every chance I got.

I finally confronted Robert at a sushi restaurant down the street from the gym. Matt was there as well.

"You know what? When you and your fucking wife get a divorce, your wife is the last person I am going to run and talk to and side with," I told Robert. "You and I are the ones that had the relationship and were supposed to be friends here."

At the same time, Robert voiced his objections to Danny opening a

Team Quest gym down in Southern California. Because Danny had lost part of his stake in the brand a couple of years before, Robert didn't think Danny had a right to use the name. Danny, Matt, and I were the original founders of Team Quest, so I wasn't pleased to hear Robert talk this way. Danny did eventually open his Team Quest gym, and it hit the ground running, becoming a notable training facility in a matter of months.

The next year, I ended up giving my shares of Team Quest to Matt and Robert. I wasn't interested in any compensation. It would cause too many complications. I just walked away. I no longer wished to be a part of the gym, though I offered to help any of its fighters. In future months, I assisted Chris Leben and Ed Herman with medicals and other details when they had fights in Las Vegas. Once you sweat and bleed together, that tie never goes away.

Meanwhile, UFC light heavyweight champion Chuck Liddell successfully defended his title against submission specialist Jeremy Horn. Our two victories allowed Zuffa to start hyping the rubber match between us, which would take place in four months on February 4, 2006, at *UFC 57: Liddell vs. Couture 3* from the Mandalay Bay Events Centre in Las Vegas.

THAT SUMMER, DOUG Crosby brought me to the East Coast to work as a stuntman on the film *Invincible*, starring Mark Wahlberg. The movie was based on the true story of Vince Papale, an unlikely rookie who got drafted to the Philadelphia Eagles through an open call. A bunch of us shot an outdoor football game in Vince's neighbourhood in the pouring rain. In the scene, Vince and his friends don't stop playing when things get muddy and grimy—they love the game so much. It was right up my alley. I can't tell you what an enjoyable time I had mixing it up on the set. I probably would have done it for free.

I also finally got the opportunity to do something I had wanted to for quite some time—give back to the military. Earlier that year, when Kim and I had attended John Bardis' medical convention, I had been very moved by a veteran recently returned from Iraq, who had lost his legs in battle. He was one of the motivational speakers at the convention and told us how he had gotten wounded. He and his spotter had been ambushed in their perch, and he was knocked unconscious. His spotter was killed instantly. He came to just as five enemy soldiers came towards him to steal his gear, and he rolled over and shot them all. He had undergone nearly twenty surgeries to correct internal injuries. He told us his whole goal had been to get enough of his rehab completed so he'd he strong enough to stand there with his prosthetic and speak at the podium. He wanted to be able to stand there and speak to us. I don't think there was a dry eye in the place when he was finished.

Don Frye had talked to me about putting together a USO tour to visit with the troops in the Middle East and offer our support. The UFC was all for it but couldn't make any headway with the USO, so the idea had temporarily fizzled. USO tours are very intricate and sometimes difficult to schedule because they require so much preparation, manpower, and coordination once the guests touch the ground overseas.

I was afraid that I might not be able to help the troops the way I wanted to when Mike Davis, a friend of mine who owned a motorcycle company called Suicide Jack Choppers, invited me to a barbeque he sponsored at a few of the stateside veteran's hospitals around Washington, D.C. My eyes lit up when he told me we could visit the soldiers in the hospitals there. I called Don Frye and Ken Shamrock— who had fought since *UFC 1*—who were now considered legends and we formed our own USO tour.

We walked the hallways of the Bethesda Naval Hospital and Walter Reed Army Medical Centre that November. I knew we were about to enter a place not readily open to the public when they handed us gowns, gloves, and masks. Cameras and video cameras were not allowed. I distinctly remember that unique, sanitised smell only a hospital can have.

Hospitals can be a disheartening place, and I knew what I saw would be sobering. Many of the soldiers we talked to had been injured by small bombs called IEDs (improvised explosive devices) which had been detonated by the enemy via cell phone from a distance. Some of the soldiers had lost their arm or a leg or had a hole blown in their torso. They were stitched and bandaged all over their bodies. Some sat up in their beds. Some were lying down. My eyes darted to the voids where limbs once were, and I half expected a leg or arm to pop out from the covers because I couldn't wrap my mind around it being gone.

It was impossible to visit every solider—Walter Reed has around 5,500 rooms alone—but I spoke with as many of these heroes as I could. I'll never forget how the vast majority of them were upbeat and wouldn't allow me to get down or feel sorry for them. They talked about their injuries matter-of-factly and all felt fortunate to be alive because some of their buddies didn't make it. I couldn't believe how calm and positive they all were.

The next day, we visited the USO mailing centre. Because of the state of security, you could no longer send packages to APO, or Army Post Office, addresses. They would have to go through the USO, so we visited the huge facility where they put together care packages and sent them to the troops. We spent the better part of the day in the assembly line, stuffing parcels for the soldiers. The UFC was kind enough to sponsor the event, and donated 500 DVDs and 300 baseball caps.

While I was there, I also participated in a meet-and-greet with the soldiers and their families stationed at Fort Belvoir, Virginia. The experience made me grateful for what I had. I'd been paid $150,000 for my second fight with Chuck Liddell, and $225,000 for my fight with Mike Van Arsdale, which included my win bonus. I wasn't short on seminar or sponsorship opportunities. Supporting the troops meant something to me, and I felt like I could do more. I told the UFC that I would be ready and able to go to Iraq or anywhere else in the Middle

East if a tour could ever be organised.

Like my childhood friend Donny, who had been forced to spend his life in a wheelchair, my trip to visit the veterans gave me the perspective and courage to make one of the most difficult decisions of my life. After handling my divorce from Trish and the subsequent end of a few of my close relationships with teammates and friends, I was certainly at a down point in my life. I didn't know if I had it in me to fight anymore. I'd thought about retirement since the final bell of the Van Arsdale fight. I knew I would be fighting Liddell next, but where would I go from there? I'd been a champion five times over. I had surpassed everyone's expectations by fighting competitively until the age of forty-two. I had tried to steer my career with dignity and pride, to be an example for others. I had achieved what I wanted to in this sport.

It honestly wasn't about the fighting. I still loved it and felt I was constantly learning and improving. My divorce was a very real battle though, and I had to fight to see my son Caden. I figured it was time to let MMA go so I could step out of that battleground and concentrate on my family.

In mid-November, I re-signed a three-fight contract with the UFC. Zuffa had been very understanding of my personal issues and had allowed me to fight Van Arsdale before re-signing again, which was not customary for them. A fighter on the last fight of his contract was always re-signed before he completed it.

The new contract was a formality. I told Dana White and Lorenzo Fertitta I would most likely be walking away after this next bout in February. Dana didn't believe me, but Lorenzo said it would be my decision to make, and they would understand whichever way I went with it.

I HAD BEEN allotted visitation rights with Caden every other weekend, so I made my way up to Oregon to see my son around Christmas. I had stopped bringing Kim with me because Trish would complain to the court, and the strain had become too much. I picked up Caden and brought him to see his grandpa Ed. I'd finally spoken with my mom and had gotten her to at least admit she'd been involved with Wally Johnson. She still adamantly denied he was my father.

Ed had hinted to my sister Yolanda earlier that summer that my mom had already been pregnant when he returned from the service. Sitting with him in the living room during Christmas, with Caden playing at our feet, we talked about him not being around during my childhood for the first time. But when it came to my mom and Wally, he wouldn't tell me anything. I got the impression that he was trying to protect my relationship with my mom, which seemed odd to me because he and my mother didn't get along. My mom hadn't gone out of her way to be mean to him, but she certainly hadn't wanted anything to do with him over the years.

My suspicions that I might not be his son certainly grew from that meeting, and I went back and forth with my feelings about it. I scrutinised the fact that I don't really look like either of my parents. My sister Yolanda looks like Ed, while Traci is clearly Marco's daughter. That left me.

At forty-two years old, I might not be who I thought I was.

14 CHAPTER FOURTEEN:
GOING OUT
ON TOP

I BELIEVE SOME THINGS DO GET BETTER WITH AGE. I know that's not the way it's supposed to go in sports. Athletes' reflexes dull, and it becomes blatantly obvious to everyone if they hang around past when they should.

In August 2005, I was determined not to become one of those guys that everyone pities. I didn't want to be that poor schlep that stuck around to get banged up a few times too many without realising it, so I decided that my third fight against Chuck Liddell would be my last.

The win over Mike Van Arsdale jetted me back up the UFC rankings, and I thought, *what better way to go out on top than to win the title back from Liddell and retire it right there in the Octagon?* That was the plan a few months out from the fight, and I can count on one hand how many people I told that secret to.

I didn't feel like my life could support fighting any longer. I had plenty of struggles to contend with outside the cage. I was in the midst of a divorce and battling for custody of my son, all during an unexpected burst of celebrity. With that came new privileges, expectations, and limitations, all rolled into one.

Moving to Las Vegas took some getting used to. Coming from the Northwest and its do-it-yourself attitude, I never hired others to do what I could do myself. In Vegas, somebody details your car. You hire people to do your yard work or clean your house once a week. It was a whole different mentality.

I will say my taste in clothing went through an upgrade. When Team Quest had cornered me for the second Liddell fight, they'd repeatedly teased me about these white-and-red velour pants a sponsor had given to me. They really weren't my style, but the guy had given them to me, so I wore them. The boys said I'd "gone Vegas." When I moved to Las Vegas permanently and was asked to appear on a few red carpets for *The Ultimate Fighter*, people assumed my style change went with my "midlife crisis," although Kim never went shopping for me. The truth is, the UFC bought a few of those earlier outfits for me to wear. I liked becoming more fashion-savvy (who wouldn't?).

I was invited back for the second season of *The Ultimate Fighter* as a consultant to develop the team challenges, then host them on-air, which kept me visible. The challenges I conceived came from my wrestling years. One of the more memorable moments of that season involved a challenge called "Scarecrow," where a welterweight fighter had to crawl around a heavyweight as many times as he could without touching the ground. Joe Stevenson, a little machine of a fighter, crawled around his partner 204 times in two hours.

Preparing for my final bout against Liddell brought stability back to my life. I had begun to train with Mike Pyle, Jay Hieron, and a group of young, twenty-something fighters that had migrated to Las Vegas from all over the country. A few of us had met at John Lewis' J-Sect Academy and then at the UFC Training Centre, but with the second season of *The Ultimate Fighter* underway there, we moved to the Xyience Training Centre, a fifteen-minute drive from the neon jungle of Las Vegas Boulevard.

Inside a strip mall, Xyience was a small gym with only a couple thousand square feet of wall-to-wall mat space and three lonely punching bags hanging in the corner. There wasn't a ring or cage, or treadmills or bikes to get your cardio work in. It seemed like a typical run-of-the-mill jiu-jitsu dojo.

When you pulled up to the gym, the front glass windows would be frosted over with steam. Opening the door, a draft of heat would slap you in the face and the sharp odour of sweat would hit your nose like a one-two combo.

It reminded me of the Sacramento training sessions. The wealth of talent that tiny gym held on some nights gave me goose bumps. On any given night, there could be a dozen "name" fighters bumping up against each other as they sparred and rolled within inches of one another. PRIDE middleweight Phil Baroni would be touching gloves with *The Ultimate Fighter* light heavyweight winner Forrest Griffin on one side of the room, while WEC welterweight champion Mike Pyle rolled with WEC featherweight champion Urijah Faber at the other end. Fighters meandered in and out of town for fights or appearances and would stop by for a few nights here and there. You never knew who would show up.

The gym became a Petri dish for sharing and exchanging techniques, and I felt very comfortable there. The fighters had exemplary attitudes, were hungry to learn, and all brought something unique to the table. Aside from his strength in submissions and striking, the gym's jester Mike Pyle kept the training light and fun and made it interesting again. I had trouble keeping a straight face around him. Forrest Griffin was the same way—he even looked like Alfred E. Newman—but he was one of hardest workers I have ever had the pleasure of being around. Forrest would be the last man out on the mats, and we had to turn out the lights to get him to leave. Jay Hieron embodied the seriousness we all felt about the sport. With only a duffle bag, he'd moved to Las Vegas with no guarantees.

We all wanted to be the most complete fighters we could be, and for two or three hours each night, we would all give everything we had to help each other get there. I found myself opening up more to this plucky new band of fighters. They were there specifically to work out with me, and I was there to work out with them. I fed off the youthful energy that pulsated through the gym. The fighters were honest and open, and we began to instinctually take care of one another. That's what you look for in teammates.

A new team of cornermen formed naturally from this group throughout the ten-week training cycle leading up to the fight, so deciding not to use Team Quest seemed like the right choice.

With a new safety net widening around me, I relaxed into a training routine. I liked to get up early in the mornings and run on the treadmill at the 24 Hour Fitness in our neighbourhood. In the weeks closer to the fight, a lot of the patrons there wished me good luck and urged me on. I usually hit the Xyience gym afterwards and then again at night for a second session. In my final weeks, I invited Andrei Arlovski, the Belarusian heavyweight I'd nearly fought at *UFC 42* in 2003, to join the team in my final preparations.

"Randy, keep your hands up. Keep moving," Andrei instructed me in his thick European accent. Andrei kept a watchful eye over me. He'd had his own share of stand-up battles in the Octagon and trained consistently in boxing at a well-regarded gym in Chicago. He exhibited fluidity in his striking rare for a man his size, so I valued his observations.

One night Andrei and I sparred, and our concentration on one another was so intense that the entire gym stopped to watch us. Andrei slapped me around a few times with the focus mitts, hitting me hard enough that I slipped on the sweat and went down. It was good, because Andrei pushed me to cover up more.

Andrei was incredibly shy around the other fighters and so sweet natured. I had to beg him to take the stipend money the UFC had given me for my cornermen to provide for their meals. He didn't want a dime for the experience.

Andrei, Brad Anderson, Mike Pyle, and Ron Frazier, a UNLV boxing coach who had followed us over from the J-Sect Academy, became my main cornermen. I felt secure going into the fray with them, though I didn't tell them that I would retire after this bout. I didn't want to put any extra pressure on them or make them feel they had to do anything different than they would have in any other fight. I didn't want my retirement to take on a life of its own. I knew the press would zoom in on it, and I didn't want the fight to be about the end of my career. I was focused on winning, just like any other fight. I believed I was prepared and could easily win.

The last night of practise at Xyience, the entire team of fighters gathered and sat in a circle on the mat to give me their final best wishes. I was touched.

I TRIED TO take in my final week as a fighter as much as I could and enjoy it. The host hotel is always bustling the week of a fight, and each day, there are a few more fans lingering in the lobby or the elevator bank with a Sharpie marker and a programme or T-shirt in hand to approach whichever fighter comes through. I signed as many things as I could.

UFC events now happen at the grandest scale in the United States, so they serve as a meeting ground for many in the industry, and are sometimes a reunion for people you haven't seen in a good while. Fighters who aren't on the card come to support teammates that are competing, and their entourages, managers, agents, friends, and family follow. As the excitement builds, everyone is along for the ride.

On Tuesday and Wednesday, Zuffa would film my pre-fight interviews for the show's opening montage, which are usually conducted by UFC matchmaker Joe Silva. I'd usually fill out any last-minute paperwork and sign an endless stack of event posters in the makeshift offices down in the underbelly of the hotel, right next to the arena.

By Thursday, the press arrives for a conference, usually held around noon, where UFC president Dana White leads the group through a question-and-answer period. This is where you get to see your opponent for the first time, and some fighters get riled up about it. With Liddell sitting on the other side of the podium just ten feet away from me, I didn't feel much of anything. Both Liddell and I had a reserved attitude before our fights, and Zuffa had given up trying to stimulate any extra hype out of us.

The week of the event has always been a waiting game for me, and the boredom and anxiousness intensifies as each day rolls by. Giving interviews with the press helped me quell the build-up and gave me something to focus on to pass the time. Many fighters refuse to do interviews the week of an event, but I thrived on them.

The morning of the weigh-ins, I did my last pre-fight interview with Maxim Radio, then headed down to the arena and jumped on the scales to see where I was at. I'd predicted I'd be 212 pounds. I was a pound and a half under that.

Many fighters dread weigh-in day, depending on how much they have to cut. Some have to pare down their eating a couple of days out and carry around bags of raw spinach leaves to snack on. Some don't eat a sliver of food or drink an ounce of water twenty-four to forty-eight hours out from the fight. Depending on the fighter's knowledge of how to cut weight or circumstances like taking fights last minute, I've heard of guys cutting up to thirty pounds the week of the fight. It can be a miserable, draining process.

I have been one of the luckier ones. I've cut weight for over half my life and my body responds well to a process I've fine-tuned over the years. I gradually trim down in the weeks leading up to the fight so I only shed a few pounds of water weight the day of. I was so on track that morning, I even had oatmeal and orange juice for breakfast.

With only five and a half pounds to go, I headed to the Mandalay Bay's spa with Brad and jumped on the treadmill, wearing long underwear, a plastic suit, and sweats over that. I have a formula where I can lose one pound every ten minutes, walking at a normal pace. I can also tell how my weight cut is going by watching the sweat stains rise up my sleeves. After fifty minutes on the treadmill, I weighed in at 203 pounds in the spa's locker room before showering and changing, then headed off to the weigh-ins, laughing and joking with

Brad and Ron on the way.

I could have been walking in on fight night. A couple of thousand people had turned up for the weigh-ins. The scales were on a stage front and centre underneath a large screen, and a black curtain behind it blocked off the majority of the arena, where the Octagon was already set up and fighters were congregating. Fans hung off the sides of the risers, and I signed as many items as I could before heading back there.

Behind the curtain, I picked up my gloves from referee John McCarthy and had one more on-site physical with the medical staff. Then I went back out onto the floor and sat with Kim and the team and waited to be called.

When my name was called, we all headed backstage and lined up. Andrei Arlovski walked me onto the platform, and the noise from the crowd grew. I felt very welcomed as I stepped onto the scales and weighed in at 203 pounds, then flexed my arms in a pose. Liddell weighed in at 204 pounds, and we stepped to the scale's left side and had our third and final staredown. Chuck Liddell and I exchanged genuine smiles.

I went back to my seat and quickly wolfed down five miniature cans of orange juice to replenish. Dana excused me from attending the fighter's meeting held backstage, and I snuck out the same side door and got back upstairs to my hotel suite. Between my family and friends, there were seventeen people in the room and everyone was buzzing. They slowly filtered out and a nurse hooked me up to an IV. I lay on the bed and let it do its job.

That night, I took my family, cornermen, and a few other teammates out to dinner at a great Italian restaurant that Kim and I like called Bootleggers. Mike Pyle and Jay Hieron battled it out for the spotlight and had us all in stitches making fun of each other.

In a room full of people that loved and supported me, it could have been easy to sit there and reflect on the great moments of my career, but I couldn't afford to dwell on how I felt about retiring before the fight. It's the same reason I barely told anybody about it. I didn't want to think or talk about it. I wouldn't allow myself to get caught up in it, so I compartmentalised those feelings to deal with them afterwards. I focused on what I needed to at the time, which was the technique and strategy necessary to go into battle.

My father Ed had come down to watch the fights, but again, my mom would not be attending, which did make me sad. I had gone to visit her in December and tried to make amends and get back on some sort of speaking terms with her. It had actually gone fairly well. I invited her to the fights and told her I had tickets for her and my stepdad, Marco. She didn't acknowledge the invitation, so I assumed that she wasn't going to come. I didn't ask her about it again. About two weeks before the fight, she asked me over the phone if I still had the two tickets.

"Yeah, Mom, I still have the tickets, but it's Super Bowl weekend," I said, a bit irritated. "The chances of you getting a hotel or even an airline ticket into Vegas this late is going to be very, very slim."

Then, the conversation turned.

"Oh, could you also tell your girlfriend to stay out of the cage?" she asked. "It makes me very uncomfortable."

"Well, if it's that big of a deal for you, why don't you just stay home?" I said. "I don't need that shit."

I didn't talk to my mom again before the fight. I hadn't told her it was my final fight, though I had told my sister Yolanda. Still, I knew it was hard for her and Marco to get up and leave Washington. They owned a bar and grill, and Marco didn't like to fly. With my life falling back into line, I was getting a handle on minimising the negative things, to make them small so they really didn't affect me.

Kim and I sat around the hotel room all day Saturday, watching TV and talking with her younger brother J.W., who was a professional rodeo roper.

Around 4:00 p.m., the team began to arrive, and the women gathered around the mirror in the bathroom, putting on their finishing touches. A vase of colourful orchids three feet high arrived, and I raced down the hallway barefoot to give the delivery guy a tip. It was from a group of club owners Kim and I knew. The card read, "Kick some arse."

Soon it was time to leave and make our way to the arena. A security guard arrived, along with some UFC cameras, and we were escorted through a service elevator that took us down into the hallway which funnelled off into the dressing rooms, adjacent to the arena. There must have been twenty of us in the group.

The commission and the UFC only approves your cornermen and a select few others to stay in the dressing rooms leading up to the bout, so I said good-bye to a large chunk of my entourage and settled in for the next five hours. There were a couple of couches lining a mat in the centre of the room and a monitor showing the fights so we could watch along. I set up my folding chair in view of the screen and plopped down.

The mood of my dressing room before the fight was crucial. I did get nervous before fights, though I like to refer to it as excitement. I liked to sit around and watch the preliminary fights with my teammates. That night, we sat around debating and critiquing the fights as if we were gathered around the TV in my living room and slamming back a few six-packs. Mike Pyle had a snappy comment for just about everything. He is one of the funniest people I've ever met, and a blessing to have in your corner because he keeps the night rolling with levity but makes sure you are warmed up and ready to go out there.

We shared the locker room with Branden Lee Hinkle, a heavyweight fighting Jeff Monson, another wrestler with a knack for submissions, in one of the undercard match-ups. Hinkle was getting cornered by Mark Coleman, the former UFC champion who I'd wrestled at the Olympic Festival back in 1989, but never met in the Octagon. We watched Hinkle and his team leave the locker room, then appear on the TV screen a few minutes later marching to the cage.

As expected, the fight spilled onto the canvas quickly, and Hinkle found himself in trouble, caught in a north-south choke, similar to the one I'd caught Van Arsdale with, at the end of the round. Hinkle lost consciousness and went limp from the hold, but came to almost immediately. A few minutes later he was back in the locker room, angry at himself and probably a bit embarrassed. I've been in locker rooms pre-fight where guys win and lose. You pause for a moment to respect your peer, but then you have to move on and concentrate on the fight at hand. You can't let it bring you down.

Finished for the night, Hinkle and his crew packed up their gear and got ready to leave. Coleman ripped a *UFC 57* poster off the wall and asked me to sign it, which I did gladly.

A few fights into the card, "Stitch" Duran, one of the cut men assigned by the UFC to work the evening, came in to wrap my hands.

"Let's get you suited up," he said, sitting down next to me. "You want the knockout wrap or the tapout wrap?"

"The knockout wrap," I answered quietly, with a wink.

The UFC cameras entered again, and I did one last interview. I told the interviewer I had nothing left to prove, though I don't think he caught my foreshadowing.

I got up and started to warm up. I like to break a good sweat, so I grappled with Mike, pummelled with Brad, then hit the pads with Ron as everyone looked on and blurted out words of encouragement. At one point, the TV camera in our locker room went live to the big screens and the fans in the arena could see me bouncing around. Mike told me to slow down, as this same feed was going to Liddell's locker room, and we didn't want to give away any of the combinations I had drilled.

Around 8:30 p.m., Dana came bursting into the locker room like a bunny hopped up on Easter candy.

"This is the deal," he said excitedly. "We've run out of fights. We're going to play the Monson-Hinkle fight, then go into the hype for you and Chuck. You have twenty minutes."

The room went silent and everyone grew more focused. I had changed into my shorts and shadowboxed around the cobalt-blue mat spattered with sweat drops. We huddled for a moving group prayer and held hands. I closed my eyes and gave praise to God for all that he had done for me in my life.

Burt, the event coordinator, came in and told us it was time to go. We lined up in the hallway, me in front, with my team stationed behind me in formation, all of us wearing the same black T-shirt plastered with my sponsors' names and gold stars. Sounds from the arena funnelled down the corridor to our ears, and I recognised the music that I'd selected: AC/DC's "Thunderstruck."

The cymbal began its tap, joined by the guitar's rambling riff, then the drums chimed in, followed by the voices that cried "Thunder!" in unison. Burt gave us the cue to start walking.

"Thunder!"

We inched up the hallway at a slow, methodical pace.

"Thunder!"

We made our way around a corner, and they stopped us again. I looked down and began to play with my fingernails. The high-pitched, screeching voice of Brian Johnson joined in.

"I knew there was no turning back," he sang. He was right.

We started the walk again and came to the black curtain separating me from 12,000 fans. The staff backstage gathered around us to wish me luck.

"You've been thunderstruck!" Johnson proclaimed, and the curtains parted at just the right second, when the lead guitar hit a chord that echoed throughout the arena. We were off, and the crowd was on fire. It was one of the most uplifting moments in my life.

I REMEMBER MAKING eye contact with Lorenzo Fertitta right before the bell rang, but I can't say why I zoned in on him. I always pick somebody across the cage from me to focus on, rather than my opponent's entrance, the crowd, and the huge noise going on around me. When I do this, everybody else goes away. One time NBA basketball star Shaquille O'Neal stood out, so I made eye contact and winked at him, which freaked him out. This time, I picked Lorenzo and gave him a confident nod.

The fight got off to a fast pace, with Liddell and me trading shots here and there, but we spent most of the time cautious of each other and kept circling. He didn't want me close enough to take him down, and I didn't want to get into enough range for him to blast me. I finally caught up to him two third's into the round right after he connected with a punch that broke my nose. It was the first of only two takedowns of the fight—a beautiful high crotch that sent us both airborne before he crashed against the cage. True to form, he popped back to his feet just as fast, but I bear-hugged him. Blood began to pour out of my nose and down his back. He grabbed the fence for balance and prevented another takedown, but I corralled him to his backside for the round's last few seconds.

I went back to my corner, thinking it was going the way I wanted it to. I was being patient. I felt like I could see most of his punches coming, and I was slipping them, while keeping him fairly ineffective. If I was a judge, I would have given myself the first round.

The second round began much like the first, with both of us doing a calculated dance. I didn't remember slipping, but watching the tape a few days later, I observed my body duck to move in with a left-right and my back leg dragged slightly. That's all that was needed to knock my timing off. At the end of my punch, my chin met Liddell's counter right hand, and my body dropped.

I never felt like I had been knocked out. I was certainly knocked down, but I still felt like I was there. I thought it looked like I was using my legs and arms to fend him off, but I guess referee John McCarthy saw it differently. The stoppage came a minute and twenty-eight seconds into the second round.

My cornermen and Kim rushed into the cage to help me up, and the cut men went to work on my nose, which was steadily trickling blood. While Liddell addressed the crowd with commentator Joe Rogan, my corner unwrapped my hands to kill the time. When you win, you usually don't shed your gloves until you get back into the dressing room, but the UFC had asked me to stick around to make a few comments. I had the black gloves in my hands, and the words just came to me.

"This is the last time you're going see these gloves and these shorts in this Octagon," I told Rogan and the audience, as a fresh trail of blood dripped onto my lip. "That's it. I'm ready to do something else."

I don't think I showed that much emotion in the cage, though people told me it sounded like the arena let out a collective gasp. I had made the decision a long time before that moment, so I was ready to share it with the world. I was emotional that I'd lost again, because I really wanted to go out on top and felt I hadn't.

It took me thirty minutes to get out of the arena. The crowd seemed to close in around me. The response was simply overwhelming. There must have been fifty people in my locker room when I finally made it back there. There were cameras and press, and many of my teammates from the Las Vegas gym, including Rashad Evans and Joe Stevenson, wrestlers who I'd helped coach a bit on *The Ultimate Fighter 2*. They'd all followed me backstage and stood around waiting for me, which showed a deep respect. The room was quiet and sober as I sat on a bench with Ron and did a few interviews.

Kim stood off to the side with tears in her eyes. I was teary-eyed as well. I think it was dawning on me that this would be my last time as a fighter. I'd kept my feelings about the retirement buried inside me, but I was ready to acknowledge them now. My nose wouldn't stop bleeding, so I kept dabbing it with a washcloth. My nose is still crooked today.

I saw Nate Quarry enter from across the room. Seeing him after a few months away from Oregon brought more emotion to the surface, and I got up and walked over to give him a hug. Nate was one of my best workout partners at Team Quest, and I'd brought him along in his career. He was there when I met Kim, and I'd confided in him during the divorce until everything with Team Quest went south. In that moment, though, I don't think any of that stuff mattered. I was glad to see him. Seeing my new and old teammates go out of their way to be with me in this moment made me even more sentimental.

Lorenzo and Dana came in and asked to speak with me privately. We walked into the showers in back, and they gave me a huge bonus cheque for hundreds of thousands of dollars, the first I'd ever gotten with the promotion. They said it didn't matter what I did; they wanted me with them. I was shocked and surprised.

Once I was examined by a doctor and gave my urine sample, I was released to leave. We packed up our gear and left, walking down the long hallway back to the service elevator to take us back upstairs. Over an hour had passed since the fight, and I couldn't believe fans were still standing outside the glass doors at the end of the hallway. A line of security guards was holding them back, but one guy broke through and ran up to me to ask me for my autograph. It was like we were at a rock concert, and I was Mick Jagger. I signed his programme, and the security guards grabbed him just as fast and dragged him away.

I never expected the response I got that night. Almost all of the fighters I'd trained with in Vegas escorted me back up to my room, and we all went out to a club together to celebrate my retirement. Despite the loss, people told me I had gone out on top that night. I had a hard time believing it, but was willing to take their word for it.

15 CHAPTER FIFTEEN: SETTLING INTO LIFE

I DIDN'T DWELL ON MY SECOND LOSS TO LIDDELL. THE next day, I threw a Super Bowl party for my friends and family at Simon's Restaurant and sat back as they all bought me beers, one by one. My cell phone's voice-mail system reset itself twice after one hundred messages poured in. Everybody must have thought I needed a job, because the offers started piling in: the World Fighting Alliance, the International Fight League, and a few other alphabet soup promotions that never even came to fruition. I certainly didn't feel unwanted.

After competing in the 205-pound division for the last two and a half years and having to watch my intake, one of the first things I did following my retirement was go out for a steak and lobster dinner, and top it off with a decadent chocolate dessert. In the next few months, I didn't limit myself to one meal when I sat down to the table; I ate two, sometimes three entrees in one sitting.

How much can one person squeeze into a year of their lives? A lot, if you're up to it. I had a list of activities I had been itching to try once I stopped fighting, and one of the first was to enter an adventure race. I had almost had my chance when I'd been selected to compete in *The Eco-Challenge* four years before, but my eye injury prevented it. Like MMA, adventure racing is a sport that combines disciplines, like kayaking, mountain biking, and running, and has its own culture and following. Kim and I found an Adventure Xtream race in Moab, Utah, and gathered four teams of four entrants each to travel there together to compete.

A treacherous seven-hour drive through mountain ranges delivered us to the world-famous location for extreme sports. My team took off paddling in the Colorado River alongside twenty-seven other teams, then biked through the mountains, rappelled down a 275-foot cliff, ran 6 miles, and biked another 20. We finished in nine hours and nine minutes, and took fifteenth place.

In April, the Secret Service invited me to teach a seminar for their counter assault team (CAT), which was basically the President's personal SWAT team. I was surprised to learn many of these officers were fight fans, and I was told even President Bush had been known to a catch a snippet of a UFC match here and there. Kim and her son Oakley came with me and toured the White House.

Later that November, the UFC sent me to Monaco for a sports TV convention. I didn't think I'd be recognised. Instead, a member of Prince Albert's private bodyguard squad hunted me down and asked me to teach a seminar for his twenty men in a tiny basement gym with Velcro mats.

In the next year, I felt like I travelled to nearly every state in the nation, teaching seminars and making appearances, which made things tough between Kim and me. My divorce from Trish had finalised, and Kim and I were thinking about getting married.

At the same time, I had hopes of jump-starting my next career in an arena just as unpredictable as fighting. I had been curious about acting for years and had taken little extras roles in Jet Li's *Cradle to the Grave* and Steven Seagal's *Today You Die*. I'd even landed a lead role in an independent film called *No Rules* in the summer of 2004. I was ready to try more.

While Jeremy renovated and prepared our Legends Gym for a fall opening in Los Angeles, I sat in on a couple of different acting classes with instructors and found one that I liked, a lady named Iris Klein. Her mother is famous in acting circles, but I had not heard of her, which was not surprising. I did not even know who Academy Award-nominated writer David Mamet was when I met him.

Without risking my reputation as a badass, I have to say that I enjoyed her classes. They were a lot different from anything I had done before. It was a little "touchy-feely" to sit face-to-face with somebody or hold hands with a perfect stranger. It required a certain focus and intensity to be able to listen to pick up your cues. Wrestling also involves a lot of listening and waiting for your sign to implement moves, and I liked that parallel.

I walked into acting class not caring about where it led. I had no expectations. In that way, it was a lot like my early days of fighting, and I was very relaxed and willing to explore, learn, and have fun with it. I think I performed better because of this, and I got positive feedback from the teacher.

That summer, I rented a condo in Los Angeles to be near the gym and my acting classes. I got a role in Rob Schneider's prison comedy *Big Stan*, where I played an inmate and had a few small lines—my first speaking role in a major motion picture.

The UFC was able to host its first USO tour in July, and I was honoured to go. I travelled to the Middle East with middleweight champion Rich Franklin and UFC Octagon Girl Rachelle Leah. We descended into the Baghdad airport in a complete nosedive (or "combat approach") to evade enemy fire. I experienced the soldiers' living conditions firsthand, sleeping in living pods no bigger than a shipping container. The desert heat was cruel, regularly hovering at 130 degrees during the day. Getting to meet the troops made it all worthwhile, and they took us around in Black Hawk helicopters to play on the shooting ranges. If given the chance to return, I would jump at it.

Legends Gym opened that August. The UFC also offered me a position commentating a couple of fights on every UFC pay-per-view broadcast and utilised me for publicity appearances and interviews. In October, I was hired as a fight analyst and host for a couple of series on

The Fight Network, a twenty-four hour combat sports TV channel based out of Toronto. I enjoyed analysis and commentary, and people said I had a knack for it. Over the years, I had become so accustomed to breaking my opponents' strength and weaknesses down that I could make a fairly educated guess as to who would win in a fight. I didn't get them all right, but I picked some doozies that nobody saw coming. Most of all, I liked to offer the athlete's perspective.

I was still an athlete myself. I continued to train a few days a week because it didn't feel right not to. Old habits, I guess. That fall, I was invited to be a part of Spike TV's *Pros vs. Joes* programme, which pitted real-life star athletes against everyday athletes. I joined a panel that included major league baseball player Jose Canseco, San Antonio Spurs standout Kevin Willis, and Dallas Cowboys wide receiver Michael "the Playmaker" Irvin. It was the first time a fighter had been invited onto the show.

AFTER NINE MONTHS' rest, the fire in my belly was burning. When my old manager Rico Chiapparelli invited me to compete in his *Professional Submission League: X-Mission* grappling event at the Veteran's Memorial Auditorium in Culver City, California, I was hungry. I wrestled Ronaldo "Jacare" Souza, a decorated Brazilian jiu-jitsu black belt who had won all the prestigious international tournaments, including the Mundials, the World Cup, and the Abu Dhabi World Submission Wrestling Championships. Fending off a cold and a little depleted in my cardio, I was winded a few minutes into the match, which didn't allow strikes of any kind and went into two overtimes. At the end of ten minutes, the match was declared a draw. I didn't mind sharing the podium with Jacare. It just felt great to be back in there with my heart racing again.

Besides giving me my first taste of combat sports competition in nearly nine months, the PSL allowed me to cross paths with Matt

Walker, a sports agent and owner of Paragon Sports. He primarily represented baseball players, including David Dellucci of the Cleveland Indians. Since my manager Jeremy and I were headed in different directions, I'd decided not to renew my contract with him and began a relationship with Matt, who joined the prestigious Gersh Agency. He agreed to take me on as an actor, though I wasn't as established as their usual clientele.

By late 2006, the UFC had hosted four seasons of *The Ultimate Fighter*, and the sport showed no signs of stopping. Kim had encouraged me to start my own brand within the sport. I wasn't sure how successful it was going to be, but she helped organise and launch the Xtreme Couture name. I don't know where I got the name from. We called our adventure race squad Team Xtreme Couture, so I guess it had been knocking around in our heads for a while. With plans for separate clothing and supplement lines well underway, Kim and I decided to open our own gym in Las Vegas. Dana had actually approached me to run a chain of UFC Training Centres, but nothing came of our talk.

The notion of fighting again started to excite me. In October, the UFC had called me with a proposed match-up against top-ranked boxer James Toney, then for a potential bout with 1996 Olympic freestyle wrestling gold medallist Kurt Angle, but both fell through. I also turned down an offer to become president of the UFC's Europe division, because the move would have kept me from my son Caden. I didn't feel like I had slowed down any in the nine months out of circulation. Kim and my wrestling friends kept encouraging me. Chuck Liddell was still the light heavyweight champion, but I had gotten knocked out by him twice in a row, so I didn't think the fans wanted to see that fight again. But UFC heavyweight champion Tim Sylvia was another story. Sitting at lunch one day, I texted Dana on his cell phone: *What if I fought Tim?*

Dana never called me back faster than that.

"Are you serious, bro?" he cooed.

"Why not?" I answered back.

On November 18, in Sacramento, California, I commentated for Tim Sylvia's title defence against Jeff Monson with Joe Rogan and Mike Goldberg from cageside at *UFC 65*. I watched his performance and thought I was just as good, if not better. I was ready to come back. I just needed the green light. Right around Christmas, I got the call.

On January 11, I met with Lorenzo Fertitta to sign a new four-fight contract. I stipulated that I would take each fight one by one, and Fertitta agreed that I would have no obligation to complete the quartet of bouts. Hearing that many of the fighters were getting signing bonuses, I requested one as well. Lorenzo told me he couldn't offer me that, but that they planned to give me the same bonus that I'd gotten after my fight with Liddell, win or lose against Sylvia, so he would take half of that and give it to me upfront. That same night, on Spike TV, I announced I was coming back.

"I just feel like I've got more fighting in me to do," I told host Joe Rogan. "I miss being able to train. I miss being able to compete. Physically, I'm very healthy and felt there were still some things to do competition-wise while I still can."

Sylvia and I were scheduled to meet at *UFC 68: Uprising* on March 3 at the Nationwide Arena in Columbus, Ohio. It was smack dab in the middle of the Arnold Classics, a national sports health and fitness expo that drew 150,000 people over three days. We all knew this could be a record-breaking weekend—and sure enough, the Nationwide confirmed it had sold out the event in record time for the UFC.

Sylvia wasn't pleased that I'd agreed to fight him. He had helped me renovate my house back in 2003 while he was there to train at Team Quest. Sylvia and I got along great, and I did consider him a friend. He called me a short time after the fight was announced.

"I thought we were friends," he said.

"We are," I told him. "This is just a fight. It's nothing personal."

Sylvia was a member of former UFC champion Pat Miletich's team, and they made it a habit not to fight any of their own teammates.

That was their credo. Other wrestlers didn't seem to have the same mentality. We spent all our time throwing each other around. Why not fight one another if we were asked? I got off the phone and couldn't help but think that this would psychologically affect Sylvia.

I didn't have any time to spare in training for Sylvia. Sylvia topped the scales at 265 pounds on weigh-in day, and usually hovered around 280 pounds the night of the fight. He had at least 45 to 50 extra pounds over me. I had to find some giants to train with or I was in big trouble.

A couple of phone calls later, I had Mark Coleman's protégé, Wes Sims; Dan Christison; Dan Evensen; Frank Mir; and Seth Woodley—all at least six-foot-four and 280 pounds—towering over me.

A few days into training, I was beginning to think that coming out of retirement might have been a mistake. It took so much extra energy to take these bigger guys down, and I didn't know if I'd be conditioned enough to get Sylvia to the mat. The first two weeks of training were murder, but I began to adjust.

The press honed in on my problems with larger heavyweights in the past. I had to leave the heavyweight division once before because I couldn't cut it. I was older now and probably slower. What made me think I could cope with it now?

The answer was simple to me. I was smarter, I trained better, and physically I thought I was in a much better place. My worst-case scenario with Sylvia was getting caught with a jab or straight punch within his monstrous range, so I practised head movement and ducking under these human tree branches coming at me to get to the clinch. I put myself underneath these mammoth athletes and practised escaping, knowing I now had the skills—which I didn't have before—that would allow me to deal with it.

More than 5,000 people turned up for the weigh-ins in Columbus. I waited backstage with my team behind the curtain and listened to the crowd erupt each time a fighter appeared and stepped onto the scales. Then it was my turn, and the noise almost blew me over. I weighed in 222.5 pounds. Sylvia weighed in at 265 pounds exactly. The look on a lot of people's face there read I was in trouble. I was too old, too slow, and too rusty—sounded like a sure underdog to me. Naturally, I smiled.

I wasn't the only one feeling good that night. Dana came into the locker room with an ear-to-ear grin. The night had broke the North American attendance record for the sport with 19,049 spectators, and boy, were they ready to see some fights.

"Wait till Father Time comes out," Dana said. "This place is going to go fucking crazy."

The opening sequence surprised me as much as it did the audience: a low left inside kick to an overhand right I'd practised with my eyes lowered so I didn't expose my chin. I didn't even get a chance to land the final component—a left hook—as I watched Sylvia slip out of my eyesight and topple to the ground.

Where is he going? I thought.

It was only ten seconds into the five-round contest, and I was within a heartbeat of taking it all. My feet touching the canvas again, I lunged forward and began to bombard him with follow-up punches as he crouched beside the fence. He scrambled to his feet, and I wrapped my arms around him, lifting him off the ground with an overhead supplex in mind. I quickly thought better of it and shrugged Sylvia to my side like a sack of potatoes before taking his back.

The crowd was on its feet, and they stayed with me as I landed punch after punch, nailed takedown after takedown, and earned round after round on the judges' cards for the next twenty-five minutes. In the final ten seconds, I could hear the audience counting down as if it was New Year's Eve in Times Square. That is when I knew I had done it.

"Not bad for an old man," I said to the crowd. *Not bad at all.* I had a UFC belt placed around my waist again for the sixth time in my career. It felt like home.

★　★　★

I ONLY HELD onto the year's biggest upset for a month.

UFC 70: Nations Collide was set in Manchester, England, between a deadly Croatian striker named Mirko "Cro Cop" Filipovic and Gabriel Gonzaga, a Brazilian jiu-jitsu black belt. I was hoping Filipovic would pull it out because the UFC had already announced that the winner would earn a title shot. Gonzaga nearly decapitated Cro Cop with a right high kick of his own in the last few seconds of round one.

The buzz began for my Gonzaga showdown.

The Sylvia fight had sent my life into its highest gear yet. At the post-fight press conference for *UFC 68* in Ohio, former UFC champion Rich Franklin said he wouldn't remember this night as the first time he got to fight in front of his hometown crowd, but would fondly look back on it as the night he got to fight on the same card as me. I'll never forget that. I can think of no higher compliment from a peer.

For some reason—whether it was Sylvia's stature, his physical size, or my age—people went nuts over that fight. The morning after, I attended the Arnold Classic, the largest sports-and-fitness expo in the country, also held in Columbus. It took me five hours to get through most of the line of well-wishers who came for autographs, and I finally had to stop so I wouldn't miss my flight home. I was very grateful for the support.

In the next few months, I made TV appearances on CBS's *The Unit* and ABC's *Dancing with the Stars*, and I gave interviews for ESPN and others. In June, Quinton "Rampage" Jackson and I were nominated for an ESPY, after they changed the "Best Boxer" category to "Best Fighter." Unfortunately, Jackson and I were double KOed by super welterweight boxing champion "Pretty Boy" Floyd Mayweather.

I also travelled to New York for a press junket, where I met a slew of the big-time editors for *ESPN The Magazine* and *Sports Illustrated*. These were mainstream outlets that hadn't even glanced at our sport before. It was a very exhilarating time.

Later I got word that *Sports Illustrated* had selected me for the cover of their first-ever feature on MMA. I was honoured. But a week before the cover was scheduled to come out, I heard they were going with the much younger Roger Huerta. Apparently Dana had herded the *Sports Illustrated* staff away from selecting me. I had nothing against Huerta, but the situation was hurtful and disappointing.

It wasn't the first time I questioned Dana's true intentions with me. A few months earlier, one of the producers of Spike TV's *Pros vs. Joes* had told me that Dana had thrown a fit because they had asked me to compete on the show without his knowledge. Dana told them he wasn't sure that I was the one he wanted representing the UFC on the show.

It added insult to injury when Dana, Lorenzo, and others from the Zuffa staff didn't attend a charity event I hosted over Memorial Day to raise money for the wounded stateside soldiers and their families through our Xtreme Couture GI Foundation. There had been an industry wedding that day, but a number of other guests made both events. Putting up a banner for the fund-raiser on the UFC website was also apparently a big hassle for them. If my staff or agent called for a request, they got no response. So I would be forced to call myself.

My discontent with Dana and Zuffa was mounting, but I tried to stay focused on the task at hand—preparing for my twenty-fourth fight against Gonzaga—while I juggled my personal life.

That summer, I asked Lori to send me a picture of Wally Johnson. It was an old photograph: Wally wore a white T-shirt and jeans, standing in front of a brown vinyl couch. The photo was a bit dark, but I showed it to a couple of people and could see the look of possibility wash over their faces. I looked at the picture many times myself and had my own reservations.

I'd decided to ask my father Ed to take a paternity test when he came to Las Vegas for the fight. I felt I was ready to know the truth, whatever it was. He had been willing to do it for me, but I had a difficult time finding a lab that did that type of test. But with so much going on leading up to the fight, I never got around to asking him. The more I thought about it, the more I thought that I should just let it go. I felt in the grand scheme of things, it didn't really matter. Ed was the only man

I'd considered my dad for my entire life, and I chose to enjoy my time with him, not dwell on the "what-ifs."

I'd also made great strides with my mom. She was planning to come to the Gonzaga fight too and had finally started to acknowledge Kim, which I was elated about. I'd been able to get them in the same room after the Sylvia fight in Ohio, though they never spoke much to each other.

I felt as relaxed and prepared as could be going into the Gonzaga fight. I was so relaxed that I forgot my mouthpiece at the gym and my teammates ran across town to grab it in the nick of time. That night in the locker room, we joked around so much, you wouldn't have guessed a few of us were going out to fight. Gonzaga's locker room was situated next to mine, and at one point, it sounded like they were banging their chairs against the wall to pump him up. We all broke out hysterically laughing.

My fight with Gonzaga went as planned. I smothered him against the cage and flustered him. I took him down in the first round with a high single-leg and broke his nose from the slam. I think I unintentionally head-butted him. That's what it sounded like, anyway, with my ear next to his face, though some say the impact of the slam caused his knee to jerk right up into his own beak and crush it.

For the rest of the fight, Gonzaga had to contend with his blood blocking his nasal passage and filling in his mouth. He fired off one of his right high kicks in the first ten seconds of the third round, but I blocked it with my arm. I found out later that I'd broken the ulna bone in my arm, but at the time I didn't feel a thing. I took Gonzaga down and began to ground-and-pound him on the fence. Referee Herb Dean halted the bout less than a minute into round three.

Once again, the geriatric, forty-four-year-old underdog had defied the odds and had taken out the twenty-eight-year-old favourite.

I should have been in high spirits, but my mind was distracted. I was about to make one of the biggest decisions of my life.

16 CHAPTER SIXTEEN:
THE RIGHT THING

THE PATH OF LEAST RESISTANCE WOULD HAVE BEEN to keep my mouth shut and finish out my contract with a smile on my face. But I'm not known for taking the easy road. Maybe it's all my years as an underdog that have hardened my sense of fear. Now all I feel is that wrench in my gut when I realise I'm about to face another challenge. I always try to concentrate on what is within my control. Part of that is the ability to step up and act upon things that I feel I have the power to change.

On October 11, 2007, at the age of forty-four, heading into the final leg of my mixed martial arts career, I resigned from the Ultimate Fighting Championship via a faxed letter to their Las Vegas offices.

"Dear Dana, I am writing to you today to officially tender my resignation from the UFC effective immediately," it read. "Working for the UFC has been a wonderful experience. I have grown in many ways here and will always treasure the opportunities provided to me by the UFC during my years of service."

It was a short letter, but my sentiment was genuine. The UFC had been my home for eleven years, and was as much a part of me as my three children. I was giving up the heavyweight crown, the two fights still available on my contract, and a second employment contract I'd signed during my eleven-month retirement to commentate on the pay-per-view cards, work with the athletic commissions in the states where the sport was still pending regulation, and make appearances anywhere I was asked to go. It was difficult to walk away from all of that, but it just felt like the right thing to do.

This wasn't a spur-of-the-moment decision. I had contemplated leaving for some time. I drafted the letter, then read it over and over. I had it with me when I met with Lorenzo and Dana over breakfast in early September at the Fertitta's Palace Station Casino in Las Vegas a couple of weeks before *UFC 76*. This was the last time I voiced my concerns to UFC management regarding my pay and their behaviour towards me, and I expected them to respond. When I didn't hear a word from them, I was certainly disappointed.

On October 10, the media reported that the number-one ranked heavyweight in the world, Fedor Emelianenko, had passed on a deal to fight in the UFC. That's when I knew it was time for me to move on. Dana had assured the public that he would recruit Emelianenko after Zuffa had purchased its biggest rival, PRIDE Fighting Championships, that March. The acquisition had caused the Japanese promotion's world-class roster to scatter when many of the contracts did not transfer over. Emelianenko, a thirty-one-year-old world sambo champion, was considered the jewel of PRIDE's crown, revered for his stoic demeanour, even as he pounded his opponents into the canvas like hamburger meat.

Emelianenko was the opponent I wanted to fight. I'd even "called" him out at the post-fight press conference at *UFC 74* in August. (Well, I politely inquired about a fight with him) At this stage in my career, I believed it made sense for me to fight the best in the world, not whoever Zuffa wanted to market as the best at that time. I left the UFC to chase after the one fight left that could cap my career.

I didn't expect my resignation to receive the attention it did, nor was I looking for the uproar it caused. Aside from the diehard MMA news websites, I didn't really expect the story to be covered as widely as it was. I'd just finished a day's shooting in Cape Town, South Africa, for my first lead role in the movie *The Scorpion King: Rise of a*

Warrior, when my assistant Val called—she said the story was spreading like wildfire and the gym's phones were ringing off the hook. A few weeks before we'd left for South Africa, Kim and my agent, Matt, had convinced me to change my cell phone number. I always had a hard time saying no to requests, and, over the years, I'd been known to give out my number to anybody who asked. In this moment, I was glad I had listened to them.

I've been told that there were no fewer than ninety articles written about my resignation in the first two days alone, making it the most covered story in the history of the sport. *ESPN, Sports Illustrated*, and The Associated Press all ran stories about my exit. The UFC had finally earned the level of attention it had craved for nearly seven years. Of course, it wasn't the type of attention Zuffa wanted and they couldn't control it. I was astounded when *SportsCenter* tracked me down halfway around the world for a phone interview to get my side of things.

I did only three interviews during those first few days. The morning of my resignation, I called Josh Gross, editor of Sherdog.com, the world's most popular English-language MMA site. Although I'd never been one for to complaining in public, I wanted to make my reasons for leaving clear and I knew my silence could leave room for others to spin the situation. Again, I wanted the fans to know that this decision hadn't come out of the blue and that I'd given the UFC every opportunity to respond. Afterwards, Dana White called my resignation a "retirement," and acted as if he wasn't surprised about it. He wasn't ready to admit things weren't quite as rosy as everyone assumed.

I'd been with the UFC for so long that my departure from Zuffa was difficult for many fans to grasp. Things are sometimes not what they seem from the outside, and no one can ever tell you how to feel about something but yourself. My decision to leave the UFC was based on seven years of feeling slighted, overlooked, used, unappreciated, and generally not wanted by the company. There were a lot of little things that happened during my time with the UFC, but to get into most of them specifically would seem kind of petty at this point. Of course, there were some larger issues at hand.

Money became a major focal point, and something I felt Zuffa tried to accentuate over the next few weeks and months to make me seem like a greedy athlete. When we'd met in September, Lorenzo and Dana had told me I was the UFC's second highest paid athlete, right behind Chuck Liddell. I had spoken to enough fighters in the industry to seriously question this, and knew that more fighters outside the UFC were being lured in with numbers bigger than the ones that I and other "company" guys had been offered.

Though we sometimes have to bash each other's heads in, fighters are generally a tight-knit group. Through sources outside the company, I'd confirmed that Emelianenko had been offered a $1.5 million signing bonus and $2 million a fight in the UFC. After ten years and eighteen appearances for the UFC, I was getting paid $250,000 a fight along with a piece of the pay-per-view revenue. Although the confidentiality provisions of my fight contract technically prevent me from disclosing what I earned from the pay-per-view revenue, I still made far less in those two fights than what the UFC was offering Emelianenko. If you worked for a company where you'd done the best you could for years and your bosses pulled in another guy from another organisation and they paid him more than you'd ever been paid, wouldn't you feel insulted and hurt?

I also knew other fighters like Tim Sylvia and Matt Hughes had been given signing bonuses—it's hard to keep much secret in this business. When I'd met with UFC owner Lorenzo Fertitta in January 2007 to renegotiate my return, I wasn't happy to hear I didn't qualify for a bonus beyond what they'd already planned to give me after the Sylvia bout, but I wanted to fight so I accepted the deal. I even showed my loyalty by turning down a $3 million offer, ironically, to fight Emelianenko in the rival BodogFIGHT promotion owned by online gambling entrepreneur Calvin Ayre.

Nine months later, it didn't seem like my gesture had mattered. It was disheartening that Lorenzo and Dana appeared less than forthcoming with me. There was a bit of a "good ol' boys' club" going on in the UFC, and that determined who got promoted, who got matched up with who, and who generally got taken care of. If you weren't in the club towing the line, you didn't get the time of day. I don't know if it was because of my shaky beginnings with them or what, but after nearly seven years, I just hadn't been able to gain entry.

Being in South Africa for the next few weeks gave me time to detach myself from the craziness back home. Our hotel didn't have Internet access and the time difference cut down on phone calls. For the first time in years, I was forced to relax and not think about fighting. I delved into acting and relished in playing the villain for once. As an evil sorcerer of sorts, I waved my hand to stop shooting arrows in their tracks (through CGI effects) and even had a small scene with my wife.

Kim and I had gotten married a year before in a small ceremony in Hawaii, but we hadn't had much time to stop and smell the roses. Our marriage had been strained by the responsibilities of running a gym, a clothing line, a nutrition line, and training and managing fighters. During our days off, Kim and I spent every moment together. This was our time to reconnect and renew our commitment to one another. We went on safaris and enjoyed fine wines and local delicacies by moonlight. I had always wanted to try shark diving, so I climbed into a steel cage and watched as the great whites hovered nearby. Kim thought I was crazy, but came on the boat to make sure I stayed out of trouble.

By the end of October, the film wrapped and it was time to get back to reality. My agent Matt had been fielding calls from nearly every major sports outlet out there and had been taking a lot of unnecessary heat from Dana, who blamed my "parasite" Hollywood agent in interviews for my sudden upheaval. Dana even told the press he'd "bitch slapped" Matt a month earlier during some negotiation. When Matt first became my agent, Dana had refused to take his phone calls. That is how Dana had shown his respect to Matt, and in turn, to me.

Later, the blame seemed to fall on Kim, the new "influence" in my life, but my decision to walk away was mine alone.

In my time away, rumours and speculation began to fly. One media outlet chose to print that I would have made somewhere between $12 to 15 million for the four bouts on my UFC contract had I stayed, a claim that was grossly inflated. I found it incredibly irresponsible for a news source to report false figures and wrongfully sway public opinion. I decided to call my own press conference to set the record straight and give the press the opportunity to ask me questions. The night before I was scheduled to face the world, Lorenzo called and asked me not to go through with it. Dana also left me a long-winded phone message. His tone was condescending, though he kept telling me I was the greatest fighter ever and I'd gotten it all wrong. But that was Dana. His emotions influenced him more than anything else and I don't think he realised the way he spoke to people sometimes.

On October 25, 2007, two weeks to the day after I'd resigned, over twenty press outlets crammed into the Xtreme Couture gym in Las Vegas. The press conference was aired online and on HDNet as well. Many of the fighters I trained with dropped their activities that morning and came to support mc. Dressed in a buttoned-down shirt and blazer, sitting at a table in the middle of the gym's boxing ring, I was more anxious in that moment than for any fight I could remember.

I started from the beginning—in 2001, when Zuffa had bought the UFC from its former owners. I spoke of my issues with the company then, how my management had refused to sign my ancillary rights over to Zuffa for nothing, and how I'd been punished for it by getting removed from the Carmen Electra ad campaign and the video games.

From that time on, I told the audience, I'd felt like I'd been counted out by Zuffa and brought in to lose. It's the little things that make athletes feel appreciated, and they just that weren't being done for me, and for others, too.

For eleven years, I had tried to represent this sport with integrity for the UFC's previous and current owners. I've never believed I was utilised appropriately to push the sport forward. And in recent months, I'd felt slighted by a company that had gotten bigger and bigger and lost sight of who had helped get it there. Though I acknowledged and thanked Zuffa for saving the sport from certain extinction, I didn't agree with the way the company had interacted with many of its athletes, including myself. Zuffa had always told us that they wanted to take care of the fighters, but it appeared as if things had changed. Their goal was to make a tonne of money.

It was easy to say my own actions were based on money, and on some level they were. There are many ways for an athlete to be respected, and I have to admit that a paycheque is one of them—especially in relation to his or her competition. But there were other reasons, too, that had nothing to do with money, and I felt it was time to take a stand.

That next week, Zuffa went on the offensive. They held their own press conference to disprove the numbers I said I'd gotten paid for my two fights in 2007. Much to their displeasure, I'd discussed the UFC's pay scale for fighters that qualified for pay-per-view revenue shares. Zuffa had taken great pains to keep these numbers in the dark, as they did with virtually all of their financial dealings with the fighters. I had told the press what I had received for those bouts thus far, and even though numerous media outlets came up with the same numbers that Zuffa verified later that day, other press didn't accurately report the information I had shared. Both Dana and Lorenzo claimed that I was a liar for underquoting the figures I had made for my two fights.

That's when I realised that this had become a game of semantics. I was a liar because they were calling me one. According to Zuffa, I hadn't "resigned." I had "retired." But there was no language in my UFC contract that could keep me from walking away if I simply turned down a bout. Zuffa and its lawyers had never considered that one of its fighters might say "no" to a fight, and, as written, the contracts couldn't penalise me for doing so. Of course, I realised I might suffer in other ways, because Zuffa was always ready for a fight. I decided to drop out of this verbal battle.

Over the next two months, Dana put on a happy face, pledging his undeterred friendship for me and his willingness to meet and work things out. Behind the scenes, it was a different story. Lawyers from both sides went back and forth. Though Zuffa preached otherwise, my lawyers and I were confident that my fight contract did not obligate me to finish out the two remaining fights and that it would run out in July. A one-year, non-compete term had kicked in with the employment contract, which meant I couldn't work for, or even promote, another organisation until October 2008.

I knew there were other offers out there waiting for me, so I approached Zuffa with a deal. If they were willing to shorten the one-year, non-compete period, I was willing to sign paperwork guaranteeing I would never fight for another promotion ever again. I was essentially giving up my chance to face Emelianenko, but I didn't really want to go to litigation. I was perfectly content to walk away and sacrifice the Emelianenko fight for the opportunity to get away from the UFC once and for all. I wanted to start anew with another organisation, working in a different capacity.

Because we had discovered a loophole in Zuffa's contracts with my "resignation" stance, Zuffa's lawyers were eager for the UFC to take the offer so we wouldn't bring our discovery to light. But Dana dragged his feet on the negotiations. After numerous drafts of an agreement exchanged hands, a question was raised: could I come out of retirement if the UFC ever did get Emelianenko under contract? This discussion sparked a new debate, and the negotiations fell apart.

In public, he Dana told the press that he and I had planned to meet around Thanksgiving. Though we had spoken, I'd made no plans to meet with him. I could have easily denied this, but I didn't see the point. Dana was going to spin things the way he wanted to, and I think he honestly thought he could meet me face to face and convince me to come back. In an effort to try and resolve our stalemate, I did eventually meet with Dana in Las Vegas, and he tried to woo me back. I wasn't buying it.

In the meantime, the M-1 Global organisation, which had secured Emelianenko's contract, sent an e-mail to Dana offering Zuffa the opportunity to co-promote a fight between the Russian and myself. Zuffa quickly turned the deal down. Their actions spoke a thousand words: If they couldn't have the fight all to themselves, nobody would.

It became clear what I needed to do. I had to make the Emelianenko fight happen outside of the UFC—not only for myself, but for the sake of the sport. The UFC had held a monopoly over the sport and unless a worthwhile event took place under a different promotion, there would be no balance. Zuffa was bound to keep treating fighters the way they did.

When negotiations crumbled, Zuffa began to play hardball. Dana went after my other business dealings to try and pressure me to cave. First, he called and threatened to ban the Affliction clothing company from UFC events because they carried my Xtreme Couture clothing brand. Though many of the fighters complained and stood up to Dana, both brand names were eventually banned from all UFC events.

In December 2007, the UFC refused to film an episode of Spike TV's *All Access* at our gym, which featured Wanderlei Silva. Silva had been training at Xtreme Couture and spoke minimal English, so when the crew took him to another gym to film the episode, he couldn't really object. The crew asked some of Wanderlei's training partners to come along and they were told they couldn't wear anything that represented the Xtreme Couture gym. It was an awkward situation for the guys at my gym—many of them were in different phases of their own contracts with Zuffa, so it was a lot of unnecessary pressure.

Stating that I still owed them two more fights, Zuffa offered me a bout in December to face former PRIDE champion Antonio Rodrigo Nogueira at *UFC 81* on February 2, 2008, in Las Vegas. I turned them down. Instead, the UFC matched the Brazilian jiu-jitsu black belt with Tim Sylvia for an interim title. Because they wanted to label my resignation a "retirement" when it went to court, I was still the champion.

At *UFC 81*, Nogueira ate two rounds of Sylvia's jabs, then came from behind to snag the submission in the third. During the broadcast, not one mention was made of me or why I was absent. In the coming months, I travelled to numerous UFC events to corner my fighters. At one point, I made eye contact with Lorenzo and he promptly turned away. If I wasn't onboard with Zuffa's plans, I apparently didn't exist.

THOUGH WE TRIED to resolve things outside the legal system, there was little doubt in my mind that we'd end up in court. That was the fate I decided when I chose the path I did. The headlines read: "UFC Sues Couture" in February 2008. Zuffa filed suit against me because they felt I'd overstepped the boundaries of my non-compete clause when I'd travelled to other events or spoke on camera of my future plans to face Emelianenko. (I was always careful to promote my fighters and not a rival event, per my agreement.) Zuffa also accused me of slander and conspiring with rival promotions to hurt their business, though they couldn't name who I was working with. I hoped that it wouldn't come to this, but I wasn't shocked that it had.

As the months passed, public reaction to my decision went back and forth. Court proceedings take time, and I know a lot of fans just wanted to see me fight again. However, I understood I was in a unique position to make an impact. UFC contracts are very favourable towards the promotion. Typically, Zuffa owns the fighters' ancillary rights and has the ability to drop a fighter at any given time if he doesn't perform up to the UFC's expectations. In the past, there was practically no other place for a fighter to go. But competition was coming.

I received an overwhelming amount of support from that competition. From the day of my resignation, my agent's phone was inundated with offers from all of the other promotions—similar to the bombardment of offers I received when I retired in 2006. Sports entrepreneur Mark Cuban was among the suitors. A self-made billionaire who'd recently begun promoting his own events on his own HDNet channel, Cuban also owned the Dallas Mavericks basketball team. He was known for taking care of his athletes and putting them first, which appealed to me right away. Cuban had a straightforward business sense and he pulled no punches during our first phone conversation. Fight or no fight with Emelianenko, Cuban asked me to get involved with promoting HDNet Fights after I had satisfied my two UFC contracts. I was intrigued.

The sport was getting flooded by big investors whose promotions tried to cash in early by signing free-agent marquee fighters and jumping into pay-per-views right away. One by one, they were all losing tonnes of money. The only pay-per-views that were selling were the UFC's, because nobody recognised or trusted any other brand.

In contrast, Cuban was taking a grassroots approach, building the stars from the ground up on HDNet, so he could move into the pay-per-view model when he felt the brand was ready. On top of that, Cuban had the finances to build up from a solid foundation. I listened to Cuban intently and I could hear a passion in his voice. He seemed genuinely interested in creating a better environment for the fighters. For the first time in a while, I felt a sense of hope.

I didn't meet Cuban in person for months, not until I travelled to Dallas to corner a few of my fighters for an HDNet Fights event. Hotel, flights, and meal money were taken care of without fuss. I also learned that Cuban financially supported fighters who were injured in his shows, so they could get healthy and compete again. A vast majority of fighters don't have health insurance, so this was really going above and beyond what most promoters were willing to do. Cuban put his money where his mouth was. And that mattered to me.

In February 2008, after Zuffa had filed the lawsuit against me in Las Vegas, Cuban requested that a Dallas court give a "declaratory judgement" regarding my fight contract with the UFC. Because Cuban's HDNet Fights was ready to go into an agreement with me, he asked the judge to read my contract and decide when it expired. Was I contractually tied to the UFC until I completed two more fights for them, or would I be free to go when my contract lapsed in July?

THIS PAST DECEMBER, I travelled out to Wisconsin. I was flattered to hear that Brett Favre watched and admired my fights. At the request of Green Bay Packers head coach Mike McCarthy, I spoke with his team the night before a big game with the Oakland Raiders. After they showed the team a reel of my highlight footage, I walked into the room. I swear you could have heard a pin drop.

I shared one of the exercises I'd used a thousand times before, since junior high. I told the team to close their eyes.

"Picture a nice big yellow lemon," I said. "See the lemon clearly. You can see the skin, the little nubs on each end of the lemon."

The room was silent.

"Picture your hand coming in now with a knife and slicing the lemon in half. The two sections fall apart, and you can see the segments in the lemons and the clear juices running out onto the counter. You can start to smell the lemon, it's sharp, tangy odour."

The players didn't budge an inch.

"Now open your eyes," I instructed. "How many peoples' mouths started moving as if they tasted the lemon?"

Everyone nodded their heads, yes.

"Do you see any lemons in here?" I asked the room. Of course, they all shook their heads.

"You have a physical response to the pictures you put in your head. You control these pictures. Put the ones you want in there, and you will have a physical response to them.

"I picture my fights, the techniques, and how I want it to go up here," I said, pointing to my head. "If you're stuck with a particular move you are trying to learn, take a break and spend a couple of days visualising it. Execute it perfectly, the way it's been taught to you, and then come back to it, and I guarantee you will execute it better when you come back."

My lemon exercise is a simple one, but it works. The Green Bay Packers must have agreed. They charged onto Lambeau Field the next day and trounced the Raiders with a score of 38-7.

When I close my eyes, I see Fedor Emelianenko. I see us staring at one another across a ring. I hear the bell sound and the crowd roar. I watch us approach each other carefully and with purpose. Our hands are up; our bodies are relaxed and tense all in the same moment. We are ready for someone to make the first move. And then we will react. That is where I see myself next—maybe in a few months, maybe a little after that, but I do see it happening.

In January, I met Emelianenko for the second time on a soundstage behind a set of train tracks in Glendale, California, right outside of Burbank. We faced off and gazed into each other's eyes, both of us unable to hide the smiles peeking out from behind our game faces. It was only for an Affliction commercial, but I found myself sizing up my competition—literally. Emelianenko didn't seem an inch taller than me, which was surprising. Once a fighter, always a fighter, I guess.

I DON'T EXPECT to compete again without going through a courtroom first. As this book goes to press, we are still awaiting word on the actions filed in Las Vegas and Texas. I only hope it doesn't take much longer past October. I turned forty-five in June. I'm not getting any younger, although I must have been blessed with some good genes because I seem to keep on ticking along.

Last summer, I participated on a National Geographic TV show called *Fight Science*. They decided to test how high the lactic acid levels would rise in my blood during rigorous physical exercise. Lactic acid is the stuff that makes your muscles ache and slows you down. I was just as shocked as the scientists when my levels actually dropped as I choked out a volunteer with all my might. I can't explain why. Sometimes there are no explanations.

For most of my life, I've eaten healthfully and taken care of my body as best as I could. I don't smoke. I don't drink excessively. I don't know what a Human Growth Hormone is, or any of those other shortcuts out there. I don't do shortcuts. I feel like I'm missing something when I don't hit the gym for a few days.

Some things have changed. I've learned to listen to my body more. I'm not as willing to come in and grind it out and push through the way I did in my late thirties and early forties. I'm a little smarter about it now. If I don't feel right, if I feel that I need a half-day off, I'm a lot more willing to take it now.

Some things in my life have come full circle. Last December, I sat down with Matt and Danny to hash out some of our differences. I'd barely spoken with Matt in the last year, and Danny and I had resorted to the sporadic phone text to wish each other good luck on our fights. I have to thank my wife Kim, because she kept encouraging the three of us to come together again. I admitted I was at fault for certain business decisions that affected Matt and Danny's Team Quest enterprises. In turn, they explained that my actions made them think that I had become someone they didn't recognise. And whether it was intentional or not, there were people that had come between the three of us and kept us apart. Though I don't have any intention of rekindling relationships with certain members of Team Quest, I love Matt and Danny, and luckily, we've been able to move forward on much surer footing. Matt's already brought his team to the Las Vegas gym to train with my new army of fighters. It was an honour to have them.

Most recently, my oldest son, Ryan, moved to Las Vegas to work alongside me in the Xtreme Couture businesses. Spending time with me, I think Ryan now has a better understanding of my life, the work I put into making him a vital part of it when he was young, and the sacrifices I made to get where I am today. He's training to fight, but whether he decides to test himself later or not, it doesn't matter to me. I feel blessed each day I get to look at his face.

I travel to see my younger son, Caden, every second and fourth weekend, and although Trish and I still don't tend to agree on much, I'm fortunate to watch my son grow into a wonderful, athletic person. My daughter Aimee recently got married, and I have never seen a more beautiful, beaming bride. My wife Kim stays firmly by my side, as we watch my twelve-year-old stepson, Oakley, inquisitively take on the world.

In the coming months, my future as a fighter will be determined, one way or another. What happens inside the courtrooms might change the sport forever, and I hope it eventually stimulates a change in the way promotions treat their fighters. There is a chance that I'll never face Emelianenko, but I know everything happens for a reason. Ultimately, my actions have affected people's perception of this still-developing sport, and if my legal battles makes things better for the athletes in the long run, then I have done my job.

My eleven-year journey through mixed martial arts has blessed my life. It's been an amazing ride. I've learned a lot along the way and I wouldn't trade any of it. There are a lot of moments I will never forget, like standing alongside trailblazers like Dan Severn and Royce Gracie at *UFC 45* in 2003, when the fans named me their favourite UFC fighter. I can still recall the rush I had raising my Hall of Fame award over my head in 2006, and the perfect experience that was *UFC 68* in Columbus, Ohio, where everything just seemed to go my way.

I have made mistakes, but I am grateful and thankful for the support the fans continue to give me. When fighters say they couldn't have done it without the fans, they do mean it. If not for our crazy, hardcore fan base, mixed martial arts would have died during its dark years, and I might not never have found my purpose in life.

I understand that my role in this sport goes far beyond what I do in a cage or ring. I have a responsibility to ensure that my sport grows and thrives for generations to come. I love what I do. I have a true passion for this sport. I love the training. I love the competition. I love being a fighter. And that's why I'm still here.

Epilogue

SO HERE WE ARE. IT'S BEEN EIGHT MONTHS SINCE MY fingers have touched a keyboard to discuss my life. A lot has changed, but you're probably expecting that from me.

I am no longer the UFC heavyweight champion, but still have a tonne of titles to live up to. I am a father and husband, a gym owner and training partner, a budding thespian and motivational speaker. I'm still a fighter too, when I can fit that in.

I think the biggest development in this time was my decision to return to the UFC in September 2008. After eleven months of back-and-forth litigation, a smidgen of mudslinging, a whole lot of public posturing, and a general feeling that I wasn't getting any closer to my goal, I re-signed with the promotion that was my beginning, my middle, and will now be my end.

In my quest to get away from the UFC and fight the world's number-one heavyweight, Fedor Emelianenko, I realised a few things along the way.

My first experience with the legal system came in 1994 with my car accident. What looked like a cut and dry case of reckless endangerment and hit-and-run, turned into something else all together. The district attorney told me that it would be an open-and-shut affair that would take half a day to complete at most. Three days later, I was still in court with this clown that had tried to use me as a tyre flap. I knew then that the system was flawed and unpredictable.

Round two with the legal system, in which I took on the UFC for my freedom, lived up to my expectations.

It became apparent to me that my chosen battle within the legal system was going to take a considerable amount of time and an even more considerable amount of money, both of which were limited on my sides of things. I couldn't continue to spend half a million dollars a year on legal fees, no matter what you think a fighter makes.

Time has never been my ally, but at the age of forty-five, I realised that it was fruitless to spend another year, or maybe two or three, not being able to compete.

If the original course of action just isn't working, you have to be ready to adjust the game plan.

I did everything in my power to secure a fight with Emelianenko, and at times, I could see our epic clash on the horizon. In July 2008, I stood across from Emelianenko minutes after his victory over Tim Sylvia at Affliction's first event in Anaheim, California, and the electricity in the air was palpable.

But by August 2008, the window of opportunity was slamming down on this old man's hands as he dangled from the edge. An attempt to have my UFC contract reviewed and ruled in Texas with help from Mark Cuban had failed. Preliminary arbitration hearings between myself and Zuffa were set to begin in February 2009, but they could easily be delayed.

Sitting with Emelianenko and his management at a swank restaurant in Los Angeles that August, reality set in. I realised there might still be some opportunity to see the fight happen in the UFC if the promotion opened a new dialogue and struck a deal with the Russian. Past negotiations had been unsuccessful, but the landscape of MMA seemed to be changing daily. Promotions were coming and going just as quickly and only the UFC seemed to have the stability needed to breathe life into this fight.

I began my renegotiations with Zuffa LLC innocently enough. Just like I'd done with the Sylvia fight, I texted Dana White with a friendly jab and he countered with the name Brock Lesnar almost immediately.

A week later, I was sitting in Zuffa's corporate offices just off the Las Vegas strip, staring at a random UFC fight poster on the wall that was staring right back at me. I wouldn't say I was totally comfortable to be there—it felt like I was entering the lion's den at lunchtime—but I was determined to make some headway. If the UFC would agree to do everything in their power to make the fight with Emelianenko happen, I'd be open to fighting Lesnar first.

It was a unique situation. The UFC had no main event for its next show and a stringent schedule to keep if it was going to make its crucial advertising deadlines. It was all down to the wire. There wasn't a lot of time to haggle or negotiate, which I almost thought was better, because we could have haggled over a whole bunch of stuff for months on end.

It wasn't like Dana and I were holding hands at a picnic either. We were cordial to one another, but there were underlying trust issues on both sides. They didn't know if they could trust me and I wasn't sure if I wanted to trust them. I'll admit I had reservations, and the thought of getting up and running out the door popped into my head once or twice. Remember how much I love confrontation.

At one point we took a break, and I walked outside rather than loiter around the hallways. I sat out in my car in the parking lot and made a few calls, then left to go fill up my gas tank. It wasn't until I returned that I realised my trip to the gas station had launched DEFCON 4 at the UFC offices when they'd assumed I'd abandoned the talks all together.

In most quarrels, both sides eat a little crow and meet somewhere in the middle. I could lie and say that I got everything I wanted, but I didn't. Life is full of give and take and we were still on opposite sides of the same table. They were still going to try and get as much as they could for as little as possible, and I was trying to do the exact opposite.

After a media teleconference call was delayed for an hour while the lawyers hashed out the final details, I was reintroduced to the press as the UFC heavyweight champion under a new three-fight contract.

Lesnar, who I'd face on November 15, 2008, joined on the phone line along with Dana. My immediate feeling was that a great weight had been lifted and a sense of relief washed over me. It had taken me only eleven months and a week to get my next fight.

At six-foot-two and some 280 pounds, Lesnar had baseball mitts for hands, but glided across the cage at a frightening pace uncharacteristic for a man his size. A side from his hulking physicality, Lesnar's wrestling background was similar to my own, which is what really attracted me to this bout.

While the media hemmed and hawed that the former World Wrestling Entertainment pro wrestling superstar hadn't earned the right to face me for the title with only three fights under his belt, I needed only look as far as Lesnar's wrestling credentials to find my own validation. A two-time NCAA All-American, Lesnar had captured the NCAA heavyweight championship in 2000 for the University of Minnesota to cap off an impressive 106-5 career record.

I knew it was this pedigree that would force me to use all the pieces of my MMA game—outside of my wrestling—to win the fight. It was my striking and jiu-jitsu, and the other skills I'd culled for the last twelve years that were going to give me the upper hand. That was what was going to make it fun for me.

Like the Sylvia fight, I searched high and low for training partners that matched Lesnar's measurements. Most of my sessions were spent finding different ways to wiggle out from underneath one 300-pound guy after another to find the sun again. Getting taken down didn't worry me; I figured it would happen. Getting marooned underneath Lesnar was my worst-case scenario.

On my feet, I couldn't afford to move just my head like I had with the lumbering six-foot-eight Sylvia back at *UFC 68*. Lesnar was just too swift and sharp. I'd have to jerk my whole body out of this tank's path or get trampled. I brought in a new boxing coach, Gil Martinez, to assist me with that.

My ten-week training camp came and went, and fight week was

suddenly upon us. The pre-fight press conference was held in the lobby of the MGM Grand Hotel and I'd almost forgotten the fanfare these events continue to draw. Hundreds of fans lined up along the dais to snap a picture or yell out an encouraging word.

I'd been to plenty of UFCs to corner some of my guys during my resignation time, but there was always the looming feeling that I wasn't welcome anymore. It was also hard to watch from cageside when I knew there was no reason I couldn't be the one in there competing.

The conference with Lesnar was also my chance to tune in on my opponent and see how he was handling the attention. As a former WWE champion, I knew Lesnar was used to the crowds and having all eyes on him. But I'd noticed that he had a bit of a temper. During our conference call with the press in September, he'd short-circuited on a hapless reporter. I'd also heard snippets here and there during training that he was saying this and that about me.

Once we hit the ground running in Las Vegas, the bravado and brashness had receded a great deal. Lesnar seemed a little nervous, to tell you the truth, and as we stood posing for pictures at the podium afterward, he told me what a great honour it would be to fight me. I thanked him for the compliment and quietly noted this change to myself.

I received a hero's welcome the next day at the weigh-ins and had all the confidence in the world as I stepped back into the Octagon come fight night. There was a 280-pound gorilla of a man in the cage with me, and even though I'd weighed in at 220 pounds myself the day before, I felt Lesnar wasn't anything I couldn't handle.

The bell sounded and Lesnar rushed me immediately, clinching and pushing me against the cage. I circled out and pinned his back against it. He flipped positions with me again, but I didn't feel like he was overpowering me. He wasn't the strongest opponent I'd faced.

Our battle for control spilled to centre stage and I nicked Lesnar with a sneaky right hand as I bounced back outside his range and waited for him to charge me. I defended the first shot, but didn't fight the second takedown attempt. I'd trained myself to be here and find an opening, and I almost took Lesnar's back as I slid out. Taking Lesnar's back had been something we'd worked on so frequently in training that the guys said I'd resembled a koala bear backpack the little kids tote around. Lesnar muscled me back to the canvas again though and tried to pin down my right arm so I'd lose half my defences. It was time to move again.

I made it back to my feet and leaned again, feeling really close to picking him up with the high single. I could feel him floating for a split second, and if he hadn't grabbed the fence, I believe I would have taken him down. I wonder how that would have affected him psychologically.

I don't remember the elbow strike Lesnar landed on my head to begin round two, but I instinctually manoeuvred him against the fence and tried to harness my monster with all of my weight. Lesnar threw a knee as we separated, and I snuck in an uppercut and another right to answer him.

I registered a small trail of blood trickle from Lesnar's right brow and he pawed at it, a little incredulous. We clinched again on the fence after Lesnar made a half-hearted double-leg attempt, and I leaned into him again before we cleared back to centre canvas.

And then it happened. One of those daddy-long-leg arms came at me and I slipped it, but it just kept unfolding. It clipped me behind my ear and I went down. Lesnar was on me in a nanosecond and his fists rained down on me like a large woman swinging a purse. No matter which way I turned, there was nowhere to go. And then it was over.

I think what surprised me the most about Lesnar was his range. He had very long arms. It seemed he could stand ten feet away from me and still knock me down if he connected. His arms seemed to keep coming and coming. I didn't seem to register that little tidbit of information beforehand, and I wasn't as prepared for it as I could have been. Don't get me wrong—I'd worked on my striking a lot. I was slipping punches, but eating a few along the way. I struggled to find my appropriate range and felt like I never quite got there.

My face was a little bruised and I'd broken one of my front teeth, but I felt fine afterward. I even went out that night to a club with my teammates and my family.

I believed I'd done a good job against Lesnar, but things just didn't line up the way they had in some of my other fights. Sometimes it goes that way.

I know what some of you may be thinking. I left the UFC, sat out for a year, and came back only to lose my title right out of the gate. How's that for karma?

I don't regret leaving the UFC when I did. I think everything served its purpose. There's a reason for everything, and I think it worked out the way it was supposed to. I may not understand it all right now, and it may not make a lot of sense, but I think at some point it will.

I made my statement with regards to the treatment of the athletes in the sport, our ancillary rights, and the pay we receive for putting our lives on the line. Other athletes followed suit and made their own statements, but ultimately, there's a serious monopoly in MMA right now. There is no other outlet outside the UFC. They're still trying to do what they need to do to maintain control of the sport and the business, and I wouldn't expect that that's going to change a whole lot. With that landscape, it's pretty hard for anybody to stand up, get any traction, and do anything, myself included. I could sit on the sidelines some more, but I don't think that helps me or the sport.

I wouldn't say my relationship with the UFC has been fully repaired. Nothing's perfect. I think we're both a little weary and I think in some ways, mistrustful, but it's kind of like an old girlfriend and boyfriend. You don't know what you're missing till it's gone, and you learn a bit more about yourself in your time away from one another. The UFC has welcomed me back and has been very supportive and appreciative, which was a bit of what I felt was lacking when I decided to go in the first place.

Even in loss, you gain something. I seem to collect new training partners. Three weeks following my loss to Lesnar, I ran into him cageside at *UFC Fight for the Troops*, a charity event held right outside Fort Bragg in Fayetteville, North Carolina, to raise money for the Intrepid Fallen Heroes Fund.

Now that we were both out of the spotlight, Lesnar's tough guy persona had melted considerably and he was a lot more relaxed. He asked if it would be acceptable for him to come out to Las Vegas and train at the Xtreme Couture gym sometime in the future. I told him that would be fine.

As for my family, it would probably make for a juicier read if I told you that Ed has taken the paternity test, and I know one way or the other who my biological father is. I'm sorry to disappoint, but I still feel it doesn't really matter or change how I feel about my father and my mother. It wouldn't settle anything for me. I continue to see Ed frequently and talk to him. He came to my last fight, and sometimes he visits me and my son, Caden, down in Oregon.

My daughter, Aimee, moved back to Las Vegas in 2008 and began working for the family business. She became the gym manager and it's been fantastic to have my daughter around again.

My oldest son, Ryan, competed in his first fight this year and won by triangle choke. It was great to have him around in training. He's a tall, rangy 155-pounder with great wrestling and jiu-jitsu skills that he's putting together with his ever-improving striking. He's a man of few words like his old man. We call him "the Silent Killer."

Already an excellent swimmer, my six-year-old son, Caden, started skiing and playing soccer and basketball. He's a stocky little bugger and coordinated to boot. There's no doubt he's an athlete.

There's a certain joy a parent takes in watching their children excel in whatever they choose to do. My three children haven't let me down with this.

We're certainly a fighting family. Even my wife, Kim, got into the game and competed in two professional bouts in 2008. Her first outing was a tough one, but she asked me to treat her like a training partner, so I did. Though she broke her jaw in the first few seconds, she made it through all three rounds and showed undeniable heart.

Her next fight in October 2008 was an arse-whipping, except this time she was the one doling out the punishment. I think having her train and fight has helped the both of us understand one another more. The life of a fighter is far from easy, and she's a bit more forgiving when I get home from training and just want to collapse on the couch and watch *CSI*.

I hardly had a chance to ponder my next fight when Hollywood came knocking again. Sylvester Stallone sent me a pretty original Christmas present—he cast me in the film *The Expendables*, about a group of mercenaries that travel to South America to overthrow a dictator. Stallone wrote the script and is slated to direct and also star in the film.

Who'd have thought the runt who lost most of his first wrestling matches would be working alongside the man that created *Rocky*, one of the big screen's original underdogs?

But it got even better. Stallone, who has always embraced his testosterone-charged persona, was looking to create the ultimate reunion of on-screen badasses. He also cast action film superstars Jet Li and my friend Jason Statham, of *The Transporter* fame, in the other two lead roles. I was cast in the role of "Toll Road," whose mantra was, "If you're gonna get past me, you're gonna have to pay." To be cast alongside these action stars is hard for me to fathom. It's a great opportunity for me.

As I write this, Stallone is currently scouting locations, and I am preparing for a nine-week shoot split between Brazil and Shreveport, Louisiana. I have two more movie offers and a potential TV series on Spike TV in the pipe as well.

Where does my fighting fit in? I'm not sure it does anymore. If all those gigs come through, I'd be happy to spend the rest of 2009 developing more tools as an actor—my next great challenge. I've realised at this point, that I can't compete at the level I have been forever. I've known that for a while, but when and where acting was going to take hold of me was the question.

I've had a great run in mixed martial arts, and if I never step into the cage again, I've found a sense of closure in my accomplishments over the last twelve years. Twenty-five is a good number to end on, don't you think?

Of course, you could be reading this now, and I've already banged heads again for the twenty-sixth time, possibly against Antonio Rodrigo Nogueira or even Fedor Emelianenko. I truly believe anything's possible. You just have to have faith in the grand plan.

I've stopped talking about retirement these days. Nobody would buy it anyway, least of all myself. For all I know I could be fighting for another championship title at the tender age of forty-six.

There's always that chance with me. Isn't there?

Appendix

RANDY "THE NATURAL" COUTURE
MIXED MARTIAL ARTS

Pro Record: 16-9

Wins: 7 (T)KOs, 2 Submissions, 7 Decisions

Losses: 5 (T)KOs, 4 Submissions

Three-time UFC heavyweight champion

Two-time UFC light heavyweight champion

UFC interim light heavyweight champion

WIN   Tony Halme – TKO 0:56 R1, *UFC 13* (May 30, 1997), Augusta, Georgia

WIN   Steven Graham – TKO 3:13 R1, *UFC 13* (May 30, 1997), Augusta, Georgia

WIN   Vitor Belfort – TKO 8:16 R1, *UFC 15* (Oct. 17, 1997), Bay St. Louis, Mississippi

WIN   Maurice Smith – Decision, *UFC Japan 1* (Dec. 21, 1997), Yokohama, Japan

LOSS   Enson Inoue – Submission 1:39 R1, *Vale Tudo Japan 1998* (Oct. 25, 1998), Tokyo, Japan

LOSS Mikhail Iloukhine – Submission 7:43 R1, *RINGS: Rise 1st*
(March 20, 1999), Japan

WIN Jeremy Horn – Decision, *RINGS: King of Kings* Block A
(Oct. 9, 2000), Tokyo, Japan

WIN Ryushi Yanagisawa – Decision, *RINGS: King of Kings* Block A
(Oct. 9, 2000), Tokyo, Japan

WIN Kevin Randleman – TKO 4:13 R3, *UFC 28* (Nov. 17, 2000),
Atlantic City, N.J.

WIN Tsuyoshi Kohsaka – Decision, *RINGS: King of Kings* Final
(Feb. 24, 2001), Tokyo, Japan

LOSS Valentjin Overeem – Submission 0:56 R1, *RINGS: King of
Kings* Final (Feb. 24, 2001), Tokyo, Japan

WIN Pedro Rizzo – Decision, *UFC 31* (May 4, 2001), Atlantic City, N.J.

WIN Pedro Rizzo – TKO 1:38 R3, *UFC 34* (Nov. 2, 2001), Las Vegas

LOSS Josh Barnett – TKO 4:35 R2, *UFC 36* (March 22, 2002), Las Vegas

LOSS Ricco Rodriguez – Submission (Strikes) 3:04 R5, *UFC 39* (Sept.
27, 2002), Uncasville, Conn.

WIN Chuck Liddell – TKO 2:39 R3, *UFC 43* (June 6, 2003), Las Vegas

WIN Tito Ortiz – Decision, *UFC 44* (Sept. 26, 2003), Las Vegas

LOSS Vitor Belfort – TKO 0:49 R1, *UFC 46* (Jan. 31, 2004), Las Vegas

WIN Vitor Belfort – TKO 5:00 R3, *UFC 49* (Aug. 21, 2004), Las Vegas

LOSS Chuck Liddell – KO 2:06 R1, *UFC 52* (April 16, 2005), Las Vegas

WIN Mike Van Arsdale – Submission 0:52 R3, *UFC 54* (Aug. 20,
2005), Las Vegas

LOSS Chuck Liddell – TKO 1:28 R2, *UFC 57* (Feb. 2, 2006), Las Vegas

WIN Tim Sylvia – Decision, *UFC 68* (March 3, 2007), Columbus, Ohio

WIN Gabriel Gonzaga – TKO 1:37 R3, *UFC 74* (Aug. 25, 2007),
Las Vegas

LOSS Brock Lesnar – TKO 3:07 R2, *UFC 91* (Nov. 15, 2008), Las Vegas

COURTESY OF SHERDOG.COM

AMATEUR WRESTLING

Weight Classes: 82kg, 90kg, 97kg

Years on Team USA: 8 (1990-96, 97-98, 99-00)

Clubs: Sunkist Kids (1989-2000), U.S. Army (1985-1988)

INTERNATIONAL COMPETITION

1988   World Military Games champion

1990   Fifth in World Cup, second in Pan American Championships, fourth in Concord Cup

1991   U.S. World team member, third in World Cup, Pan American Games champion, second in Concord Cup, fourth in Trofeo Milone (Italy)

1992   World Cup team member, second in Pan American Championships

1993   U.S. World team member, second in Concord Cup, fourth in German Grand Prix, Michigan WC International champion

1994   Fourth in Concord Cup

1995   U.S. World team member, fourth in World Cup, Polish Grand Prix champion, fourth in Concord Cup

1996   Sunkist Kids International Open champion

1997   Ninth in World Championships, third in Pan American Championships, second in Granma Cup (Cuba), Sunkist Kids International Open champion

1998   Fourth in Henri Deglane Challenge (France), second in Pan American Championships, third in Trofeo Milone (Italy), sixth in Hungary Grand Prix, eighth in Vebhi Emri Tournament (Turkey)

1999   Fifth in Nordvest Cup (Sweden)

2000   Second in Dave Schultz Memorial International, sixth in 2000 Takhti Cup (Iran)

U.S. COMPETITION

1983   First in Fifth Core Regional Championships (Armed Forces) in freestyle and Greco-Roman, first in USAREUR (U.S. Army Europe) tournament in freestyle, second in USAREUR (U.S. Army Europe) tournament in Greco-Roman

1984   First in Fifth Core Regional Championships (Armed Forces) in freestyle and Greco-Roman, first in USAREUR (U.S. Army Europe) tournament in freestyle, second in USAREUR (U.S. Army Europe) tournament in Greco-Roman

1985   Second in Armed Forces in freestyle, All-Army team member

1986   All-Army team member

1987   Second in Armed Forces in freestyle, All-Army team member

1988   Fourth in Olympic Team Trials, third in Final Olympic Qualifier, fourth in U.S. Nationals, Armed Forces champion, All-Army team member

1989   Fourth in U.S. Olympic Festival, seventh in U.S. Nationals

1990   Second in World Team Trials, U.S. Nationals champion, Outstanding Greco-Roman Wrestler at U.S. Nationals

1991   World Team Trials champion, second in U.S. Nationals

1992   Second in Final Olympic Wrestle-off, Olympic Team Trials champion

1993   World Team Trials champion, U.S. Nationals champion

1994   Second in 1994 Winter Classic, third in World Team Trials

1995   World Team Trials champion, third in U.S. Nationals

1996   Fourth in U.S. Olympic Team Trials, second in U.S. Nationals, West Regional Olympic Trials champion

1997   World Team Trials champion, U.S. Nationals champion, Winter Classic champion, Outstanding Greco-Roman Wrestler at U.S. Nationals

1998   Fifth in World Team Trials

1999   Second in World Team Trials, U.S. Nationals champion

2000   Sixth in U.S. Olympic Team Trials, West Regional Olympic Trials
        champion

OKLAHOMA STATE UNIVERSITY

1989   Div. 1 National Championships team member

1990   Div. 1 National Championships team member, sixth in NCAA
        Championships, All-American

1991   NCAA Div. 1 runner-up, All-American, Big Eight Conference
        champion

1992   NCAA Div. 1 runner-up, All-American

LYNNWOOD HIGH SCHOOL

1981   Class 3A state high school champion

COURTESY OF USA WRESTLING

Acknowledgements

THE AUTHORS WOULD like to thank Gerry Anderson and David Dunn, whose enthusiasm about my life story sparked this project, and Matt Walker, for introducing me to everyone at the Gersh Agency. They were instrumental in making the final corrections to see this project through. Our editor, Ursula Cary, was a vital member of the team, along with Trisha Boczkowski, Jennifer Robinson, and Sam Spira.

Our gratitude goes to Valerie and Scott Haney, who handled any obstacle, big or small, with the gusto of an army.

And to our agent, Margaret O' Connor, whose dedication, professionalism, and willingness to go the extra mile has made her a guardian angel.

★　★　★

RANDY, THANK YOU for believing in this underdog and letting me come along for the ride. You inspire all.

To my brother, Jim, who put me on the path.

To my husband, Shane, you are my everything.

-Loretta Hunt

About The Authors

RANDY COUTURE

Randy is widely acknowledged as the greatest and most popular UFC and mixed martial arts fighter in history. A member of the UFC Hall of Fame, he is the only athlete to have held championship titles in both the heavyweight and light heavyweight divisions of the UFC. He lives in Las Vegas, and is currently pursuing an acting career in Hollywood.

LORETTA HUNT

Loretta is the first and only female to be internationally recognised as a full-time mixed martial arts journalist. She has covered the fast-growing sport for nearly a decade.

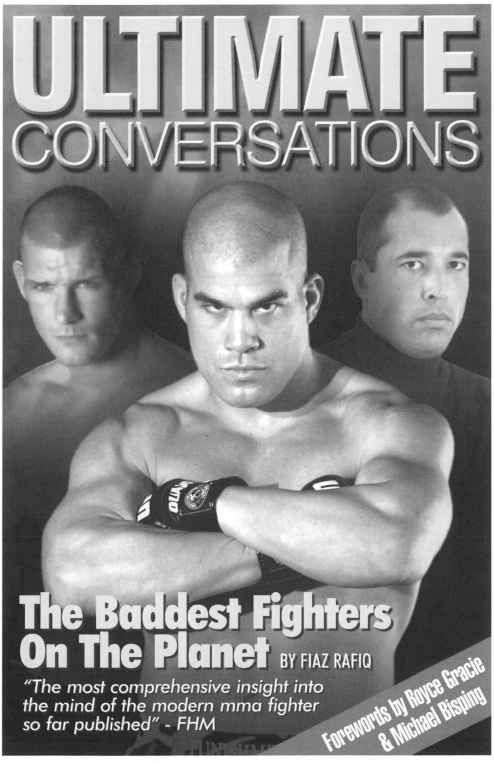

ULTIMATE
CONVERSATIONS

The Baddest Fighters
On The Planet BY FIAZ RAFIQ

*"The most comprehensive insight into
the mind of the modern mma fighter
so far published"* - FHM

Forewords by Royce Gracie
& Michael Bisping

AVAILABLE FROM ALL GOOD BOOKSTORES

CAGE TALK

CAGE TALK

INSIDE THE WORLD'S TOUGHEST SPORT

BY JIMMY PAGE

AVAILABLE FROM ALL GOOD BOOKSTORES

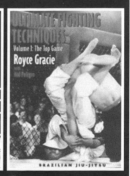